Keep the
Faith !

E
"Mr Awesome"

13 STEPS TO RICHES

Featuring
Erik Swanson & Sharon Lechter

#1 BESTSELLER

FAITH
VOLUME 2

HABITUDE WARRIOR

Foreword by Larry Wilcox

Orders by U.S. trade bookstores and wholesalers.
Email info@ BeyondPublishing.net

Manufactured and printed in the United States of America and distributed globally by BeyondPublishing.net

BEYOND

Library of Congress Control Number: 2021918893

Hardback ISBN: 978-1-63792-117-3

Paperback ISBN: 978-1-63792-122-7

TESTIMONIALS
THE 13 STEPS TO RICHES

"What an honor to collaborate with so many personal development leaders from around the world as we Co-Author together honoring the amazing principles by Napoleon Hill in this new book series, *The 13 Steps to Riches*, by Habitude Warrior and Erik "Mr. Awesome" Swanson. Well done "Mr. Awesome" for putting together such an amazing series. If you want to up-level your life, read every book in this series and learn to apply each of these time tested steps and principles."

Denis Waitley ~ Author of *Psychology of Winning & The NEW Psychology of Winning - Top Qualities of a 21st Century Winner*

"Just as *Think and Grow Rich* reveals the 13 steps to success discovered by Napoleon Hill after interviewing the richest people around the world (and many who considered themselves failures) in the early 1900's, *The 13 Steps to Riches*, produced by Habitude Warrior and Erik Swanson takes a modern look at those same 13 steps. It brings together many of today's personal development leaders to share their stories of how the 13 Steps to Riches have created and propelled their own successes. I am honored to participate and share the power of Faith in my life. If you truly want to accelerate reaching the success you deserve, read every volume of *The 13 Steps to Riches*."

Sharon Lechter ~ 5 Time N.Y. Times Best-Selling Author. Author of *Think and Grow Rich for Women*, Co-Author of *Exit Rich, Rich Dad Poor Dad, Three Feet from Gold, Outwitting the Devil* and *Success and Something Greater* ~ **SharonLechter.com**

"The most successful book on personal achievement ever written is now being elaborated upon by many of the world's top thought leaders. I'm honored to Co-Author this series on the amazing principles from Napoleon Hill, in *The 13 Steps to Riches*, by Habitude Warrior, Erik "Mr. Awesome" Swanson."

> *Jim Cathcart* ~ Best-Selling Author of *Relationship Selling* and *The Acorn Principle*, among many others. Certified Speaking Professional (CSP) and Former President of the National Speakers Association (NSA)

"Where else can you find 13 leaders sharing their amazing insights and principles of success, while honoring one of the best books ever published in *Think and Grow Rich* by Napoleon Hill? I know... right here! Pick up your copy of *The 13 Steps to Riches* book series and follow these time tested steps and principles that will change your life if you take action on them."

> *Steve Sims* ~ N.Y.Times Best-Selling Author of *Bluefishing - The Art of Making Things Happen*

"Some books are written to be read and placed on the shelf. Others are written to transform the reader, as they travel down a path of true transcendence and enlightenment. "*The 13 steps to Riches*" by Habitude Warrior and Erik Swanson is the latter. Profoundly insightful, it revitalizes the techniques and strategies written by Napoleon Hill by applying a modern perspective, and a fearsome collaboration of some of the greatest minds and thought leaders from around the globe. A must read for all of those who seek to break free of their current levels of success, and truly extract the greatness that lies within. It is an honor and a privilege to have been selected to participate, in what is destined to be the next historic chapter in the meteoric rise of many men and women around the world."

> *Glenn Lundy* ~ Husband to one, Father to 8, Automotive Industry Expert, Author of "The Morning 5", Creator of the popular morning show "#riseandgrind", and the Founder of "Breakfast With Champions"

"How exciting to team up with the amazing Habitude Warrior community of leaders such as Erik Swanson, Sharon Lechter, John Assaraf, Denis Waitley and so many more transformational and self-help icons to bring you these timeless and proven concepts in the fields of success and wealth. *The 13 Steps to Riches* book series will help you reach your dreams and accomplish your goals faster than you have ever experienced before!"

> *Marie Diamond* ~ Featured in *The Secret*, Modern Day Spiritual Teacher, Inspirational Speaker, Feng Shui Master

"If you are looking to crystalize your mightiest dream, rekindle your passion, breakthrough limiting beliefs and learn from those who have done exactly what you want to do - read this book! In this transformational masterpiece, *The 13 Steps to Riches*, self-development guru Erik Swanson has collected the sage wisdom and time tested truths from subject matter experts and amalgamated it into a one-stop-shop resource library that will change your life forever!"

> *Dan Clark* ~ Speaker Hall of Fame & N.Y. Times Best-Selling Author of *The Art of Significance*

"Life has always been about who you surround yourself with. I am in excellent company with this collaboration from my fellow authors and friends, paying tribute to the life changing principles by Napoleon Hill in this amazing new book series, *The 13 Steps to Riches*, organized by Habitude Warrior's founder and my dear friend, Erik Swanson. Hill said, 'Your big opportunity may be right where you are now.' This book series is a must-read for anyone who wants to change their life and prosper, starting now."

> *Alec Stern* ~ America's Startup Success Expert, Co-Founder of Constant Contact

"Finally a book series that encompasses the lessons the world needs to learn and apply, but in our modern day era. As I always teach my students to "Say **YES**, and then figure out how", I strongly urge you to do the same. Say YES to adding all of these 13 books in *The 13 Steps to Riches* book series into your success library and watch both your business as well as your personal life grow as a result."

> *Loral Langemeier* ~ 5 Time N.Y. Times Best-Selling Author, Featured in *The Secret*, Author of *The Millionaire Maker* and *YES! Energy - The Equation to Do Less, Make More*

"Napoleon Hill had a tremendous impact on my consciousness when I was very young – there were very few books nor the type of trainings that we see today to lead us to success. Whenever you have the opportunity to read and harness *The 13 Steps to Riches* as they are presented in this series, be happy (and thankful) that there were many of us out there applying the principles, testing the teachings, making the mistakes, and now being offered to you in a way that they are clear, simple and concise – with samples and distinctions that will make it easier for you to design a successful life which includes adding value to others, solving world problems, and making the world work for 100% of humanity... Read on... those dreams are about to come true!"

> *Doria Cordova* ~ CEO of Money & You, Excellerated Business School, Global Business Developer, Ambassador of New Education

"Success leaves clues and the Co-Authors in this awesome book series, *The 13 Steps to Riches*, will continue the Napoleon Hill legacy with tools, tips and modern-day principals that greatly expand on the original masterpiece... Think and Grow Rich. If you are serious about living your life to the max, get this book series now!"

> *John Assaraf* ~ Chairman & CEO NeuroGym, MrNeuroGym.com, New York Times best-selling author of *Having It All, Innercise,* and *The Answer.* Also featured in *The Secret*

"Over the years, I have been blessed with many rare and amazing opportunities to invest my time and energy. These opportunities require a keen eye and immediate action. This is one of those amazing opportunities for you as a reader! I highly recommend you pick up every book in this series of **The 13 Steps to Riches** by Habitude Warrior and Erik Swanson! Learn from modern day leaders who have embraced the lessons from the great Napoleon Hill in his classic book from 1937, **Think and Grow Rich.**"

Kevin Harrington ~ Original "Shark" on *Shark Tank*, Creator of the Infomercial, Pioneer of the *As Seen on TV* brand, Co-Author of *Mentor to Millions*

"When you begin your journey, you will quickly learn of the importance of the first step of *The 13 Steps To Riches*. A burning desire is the start of all worthwhile achievements. Erik 'Mr. Awesome' Swanson's newest book series contains a wealth of assistance to make your journey both successful and enjoyable. Start today... because tomorrow is not guaranteed on your calendar."

Don Green ~ 45 Years of Banking, Finance & Entrepreneurship, Best-Selling Author of *Everything I know About Success I Learned From Napoleon Hill* & *Napoleon Hill My Mentor: Timeless Principles to Take Your Success to the Next Level* & *Your Millionaire Mindset*

Our minds become magnetized with the dominating thoughts we hold in our minds and these magnets attract to us the forces, the people, the circumstances of life which harmonize with the nature of our dominating thoughts.

(Napoleon Hill)

NAPOLEON HILL

I would like to personally acknowledge and thank the one and only Napoleon Hill for his work, dedication, and most importantly believing in himself. His unwavering belief in himself, whether he realized this or not, had been passed down from generation to generation to millions and millions of individuals across this planet including me!

I'm sure, at first, as many of us experience throughout our lives as well, he most likely had his doubts. Think about it. Being offered to work for Andrew Carnegie for a full 20 years with zero pay and no guarantee of success had to be a daunting decision. But, I thank you for making that decision years and years ago. It paved the path for countless many who have trusted in themselves and found success in their own rights. You gave us all hope, desire, and faith to bank on the most important energy in the world - ourselves!

For this, I thank you Sir, from the bottom of my heart and the top of all of our bank accounts. Let us all follow the 13 Steps to Riches and prosper in so many areas of our lives.

~ Erik "Mr. Awesome" Swanson

10 Time #1 Best-Selling Author & Student of Napoleon Hill Philosophies

SGT. NICOLE L. GEE, 23

It is our distinct honor to dedicate each one of our *13 **Steps to Riches*** book volumes to each of the 13 United States Service Members who courageously lost their lives in Kabul in August, 2021. Your honor, dignity, and strength will always be cherished and remembered. ~ Habitude Warrior Team

Sgt. Nicole L. Gee, 23, of Sacramento, California, assigned to Combat Logistics Battalion 24, 24th Marine Expeditionary Unit - II Marine Expeditionary Force, Camp Lejeune, North Carolina. Gee entered active duty in the Marine Corps in 2017. She was a ground electronics transmission systems maintainer assigned to Combat Logistics Battalion 24, a subordinate unit of Combat Logistics Regiment 27, 2nd Marine Logistics Group - II Marine Expeditionary Force.

Her previous assignments include recruit training at Parris Island, South Carolina; School of Infantry–East in Camp Lejeune, North Carolina; Aviation Accession & Primary Military Occupational Specialty School in Pensacola, Florida; and Marine Corps Communications. Her military awards include the Marine Corps Good Conduct Medal and the National Defense and Global War on Terrorism Service Medals.

JACKSON SWANSON

I would like to dedicate this volume of The 13 Steps to Riches - FAITH, to my one and only Jackson! "What a gentleman!" ~ "He is so polite!" ~ "Can he come over and train all of my pets and maybe if he has time he can also train my husband?" ~ "How in the world is your dog that well behaved with so much going on around him?" These were just a few of the comments he and I would hear every single day when we would take our daily morning walk to go grab some green iced tea and puppuccinos. Jackson truly showed me the way to enlightenment. He showed me how to be curious. He showed me how to investigate and learn about new things each and every day. He showed me how to become friends with the world. He showed me how to stay calm, no matter what is going on around us. He showed me how to teach people how we should be treated. He showed me love and affection and unconditional awesomeness! You have given me the best 12 years of my life. I love you and miss you Jackie!

~ Your Dad, Erik

THE 13 STEPS TO RICHES
FEATURING:

DENIS WAITLEY ~ Author of *Psychology of Winning & The NEW Psychology of Winning - Top Qualities of a 21st Century Winner*, NASA's Performance Coach, Featured in *The Secret* ~ www.DenisWaitley.com

SHARON LECHTER ~ 5 Time N.Y. Times Best-Selling Author. Author of *Think and Grow Rich for Women*, Co-Author of *Exit Rich*, *Rich Dad Poor Dad*, *Three Feet from Gold*, *Outwitting the Devil* and *Success and Something Greater* ~ www.SharonLechter.com

JIM CATHCART~ Best-Selling Author of *Relationship Selling* and *The Acorn Principle*, among many others. Certified Speaking Professional (CSP) and Former President of the National Speakers Association (NSA) ~ www.Cathcart.com

STEVE SIMS ~ N.Y.Times Best-Selling Author of *Bluefishing - The Art of Making Things Happen*, CEO and Founder of Bluefish ~ www.SteveDSims.com

GLENN LUNDY ~ Husband to one, Father to 8,

Automotive Industry Expert, Author of "The Morning 5", Creator of the popular morning show "#riseandgrind", and the Founder of "Breakfast With Champions" ~ www.GlennLundy.com

MARIE DIAMOND ~ Featured in *The Secret*, Modern Day Spiritual Teacher, Inspirational Speaker, Feng Shui Master ~ www.MarieDiamond.com

DAN CLARK ~ Award Winning Speaker, Speaker Hall of Fame, N.Y. Times Best-Selling Author of *The Art of Significance* ~ www.DanClark.com

ALEC STERN ~ America's Startup Success Expert, Co-Founder of Constant Contact, Speaker, Mentor, Investor ~ www.AlecSpeaks.com

ERIK SWANSON ~ 10 Time #1 International Best-Selling Author, Award Winning Speaker, Featured on Tedx Talks and Amazon Prime TV. Founder & CEO of the Habitude Warrior Brand ~ www.SpeakerErikSwanson.com

LORAL LANGEMEIER ~ 5 Time N.Y. Times Best-Selling Author, Featured in *The Secret*, Author of *The Millionaire Maker* and *YES! Energy - The Equation to Do Less, Make More* ~ www.LoralLangemeier.com

DORIA CORDOVA ~ CEO of Money & You, Excellerated Business School, Global Business Developer, Ambassador of New Education ~ www.FridaysWithDoria.com

JOHN ASSARAF ~ Chairman & CEO NeuroGym, MrNeuroGym.com, N. Y. Times best-selling author of *Having It All, Innercise,* and *The Answer.* Also featured in *The Secret* ~ www.JohnAssaraf.com

KEVIN HARRINGTON ~ Original "Shark" on the hit TV show *Shark Tank,* Creator of the Infomercial, Pioneer of the *As Seen on TV* brand, Co-Author of *Mentor to Millions* ~ www.KevinHarrington.TV

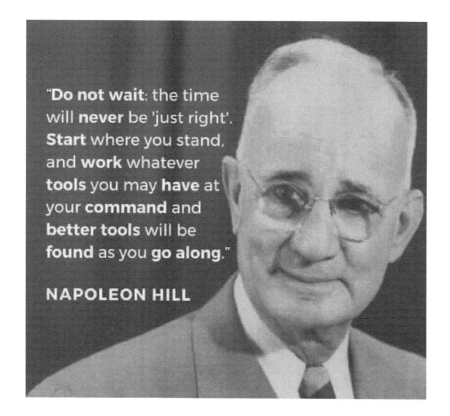

"**Do not wait**: the time will **never** be 'just right'. **Start** where you stand, and **work** whatever **tools** you may **have** at your **command** and **better tools** will be **found** as you **go along**."

NAPOLEON HILL

CONTENTS

INTRODUCTION

by Don Green

ERIK SWANSON & DON GREEN

Once you give yourself the gift of reading Erik Swanson's newest book series, *The 13 Steps to Riches*, you are sure to realize why he has earned his nickname, *"Mr. Awesome."* Readers usually read books for two reasons – they want to be entertained or they want to improve their knowledge in a certain subject. Mr. Awesome's new book series will help you do both.

I urge you to not only read this great book series in it's entirety, but also apply the principles held within into your our life. Use the experience Erik Swanson has gained to reach your own level of success. I highly encourage you to invest in yourself by reading self-help materials, such as *The 13 Steps to Riches*, and I truly know you will discover that it will be one of the best investments you could ever make.

Don Green
Executive Director and CEO
The Napoleon Hill Foundation

FOREWORD

by Larry Wilcox

The term "Riches" has so many synonyms and one hopes that we embrace all of them as we read this wonderful book concerning "Faith" as faith provides so many keys to so many padlocks in life while rewarding us with a very personal and subtle gift of richness and freedom. Faith is a choice!

I have a humble opinion that "faith" was always available to all of us as a provocative truth that is served early in life but often blocked by the maturation process of emotions that vacillate in the extremes during the adolescent spectrum of life and often shield one from critical thinking and it's foundational offspring. However, when faith comes forward, in front of the cyclorama of emotions, life becomes richer and deeper.

I have often felt you have several choices of thought with respect to faith. My sense of faith has allowed me to have many arrows in my faith quiver if you will. My favorite faith arrow is the belief in oneself. Of course it is easy for one to rhetorically quip…"hey, just believe in yourself" and the doors will open. However, like other choices of thought, faith requires a foundation and a maturation and it becomes layered with prongs of wisdom and a deep foundation from which one can distill thoughts, choices, logic, responsibility and consequences. Faith in yourself, as a person who reasons from principle is key for me. I like to believe that my faith in my ability to reason from principle instead of emotional indulgence has been my pillar, my compass in my rich life. Faith in my ability to survive at all costs assists me with preparation, simulation, and the predisposition of shadow boxing in life. Faith is a theme in my life tapestry which is made up of disciplined and practiced daily rituals so that my "muscle memory" understands this without having to engage in the parasitic drag of an inner debate. Faith in my wife and our relationship, and faith in my business partners so all can operate in a non-oppressive environment and succeed accordingly. Faith in my God who navigates my stream of consciousness and its polarity. I could write many paragraphs on the arrows of faith as they are deep and voluminous. It takes a lifetime to hone the wonderful arrows of faith but the process and the timeline will always reflect on the rich hues and spiritual depth of your character and legacy. I will attempt to share just a snippet of the all powerful "faith" in my own humble life. Sometimes faith just beckons you, in such a beautiful customized sheet of music. I hope you are listening as all forms of joy and success are beckoning your soul through faith.

In 1967 I joined the United States Marine Corps during Vietnam. I joined the Marines because I expected I would go to Vietnam and even though I had major reservations and some fears, I wanted to be trained by what I construed as the best, the Marines. I had many experiences of fear and vulnerability, and yet, I knew I would eventually win as I had faith in myself. I found ways to escape the pain of physical and emotional abuse that was part of the Marine Corps Drill Instructor training, which was meant to break a person down and then re-build them. I can remember them having us swim in pure mud on a very hot day and then tell us we could not shower while hitting us in the trachea when we talked. They would put our thumbs in the chamber of an M-14 and let the chamber slam home on your thumb and laugh at the bloody and swollen thumb. You see, you could choose faith or you could wallow in your misery. I chose faith, because I had faith in my ability to re-interpret their abuse as entertainment and comedy. I imagined that these idiots were enjoying watching my side stroke or breast stroke in the mud because they were the ones that needed a psych exam and an assigned disorder or two. Later, I was made the Platoon Leader as the Guide and the Guide is supposed to train his Platoon and to hit them or give a blanket party to the twenty percent who they deemed, should not be in the Marine Corps. They would call these guys, wannabe Marines and Private Pukey or other derogatory and profane names. They wanted these guys to be slugged and to be reprimanded by the entire platoon so they would learn a lesson or leave the Marines. So, I had faith in these guys and I began to train them privately. I often say, everyone is a diamond, just some are more camouflaged than others. So, when we would be standing in formation, I would tell them that I would be slugging them in the stomach when the Drill Instructor came out of the mess hall. I would obviously pull my punch so it would not hurt them but it was important they faked the injury a bit so it looked real. That way no one suffered, and the D.I. was happy to see the discipline and we could avoid a little abuse from them. We had one particular kid who was red headed, wore glasses, and was rather obese. They hassled this poor kid every day and at night they would march him out to the fence that separated the Marines from the Navy and they would tell him they wanted him to go AWOL (Absent Without Leave) that night because he was a puke, and he was an embarrassment to the Marines and they told him he better be gone tonight and joing the Navy, the swabbies where he belonged. Each night Private Pukey, which was one of his names, but they also called him the four eyed Mother.Fer, and he would undergo more daily abuse. They made him write letters to his mom, and before he could send them, they told him he had to read them out loud to the entire Platoon while they mocked him like he was a coward and a sissy. I took him aside and told him that he needed to not allow his mind to engage in their ignorance and that he needed to beat them at their own game. He asked how he could do that, as he was having a hard time surviving, as that day, he fainted in the forced march in the heat and they poured warm coffee on his face and berated him even more. I told him to have faith in his choice of thoughts. I told him to choose his reality with faith and not to allow them to dictate his reality. I told him to have faith not only in his choice of thoughts but in himself and he would win. I gave him examples of these choices of thought so it was not some esoteric mental masturbation but would in fact help him. Soon thereafter, I never saw him for the rest of bootcamp because the Drill Instructors sent him to the dreaded Fat Farm where all day in the heat you worked with hard physical fitness while carrying and using a sledge hammer. I felt so bad for him and wondered if his faith was his golden arrow that would get him through boot camp. The problem with being sent to the fat farm is that you have do begin boot camp all over so he probably missed a few weeks, meaning, that if boot camp was 14 weeks long his was now 16 weeks of hell.

During the next few months of training, I took every test the Marine Corps offered and I was chosen to go to Officer Candidate School but that meant I had to stay in another 6 years and I passed. I also was the only one chosen to go to foreign language school but the good ole Marine Corps lost my orders. October 1967, I landed in Vietnam, trained as a forward observer, a Fire Direction Control Artillery person and a survey expert using the Theodolite T-16. All Marines were trained as rifleman and in jungle training. While I was sitting in Da Nang, watching all the wounded marines getting off a C-130 to go home I listened to their short timer crass insults to all of us….the "cherries" as we were called. They would yell…. "hey Marine," what is your MOS (Military Occupation) and I would say FO and FDC. They would laugh and laugh… "16 second life expectancy there Mr. Forward Observer Cherry!" I finally disengaged with their ridicule and began reading a Life Magazine article about the DMZ and it showed photos of Marines wrapped in bandages on top of a mountain area called Con Thien. I hoped I would not be going to the DMZ. A few minutes later the loudspeaker came on again and announced names and serial numbers. I was one of the names and serial numbers, going to the DMZ. I felt a sudden gloom come over me and I grabbed my Saint Christopher Medal and said a simple prayer to God and asked him to protect me with a golden shield and I would attempt to do the rest in good faith. I got on a C-130 Airplane and landed in Dong Ha, Vietnam. Next, I got on the plane and got into a Personnel Carrier (PC) and we were told to lay down as we would be taking sniper fire. I thought wow.....I have no flak jacket yet and no rifle or anything. We drove north on the dirt road called Highway 1. We arrived at an artillery base, and drove through the Constantine wire barricade. The noise was deafening and made one shaky as 105mm and 155mm Howitzers were shooting all night long. I was told where to sleep and I was freezing cold as the Monsoons were starting. I woke up the next morning with very little sleep and followed other Marines to the chow hall. I stood in line with my tray wondering where I was going next, probably a lot closer to the DMZ and I looked up and almost started to cry. I stared, making sure I was not hallucinating and then squinted at the red hair, a survivor, a hero, a true MARINE who had gone through hell, Private Pukey. I went up to him and gave him a big hug and asked him what he was doing here in the Nam. He said he graduated finally from boot camp and was a cook. He told me thanks for the lessons in Faith. I hugged him again, and thanked God for such a cool reward. The red headed, 4 eyed, private pukey made it and he made it like no other. His faith carried him through hell and he can be proud his whole life. I spent the next 13 months clinging to the memories of my hero, and of course, my "faith arrows" and I knew I would make it home to the USA. I was honorably discharged a E6, Staff Sgt and I am glad my faith helped me and helped others. I have so many stories of faith; faith made my acting career in Hollywood where I starred in two Television series and produced an award- winning TV series on HBO. Faith blessed me when I was flying war games in an A-7 fighter Jet fighting F-16s from the Air Force Academy. We had to eject but at the last minute we decided to try and catch the famous trip wire and we were successful, because of faith. It is a long exciting story but too long for this narrative. I raced and wrecked my race cars from time to time at Riverside, Phoenix, Baja and Laguna Seca. I set International Land Speed records at the Bonneville Salt Flats and yet, faith was the true winner. I have five children, all better than myself, and faith in them has been a journey, a blessing.

 Never forget your maturation process of faith, and never forget your reality is a choice of thoughts and I humbly recommend the choice of faith. I hope you embrace this book and its contents and that it provokes a deeper consciousness in your choice of a faithful success. Make sure you choose to place these arrows in your quiver.

To your success,
Larry Wilcox
Actor, Producer, Speaker, Retired Marine

LARRY WILCOX

About Larry Wilcox: Lary Wilcox is a Wyoming native who is a well known actor who starred in Lassie and also played the role of John in *CHiPs* for NBC. He produced the movie, *FLIPPER* and the award-winning TV Series, *The Ray Bradbury Theater* on HBO for 5 years. Larry served in the U.S.M.C. and was honorably discharged after serving 13 months in Vietnam in 1967-1968 on the DMZ. He is a member of SAG, DGA, and the WGA and has been developing movie and TV shows and series while enjoying the mergers and acquisitions of technology. Wilcox is also a pilot, an International Land Speed Record Holder from the Bonneville Salt Flats, a Baja 1000 Truck Race Driver, a Professional Rodeo Cowboy and is now working on his Autobiography. He is married and his wife of 35 years (Marlene Harmon) is a former 1980 Olympic Track and Field team member. Wilcox has five children and he cherishes every moment he has with each of them.

SHARON LECHTER

About Sharon Lechter: As an Entrepreneur, International Speaker, Best-Selling Author, Mentor, Philanthropist, Licensed CPA for 35 years and a Chartered Global Management Accountant, Sharon Lechter is the premier expert for financial literacy and entrepreneurial success. A lifelong education advocate, in 1989, Sharon joined forces with the inventor of the first electronic 'talking book' and helped him expand the electronic book industry to a multi-million dollar international market.

In 1997 Sharon co-authored the international bestseller *Rich Dad Poor Dad*, and has released 14 other books in the Rich Dad series. Over 10 years as the co-founder and CEO, she built the empire into the world's leading personal finance brand.

In 2008, she was asked by the Napoleon Hill Foundation to help re-energize the powerful teachings of Napoleon Hill just as the international economy was faltering. Sharon has released three bestselling books in cooperation with the Foundation, including *Think and Grow Rich- Three Feet from Gold*, *Outwitting the Devil* and her latest project, *Think and Grow Rich for Women*, released in June of 2014. She is also featured in the 2017 movie Think and Grow Rich: The Legacy and has released the book *Save Wisely, Spend Happily* in cooperation with the American Institute of CPAs.

Sharon is a highly sought-after mentor and has worked with major brands like Disney and Time Warner and served two U.S. Presidents as an advisor on the topic of financial literacy. As CEO of Pay Your Family First, she has dedicated her entrepreneurial efforts to the creation and distribution of financial education books, games, curriculums, and other experiential learning projects. Everything about Sharon's career centers around impacting others to improve their financial IQ, access untapped potential personally and in business, and create their own legacy.

But everything changed in 2012 when Sharon's son unexpectedly died. All of Sharon's successes seemed to fade into the background. She kept working, but on autopilot. She stopped playing at the level she always had and just started coasting. Until now!

Now, Sharon is back and playing big again, and she wants you to as well with the Play Big Movement. It's time to shed the limitations that have stopped you in the past. It's time to play big, master your money and time and create maximum impact.

Sharon lives in Paradise Valley, AZ with her husband and business partner, Michael Lechter, a powerhouse in the area of Intellectual Property, Organizational Architecture, and Publishing. Together, they love spending time with each other and especially like to get away to their dude ranch, Cherry Creek Lodge, where they can get "off the grid" (literally) and get recharged for their next big play.

Sharon continues to be a committed philanthropist by giving back to world communities both as a benefactor and a volunteer and has been honored with numerous awards.

Author's website: *www.SharonLechter.com*
Book Series Website & author's Bio: *www.The13StepsToRiches.com*

Sharon Lechter

HAVE YOU ADDED VALUE TO SOMEONE'S LIFE TODAY?

What role has FAITH played in your life and in your success? Try to remember a time when you "powered through" a difficult period in your life. How did FAITH show up and help you through?

When I asked myself this question, I first think about the spiritual aspect of faith and my trust in a higher power…but I also think about the faith I have in myself. It reminds me of my father and a simple question he would ask me each night.

"Have you added value to someone's life today?"

My dad used to ask me that question every night when I was growing up. He has been gone for 15 years, but I still ask myself this same question every evening.

As a child, I didn't understand how dramatically this simple question would impact my life. By concentrating on adding value to others' lives, you don't focus on just yourself or your personal desires. But even more importantly, when you see the positive impact your actions make in the lives of others, it makes you feel better about yourself. It builds your self-confidence, or faith in yourself by helping others find faith in themselves. That is truly adding value to the world.

When most people hear the word faith, they think of faith from a spiritual perspective. Spiritual faith in God or a higher power is incredibly important and creates a fundamental belief system that shapes who we are and who we become as adults.

It is also important not to neglect the faith that we can build in ourselves and in each other every single day through the thoughts, words and actions that we choose. I realize that the nightly question from my father and my desire to help others helped me build faith and self- confidence as a result of my service to others.

In addition to spiritual faith and faith in yourself you can have faith in others, faith in your endeavors and faith that you will succeed.

What is the first thought the word FAITH triggers in your mind?

Many of history's greatest thought leaders have highlighted the importance of faith.

Faith consists in believing when it is beyond
the power of reason to believe.
~ Voltaire

He who has faith has... an inward reservoir of courage, hope,
confidence, calmness, and assuring trust that all will come out well -
even though to the world it may appear to come out most badly.
B. C. Forbes (founder of Forbes Magazine)

Faith is the strength by which a shattered
world shall emerge into the light.
~ Helen Keller

When you focus on being a blessing, God makes sure
that you are always blessed in abundance.
~ Joel Osteen

In faith there is enough light for those who want to believe and enough
shadows to blind those who don't.
~ Blaise Pascal

Keep your dreams alive. Understand to achieve anything requires
faith and belief in yourself, vision, hard work, determination,
and dedication. Remember all things are possible
for those who believe.
~ Gail Devers

In *Think and Grow Rich*, Napoleon Hill himself challenged the notion that faith is only about religious belief. Faith becomes the beacon of light that provides a path forward and engages your subconscious mind. Without faith, negativity fills your subconscious and multiplies more negativity. On the other hand, optimism, positivity, and faith create the foundation that shields your mind from negativity and from which success can be built.

Let's review Hill's definition of FAITH and the role it plays in creating success in your life:

Have Faith in yourself: Faith in the Infinite.

FAITH is the "external elixir" which gives life, power, and action to the impulse of thought!

FAITH is the starting point of all accumulation of riches!

FAITH is the basis of all "miracles" and all mysteries which cannot be analyzed by the rules of science!

FAITH is the only known antidote for FAILURE!

FAITH is the element, the "chemical" which, when mixed with prayer, gives one direct communication with Infinite Intelligence.

FAITH is the element which transforms the ordinary vibration of thought, created by the finite mind of man, into the spiritual equivalent.

FAITH is the only agency through which the cosmic force of Infinite Intelligence can be harnessed and used by man.

The importance of faith became very clear to me during the writing process for *Three Feet From Gold*, my first *Think and Grow Rich* series book with the Napoleon Hill Foundation co-authored with Greg Reid. As we interviewed successful business men and women, we found they shared common traits that drove them to success. But even more importantly we found the common attributes that helped them drive and persevere through the tough times.. turning obstacles they faced into opportunities. As a result of our research we formulated the Personal Success Equation to share the common elements of their success stories.

It is as follows:

$[(P + T) x A x A] + F = Personal Success Equation$

[(**P**assion + **T**alent) x **A**ssociation x **A**ction] + **F**aith = Personal Success Equation

Just as Hill discovered the principles of success by research and study of the most successful people of his time and shared them in *Think and Grow Rich*, the personal success equation was derived by analysis of what was key to the success of modern industry leaders and their ability to overcome obstacles. When you combine your Passion and your Talent with the right Associations and then take the right Actions you are well on your way to success. Your Passion and Talents are personal to you, often learned in school or from life experience. But true success is achieved through the Power of Association and taking action towards your goals. And we almost went to print with *Three Feet From Gold* with that as the formula but I recognized that a huge common element with these industry leaders that was missing was their incredible Faith. Faith in themselves, faith in what they were doing, faith that it was needed and necessary and faith that they would succeed. That faith kept them moving and persevering even during tough times when others would have easily quit "three feet from gold!"

In addition, we discovered that for many business owners that "F" actually stood for Fear, not Faith. And it was that Fear that make it easy for them to give up and quit, choosing NOT to persevere. This fear prevented them from achieving the success they deserved.

It is impossible to have Faith and Fear in your mind at the same time. Having faith helps you keep fear under control. Fear does one of two things - it paralyzes us or motivates us. The vast majority of us are paralyzed by fear so we fail to take action. We hide away and isolate and end up missing opportunities that are right there in front of us. This fear stops us and keeps us from moving past the obstacle that caused the fear.

When we internalize that fear it becomes destructive. We start thinking things like, "I am not good enough, I am not qualified, I am not thin enough, I am just not as lucky as he is." In each of these statements we are giving up our own power and judging ourselves through the eyes of others. This negativity eats away at our self-confidence and destroys our faith in ourselves. If we can learn to identify the fear and turn it into energy and action, we can overcome it, stand tall in our own power and place ourselves in the position of greatest potential.

Hill provides us with a roadmap to overcome fear in *Outwitting the Devil,* which he actually wrote in 1938, intending it to be the sequel to *Think and Grow Rich.* But it was kept in a vault until I had to honor to annotate it and share it in 2015. (Why was it kept in the vault? His wife was afraid of the title!) In this manuscript, Hill provides incredible insights into why we hold ourselves back and fail to reach the level of success we deserve. He takes on every taboo of our times... sex, politics, education, religion, diet, alcohol, cigarettes just to name a few...and shares how fear manipulates us in each one of these areas and prevents us from achieving the success we deserve.

This fear robs us of the ability to think for ourselves. To have control over our own thoughts. He talks about fear of poverty, fear of death, fear of criticism, fear of old age, fear of loss of love. I believe the fear of criticism is pervasive in society today and prevents us from finding our own voice. We are so afraid of what others will think of us, of being embarrassed or being different that we "go with the flow" and don't carve our own path.

Outwitting the Devil shows you how to break the paralysis of fear and take control of your thoughts, your actions and your results. It all starts with Definiteness of Purpose. When you know what your definiteness of purpose is, it gives you courage and energy to move forward. Just as asking myself if I have added value to someone's life today does, it takes you out of yourself and allows you to focus on being of contribution to the world.

In fact, every successful business defines its definiteness of purpose by the problem it solves or the need that it serves. It is the mission of the business. As an individual you should also incorporate your personal mission statement that allows you to stay focused your definiteness of purpose.

The next step is Mastery over Self which is creating the self-discipline that creates positive habits that allow you to keep focused and demonstrates that you truly are in control of your thoughts and actions.

But in his wisdom, Hill also recognized that we all make mistakes, so we need to acknowledge them and learn from them. Too often when we make mistakes, instead of learning from them, we carry them around with us like heavy baggage defining ourselves as failures. It is important to understand that mistakes happen to all of us and when they do it is important to ask yourself what the lesson is…so you don't repeat the mistake. *It is important to remember that mistakes are occurrences…not definitions.*

But Hill also recognized that even the strongest faith can be tested by everyday life. He shared the importance of controlling our environment. What are you listening to? What are you reading? Who are you spending time with? Who are you listening to? Just imagine entering a room that is full of people crying at the funeral of a child…do you feel the emotional pull of sadness? Now imagine entering a room of people singing and dancing…where you immediately smile and feel the beat of the music. That small example demonstrates the impact of our environment on our attitude and emotional well-being.

It is very important to surround yourself with people who support you and want you to succeed. And it is even more important to limit your exposure to people who try to hold you back or pull you down. Environment includes what you and those around you feed your subconscious. *In Think and Grow Rich*, Hill shares the importance of Autosuggestion, feeding your mind and subconscious with positive messaging to bolster your outlook, your confidence and faith in yourself. It not only helps nurture your faith but gives you energy and motivation to move forward toward accomplishing your definiteness of purpose. When the pandemic stopped us in our tracks, I was distressed by all the negative messaging and the amount of fear and hopelessness it was generating. I took action and started sharing a daily message of hope and positivity, called daily ATMs (Abundance, Tips and Mentorship). The ATMs are an autosuggestion tool for you if you are looking for positive messaging and environment. I end each message every day with the same exercise. I ask you to repeat in the mirror, "I am fabulous!" And then I respond, "Yes you are!" (**atm.sharonlechter.com**)

Going hand in hand with controlling your environment, and equally as important is controlling your time. So often we know what we need to do…we just don't do it! (Are you feeling busted right now?) It could be fear that is holding you back or a lack of motivation. Start by analyzing your calendar. Are you spending time…or are you investing time? You can make money, lose it, and make it back. But time is your only truly precious resource. Once it is gone…you don't get it back. Commit to investing your time in the pursuit of your Definiteness of Purpose and you will feel the faith and confidence in yourself grow.

When I start working with new clients, I carefully review the Personal Success Equation with them. Entrepreneurship can be very lonely because entrepreneurs are trying to do everything themselves relying solely on their own passion and talent. This comes from being taught to work alone in school. But business is a team sport and collaboration is essential for innovation and success. While my clients are strong in their passion and talents, the areas that are often weakest for them in their Personal Success Equations are usually the Associations they have as well as the lack of Faith in themselves.

After years of mentoring clients, I can honestly say having the right Associations are the best and quickest way to build your Faith and confidence in yourself. Those new associations can include having the right mentor, people on your team who are strong where you are weak, the right advisors, and the right industry collaborators. When you have the right people around you and you have a bad day, they step up to bolster you and keep you focused on the big picture. They help transform your fear into faith. Having the team moving together toward your definiteness of purpose is much more fun and rewarding that trying to do it all alone.

To ensure you truly succeed and overcome any obstacles that may stand in your way, you definitely need the right association and faith. Having faith in yourself, your mission and your ability to succeed, will help you persevere when times are difficult and propel you to even greater heights of success.

When I wrote *Think and Grow Rich for Women*, I asked Sara O'Meara and Yvonne Fedderson to share their thoughts on Faith and I was so impressed with what they shared that I am including it here as well. Sara and Yvonne are the founders of Childhelp, the largest non-profit dedicated to the prevention and treatment of child abuse saving over 11 million children from the horrors of abuse. (**www.childhelp.org**) They have been nominated for the Nobel Peace Prize ten times. They are dear friends, mentors of mine, and true angels on earth. Here is some of what they shared:

The Faith Tree: Growing, Surviving and Thriving

Growing

Money doesn't grow on trees but faith does. Worry is interest paid on trouble before it is due but Faith is like money in the bank. Napoleon Hill wrote, "Faith is the starting point of all accumulation of riches." We often find we are where we choose to be. Faith gives us the courage to make necessary changes in our lives and allows us to grow in a clear and positive manner. Every dream shaped into a goal begins with the faith that if we plant a seed of hope, tend our garden with care and survive the storms that are sure to come our way, a thriving success will bloom.

When we began building our nonprofit, Childhelp, faith was the foundation; it became the soil in which we planted each advocacy center, residential treatment facility, hotline, adoption agency, foster care and group home. Soon we saw the fruits of our labor branching into national legislation and flowering into prevention education. We knew that advocating for abused children was part of God's plan and we would be guided through each season. We worked hard in the field every day but never doubted that a Higher Power was enriching our soil, nourishing our vision and ensuring the sun shone on our children.

But what if you have no faith? What if difficult times and disappointment leave you lacking the belief that you can be successful? The good news is that you can grow and know that you are growing. You can become stronger in faith, more knowledgeable in spirit and see it in yourself. A popular biblical parable posits that the smallest grain of faith, as miniscule as a mustard seed, can uproot trees and move mountains. Before you plant your tree, define successful growth and determine what will make your soil "rich."

When you choose to live your life in faith, desires and hopes will magnetize to you and you will begin to rise above the clouds. You will see beyond all seeming limitations and value yourself and others more. So ask yourself: Are you solely seeking monetary wealth or the richness of spirit that comes from being in the service of others?

Surviving

After the devastating attacks on America on September 11, 2001, a scorched tree with broken branches was discovered in the rubble at Ground Zero. It was a small Callery pear tree that had managed to sprout a few leaves beneath the destruction. Its discovery rejuvenated the spirits of weary rescue workers and became a symbol of recovery. They were determined to keep the tree alive and worked with local parks & recreation professionals to plant it at the site where so much had been lost. Even when a terrible storm uprooted it, the tree was replanted and once again flowered with white blossoms of hope. It was named "The Survivor Tree."

Children who have been abused and neglected come to us with their spirits scorched and their lives uprooted. At each Childhelp Residential Treatment Village, there is a garden where the little boys and girls in our care nurture fruits and vegetables from seed to plate, learning the cycle of growth but embodying the importance of survival. We teach that there is no challenge of the past that can stop the fulfillment of a fruitful future. Like "The Survivor Tree", they learn that a small seed can create something great that may be uprooted time and time again but always has the chance to branch out and become whole.

What if your past is blocking your progress or you keep experiencing setbacks? There is no need to look back except to acknowledge the lessons you have learned, taking only the positive from these experiences to draw upon in your future. Sorrow looks back, worry looks around and faith looks up. Napoleon Hill asserts, "Faith is the only known antidote to failure" and 2 Corinthians 4:13-18 promises, "Though outwardly we are wasting away, yet inwardly we are being renewed day by day. Four our light and momentary troubles are achieving for us eternal glory that far outweighs them all. So we fix our eyes not on what is seen, but what is unseen. For what is seen is temporary, but what is unseen is eternal." When you release your struggle to a Higher Power, you not only survive, you plant roots that will keep you strong forever.

Thriving

Once you have grown in trust and survived the tests of your faith, you will enter a period of great power and responsibility. You will be victorious over your environment, weaknesses and all obstacles in your life when you follow God's path. This is your time to thrive! You have become confident in overcoming struggles and watched your dreams manifest. Suddenly, you can see the way in which a bright idea becomes a concrete reality.

This is the final plateau of faith that Napoleon Hill so deftly defines, "Faith is the 'eternal elixir' which gives life, power, and action to the impulse of thought."

It is important to live and do your work in such a way that when others see you, their evaluation is the evidence of Faith. When that happens, you reap the rewards you rightfully deserve. One of the most important lessons we have learned is that success is not an endpoint and our thoughts shape each and every day. Our thoughts are our actions so positive thinking begets positive results. What's another word for positive thinking? Faith.

Matthew 12:33-37 speaks about using success responsibly, "The good person out of his good treasure brings forth good, and the evil person out of his evil treasure brings forth evil." The verse sums up perfectly, "Either make the tree good and its fruit good, or make the tree bad and its fruit bad, for the tree is known by its fruit." Thriving, then, is not just about how high you grow, it is ensuring that your branches never sprout poison bitter blossoms but rather that your fruit is always healthy and sweet.

Sara and Yvonne's Faith Tree certainly shows the depth of their giving natures, as well as their FAITH in each and every one of us. Let's review just a couple of their thoughts followed by how we can apply them to ourselves:

"Every dream shaped into a goal begins with the faith that if we plant a seed of hope, tend our garden with care and survive the storms that are sure to come our way, a thriving success will bloom."

Your definiteness of purpose (goal) when nurtured with action and faith will overcome obstacles and create the success you deserve.

"We worked hard in the field every day but never doubted that a Higher Power was enriching our soil, nourishing our vision and ensuring the sun shone on our children."

Work hard every day but never doubt that a higher power is enriching your soil, nourishing your vision and ensuring that the sun will shine on your endeavors.

If you are struggling to find ways to cultivate your own garden of faith, review the passage from Napoleon Hill and begin to harvest confidence in yourself.

Self-Confidence Formula

Resolve to throw off the influences of any unfortunate environment, and to build your own life to ORDER. Taking inventory of mental assets and liabilities, you will discover that your greatest weakness is lack of self-confidence. This handicap can be surmounted, and timidity translated into courage, through the aid of auto-suggestion. The application of this principle may be made through a simple arrangement of positive thought impulses stated in writing, memorized, and repeated, until they become a part of the working equipment of the subconscious faculty of your mind.

First. I know that I have the ability to achieve the object of my Definite Purpose in life; therefore, I DEMAND of myself persistent, continuous action toward its attainment, and I here and now promise to render such action.

Second. I realize the dominating thoughts of my mind will eventually reproduce themselves in outward, physical action, and gradually transform themselves into physical reality; therefore, I will concentrate my thoughts, for thirty minutes daily, upon the task of thinking of the person I intend to become, thereby creating in my mind a clear mental picture.

Third. I know through the principle of auto-suggestion, any desire that I persistently hold in my mind will eventually seek expression through some practical means of attaining the object back of it, therefore, I will devote ten minutes dialing to demanding of myself the development of SELF-CONFIDENCE.

Fourth. I have clearly written down a description of my DEFINITE CHIEF AIM in life, and I will never stop trying until I shall have developed sufficient self-confidence for its attainment.

Fifth. I fully realize that no wealth or position can long endure, unless built on truth and justice; therefore, I will engage in no transaction which does not benefit all whom it affects. I will succeed by attracting to myself the forces I wish to use, and the cooperation of other people. I will induce others to serve me, because of my willingness to serve others. I will eliminate hatred, envy, jealously, selfishness, and cynicism, by developing love for all humanity, because I know that a negative attitude towards others can never bring me success. I will cause others to believe in me, because I will believe in them, and in myself.

I will sign my name to this formula, commit it to memory, and repeat it aloud once a day, with full FAITH that it will gradually influence my THOUGHTS and ACTIONS so that I will become a self-reliant, and successful person.

As I end this chapter on Faith, I want to share how I acknowledge and request support from a higher power. I have strong faith in God and believe in his abundant love. My faith was dramatically tested in December of 2012 when my youngest son died. We are not supposed to outlive our children. My life went into neutral, or into the land of numb, for several years. In fact, I almost retired because I was unable to find the joy in life. It was the people around me that challenged me, and yes, I believe my son even whispered in my ear, "Get over it Mom...you are still here for a reason. There is more for you to do." At the same time someone sent me the book, *The Prayer of Jabez* by Bruce Wilkinson

The Prayer of Jabez is a simple 4 line prayer found in the Old Testament 1 Chronicles 4: 9-10 that reads:

> **'Oh, that You would bless me indeed,**
> **and enlarge my territory,**
> **that Your hand would be with me, and that**
> **You would keep me**
> **from evil, that I may not cause pain.'**

This prayer has brought me great peace and faith. I say it every day and before every interview or speech so that I may add the greatest value each and every time. Below I share how each line impacts me each time I say it.

Oh, that you would bless me indeed – Dear God, thank you for blessing me with this opportunity

Enlarge my territory – Allow me to reach a larger audience than I can imagine

Your hand would be with me – Use me as your vessel and help me deliver the right message for the people before me

Keep me from evil, that I may not cause pain – Help me make sure the message is a force for good and adding value.

In closing, I want to remind you that you are FABULOUS! No matter what you have been through, or what may have stopped you in your tracks…you are still here for a reason! And you can help others going through what you have survived. Have faith in yourself and use that faith to help others find the faith in themselves. And then ask yourself

Have you added value to someone's life today?

I have faith in you!

Sharon Lechter www.sharonlechter.com

Author of *Think and Grow Rich for Women*, Co-author of *Exit Rich, Three Feet From Gold, Outwitting the Devil, Success* and *Something Greater, The 13 Steps to Riches, Rich Dad Poor Dad* and 14 other Rich Dad books.

Erik "Mr. Awesome" Swanson

FAITH REMOVES LIMITATIONS AND OPENS UP OUR WORLD

The late, great Napoleon Hill once wrote, "Riches begin in the form of thought! The amount is limited only by the person in whose mind the thought is put into motion. Faith removes limitations!"

What is Faith? Where does Faith come from? How do we sustain Faith in our lives?

I believe that Faith is an 'all-knowing' entity that lives deep in our souls. It is what I also refer to as our "Internal Belief System," or "IBS." We all have an internal belief system in which we call upon each and every day. We may not actually notice or realize we are calling upon it. But we are. Have you ever noticed yourself actually talking to yourself maybe not out loud, but under our breath or even quietly in our heads? And, you actually answer yourself as well in that same fashion. *That* is the voice of Faith!

When I was traveling to speak on various stages throughout the world and sharing the stage with the one and only Jim Rohn, I recall he and I sitting down from time to time, having deep philosophical conversations.

One of those conversations with Mr. Rohn was focused around Faith and our belief systems. He shared with me that he believed all of the 'answers' were all already inside of us. I asked him, "What do you mean?" He replied, "I believe that we all simply need to adjust our thinking patterns.

Rather than searching 'outside' of us, we should be searching 'inside' of us." He explained that he believed God ensured all of the answers we seek deep inside of each and every one of us. The goal is to search internally, rather than externally and we shall all find the answers we truly seek.

But the issue most people around the world have is that they are always seeking and searching for answers externally. The grass seems to always be greener across the street. This mindset is detrimental to success for those individuals. It's time for people to have Faith in themselves, knowing that our higher source has given each of us the tools to excel in our lives beyond our wildest and amazing dreams. In fact, the world and planet grows in such a positive way as one community and entity when everyone is in alignment with this mindset theory.

Have you ever heard of the saying: "If you want to go fast, go alone. If you want to go far, go with a team!?" Once we all, as a community, vow to be in alignment with the Faith mindset or "IBS," a movement starts to form! This is so powerful and vital for our world as a whole. And it all starts with Faith!

Think of a team; for instance, a football team. Once you have the alignment of the Faith mindset embodied not only in the minds, but also in the souls of each and every player on the team, you start to form a community that is unstoppable. And, on the flip side of that coin, once you allow a "bad apple" mindset to spread within the community, or in this case the football team… it starts to corrupt the other team members' mindsets. This negative mindset or non-faith mindset will slowly and ultimately bring down the rest of the team or community unless two things happen: 1) You change the negative individual's mindset into the positive mindset embodied by the other members of the community. 2) You extract or cut the negative "bad apple" individual out of the group or community.

This concept shows up in many areas of our lives. Yet, most people never make those decisions to actually do one of those two actions. Most people simply hope things will change. You can't change the people around you, but you can change the people around you! Let me be one to tell you the simple truth in that most people never change. It's what my mentor, Brian Tracy, would always tell me in that people show you their true colors if you actually pay attention. So, pay attention! Success leaves clues - so does failure.

Your goal should be to seek out or build communities in which the Faith alignment mindset will be prevalent, consistent, and sustainable. This is what I set out to do once I had my "satori" moment. A satori moment is what you have an awakening... or what the Japanese call "instant enlightenment." Years ago, I never really considered the fact that who I was surrounding myself with made a difference in my success equation. It does! Now, and for the past 10 years, I have been extremely conscious and aware of who I allow to be in my space, community, businesses, and even personal world. I only seek out those who have the Faith mindset.

So, where does this Faith mindset ultimately come from? That's easy, it comes from within! It's like I said before... it's a knowing, it's a belief system, and it's an understanding in yourself through your higher source. Give yourself permission to allow it into your life. Give yourself permission to enjoy the success benefits in which having Faith will gift to you.

I recall many of my friends throughout the years commenting to me that they love the fact that I always seem to have an abundance mindset. They see that I always have a calmness about me and a knowing that things will always work out. It truly comes from having Faith! I believe having Faith in yourself is absolutely vital. I believe our higher source gave all of us this ability to tap into Faith at any given moment of the day. In fact, once you truly master the art of tapping in to your Faith, you start to experience what I call the "Ultimate Belief System," or "UBS." This is a **knowing** that it will all work out for the best. Having "UBS" is so powerful as you start to turn it on more and more throughout the day. Your decisions tend to get easier and always seem to land in the success field rather than the failure field. This is how you sustain your Faith... by continuing to use it daily. Consistency is key!

As Napoleon Hill explained to us early on, Faith removes limitations, it truly does! Whenever I tap into my "UBS," I start to notice that success started to flow towards me rather than away. Once I started seeing this on a regular basis, I started to test it out. I would consciously be aware of the outcome when I chose different decisions...especially when there was a fork in the road. You know those for kin the road decisions when you feel the pressure of making a right or wrong decision? Those can be brutal. But I decided to tap into my "UBS" mindset and track the outcomes. Wow, the results were amazing! I actually found out that I was making *right* decisions on about a 90% rate! This was crazy, I thought! But I kept on testing this theory and guess what happened? 90% is what kept on happening! Ok, I'm on to something here. Ladies and gentlemen, Faith and my "UBS" theory is here to stay. I'm sold on it now!

I suggest you give it a go as well in your life. You literally have nothing to lose by incorporating Faith into your daily habits. It's truly one of my habitudes now and is here to stay forever.

Oh, and if you are still wondering if I ever ended up kissing my kindergarten crush, Kirsten, well, I can't tell you that yet. But what I can tell you is that I had so much Faith that she would at least accompany me to the schoolground swing sets during at least one of the recess breaks coming up. I mean, if I didn't believe in myself or have Faith then I was doomed to succeed right from the start. So, what do I have to lose? - absolutely nothing! Onwards to ask Kirsten to walk with me and swing on the playground swing sets. Ugh, I'm so nervous to ask her. But I reminded myself that she may be nervous as well. And heck, maybe she won't notice that I'm so nervous. Hmmm, fat chance for that mainly because of the sweat pouring down my face and my sweaty palms. Ok, new plan, don't let her touch my hands cause that would be a sure giveaway that I'm super nervous. Ok, here goes! Wish me luck... or better yet, wish me Faith!

ERIK SWANSON

About Erik "Mr. Awesome" Swanson: As an Award-Winning International Keynote Speaker and 10 Time #1 International Best-Selling Author, Erik "Mr. Awesome" Swanson is in great demand around the world! He speaks to an average of more than one million people per year. He can be seen on Amazon Prime TV in the very popular show *SpeakUP* TV. Mr. Swanson has the honor to have been invited to speak to many universities such as University of California (UCSD), California State University (Cal State Fullerton), University of Southern California (USC), Grand Canyon University (GCU), and the Business and Entrepreneurial School of Harvard University. He is also a Faculty Member of CEO Space International and is a recurring keynoter at Vistage Executive Coaching. Erik also joins the Ted Talk Family with his latest TEDx speech called "A Dose of Awesome."

Erik got his start in the self development world by mentoring directly under the infamous Brian Tracy. Quickly climbing to become the top trainer around the world from a group of over 250 hand picked trainers, Erik started to surround himself with the best of the best and soon started to be inviting to speak on stages along side such greats as Jim Rohn, Bob Proctor, Les Brown, Sharon Lechter, Jack Canfield, and Joe Dispenza... just to name a few. Erik has created and developed the super-popular Habitude Warrior Conference, which has a two-year waiting list and includes 33 top named speakers from around the world. It is a 'Ted Talk' style event which has quickly climbed to one of the top 10 events not to miss in the United States! He is the creator, founder, and CEO of the Habitude Warrior Mastermind and Global Speakers Mastermind. His motto is clear... "NDSO!": No Drama – Serve Others!

Author's Website: *www.SpeakerErikSwanson.com*
Book Series Website & Author's Bio: *www.The13StepstoRiches.com*

Jon Kovach Jr.

THINK HIGH TO RISE

"Faith is the 'eternal elixir' which gives life, power, and action to the impulse of thought." ~**Napoleon Hill**

We arrived at the trailhead, preparing for the 8-mile hike ahead of us. In my short eight years of living, I was sure about two things: first, my family had hiked these mountains for decades because at the end of that trail was a secret lake (still secret today) where my ancestors caught the most incredible fish in the country, and the second surety was that it's Kovach tradition that each family member has the distinct honor to fish from our special spot at the secret lake.

It was my first time hiking these mountains. I was so excited and only had one thing on my mind: fulfilling our family legacy. I naively hopped out of the car to begin a journey that I was gravely unprepared to endure.

Instead of training for this hike and packing only the essentials—as any intelligent outdoorsmen would—I procrastinated in my preparations. I thought it would be wise to fill my backpack with the eight-year-old essentials for a campout. The list must have included Cheetos, beef jerky, candy, lots of hot cocoa, a cassette Walkman to listen to my music, and the thickest, most durable hiking and backpacking equipment I owned. All of those things accumulated to weigh in far above the suggested weight limit for a young backpacker.

We started up the trail. Not even one hundred feet into the journey, I glanced up the mountain and witnessed that the first two miles were completely uphill and consisted of switchbacks (a trail that winds back and forth, designed for elevation gain). I immediately regretted my choices as the weight of an oversized and disproportionate backpack dug into my shoulders. With eight miles still to go, I knew I was doomed and had made a colossal mistake.

With each step, my backpack grew heavier. The pain in my shoulders intensified. I felt cramping and soreness in my feet, calves, hips, and back. My legs were weak. I reacted how any other eight-year-old might in this exact scenario—I cried, whimpered, whined, and complained. Every second in this pain magnified the negativity I was spewing. The childish swear words were flowing like a freshly-opened fire hydrant—the foulest vulgarity including shoot, darn, dang, dagnabbit, fudge, and any other inconceivable superlative could be heard by anyone within earshot.

Fed up by the whining and complaining, my father sat me down on a rock on the side of the trail. He looked into my eyes and paused. I knew he was frustrated and wanted to rip into me with chastisement. Instead, he firmly reminded me of something I had misunderstood in all the stories of my family's tradition. He said, "We (Kovaches) work hard and never complain. We're honest, and we always do our best." He didn't offer to carry my backpack or lighten the load. He didn't even ask if I was ok. It's like he knew that because I was his son, I could overcome this painful trial. My father offered support, but ultimately wanted me to deal with the consequences of my decisions.

Out of all the fatherly things he could have said and done to me, he chose to remind me of who we were as Kovaches. I wasn't expecting a pep talk or reminder of our family mantra, but his words sank deep, and I'll never forget how his expectations and beliefs in who we were made me believe that no matter the difficulty ahead, I was to proceed by working hard, never complaining, being honest, and doing my best.

Before standing up to give the trail another go, my father grinned and reminded me of another family tradition I had overlooked. He said, "Don't forget that after you make it to the lake, you must drop your pack and run back down the trail and help me carry my backpack. That's been a family honor for years." I WAS SHOCKED! Not only do we hike the eight miles to our secret lake, we then go back down the trail to carry our elder's backpack too! "But if you don't think you can do it, then I guess you'll just break that tradition too," he said. Reluctantly, I replied, "No, no. I can do it. If you did it, then I can do it."

I had never witnessed this tradition. I had no proof that my father had ever run up the trail, dropped off his backpack at the secret lake, then ran back down the path to assist his father with his heavy backpack as well. It seemed absurd that they'd expect me, the unprepared, distracted, and naive eight-year-old, to carry out these wishes. Without any evidence of these claims, I still proceeded with Faith up the trail. There was no way I would ever break tradition or disappoint my family legacy.

The expectation and belief now planted in my heart somehow gave me a new gear of energy and determination. Instead of whining and whimpering with every step I took on the trail, my complaining lessened to every other step. Then every third. Even though I felt hot spots on my feet where blisters were developing and the weight of the backpack was piercing my tiny shoulders, I slowly made my way up the switchbacks. Repeating in my mind my father's words, "Work hard. Don't Complain. Be Honest. Always do your best," I crawled up the trail and inched closer to the secret lake. Even though each step was excruciating, I repeated that mantra out loud.

Work hard. Don't Complain. Be Honest. Always do your best. Those words fueled me. The more I repeated them, the less pain I felt. My attitude changed. I was more enamored by the power of a Kovach who could make it up to the secret lake only to turn around and help others on the trail as well. The focus was never on me as I thought; if my backpack hurts, I can't imagine how others are feeling. I repeated this mantra so much, it became a song. Minutes on the trail converted into hours of hiking. Completely engrossed in the singing and repeating that mantra, I reached the secret lake. I almost walked right into the lake because I was so focused!

I quickly dropped my backpack, tightened my tiny shoelaces, sprinted back down the trail, and met my father about halfway up the mountain. He smiled at me, removed his backpack, and handed it to this newly-transformed super kid who was on a mission to perpetuate his family's legacy. I put his pack on and immediately realized how much heavier his bag was than mine. I sang confidently, "Work hard. Don't Complain. Be Honest. Always do your best." And up the trail, we went until I dropped off his pack at the secret lake. LEGACY ACHIEVED!

It was the most challenging thing I had ever done. But what surprised me the most is that I didn't die, collapse, or even suffer for days on end. Instead, I lived and had the most incredible time of my life, making memories of fishing with my father from our secret spot. The fish were definitely worth it and I had expanded what I knew I could achieve.

My father taught me the importance of reaping what you sow. If you believe in greatness and overcoming difficult things, then you will do just that. If you focus on positive things and serving others, your life will be exponentially better. If you believe in greatness, you will acquire it too.

I had Faith that if I could take one step forward, then that was one more foot in the right direction of our secret sport-fishing spot.

Faith and belief are the formulae for curating something into existence. Faith is the second step to riches because it's the visualization and belief in attaining desire.

An old verse by Walter D. Wintle reads:

> *...You've got to think high to rise*
> *Life's battles don't always go*
> *To the stronger or faster man,*
> *But soon or late the man who wins*
> *Is the man who thinks he can!*

You can be the creator of your own fortunes by developing Faith in positive beliefs. Then your mind will translate that Faith into its physical equivalent. I invite you to read the following chapters submitted by our contributing authors with an open heart and seek to expand your understanding and application of the second step to riches—Faith.

Every year, my family carries out the same tradition, and I repeat the mantra as I sprint up the mountain, drop my pack off at the secret lake, and then hike back down the trail to assist others walking up the path. There have been times where I've hiked over twenty miles in one day, repeating this process. Mastering this positive habitude (habit and attitude) of Faith has given me an unfair advantage over others in achieving personal goals, overcoming challenges, and accelerating my successes in every area of my life. It's become my ultimate secret to success.

Now that you know my secret, you'll need to read the next volume in this series (*The 13 Steps To Riches: Volume 3 Auto Suggestion*) to discover how my desire and Faith transmuted into me competing in the decathlon.

JON KOVACH JR.

About Jon Kovach Jr.: Jon is an award-winning and international motivational speaker and global mastermind leader. Jon has helped multibillion-dollar corporations, including Coldwell Banker Commercial, Outdoor Retailer Cotopaxi, and the Public Relations Student Society of America, exceed their annual sales goals. In his work as an accountability coach and mastermind facilitator, Jon has helped thousands of professionals overcome their challenges and achieve their goals by implementing his 4 Irrefutable Laws of High Performance.

Jon is Founder and Chairman of Champion Circle, a networking association that combines highperformance based networking activities and recreational fun to create connection capital and increases prosperity for professionals.

Jon is the Mastermind Facilitator and Team Lead of the Habitude Warrior Mastermind and the Global Speakers Mastermind & Masterclass founded by Speaker Erik "Mr. Awesome" Swanson.

Jon speaks on a number of topics including accountability, The 4 Irrefutable Laws of High Performance, and The Power of Mastermind Methodologies. He is a #1 Best-Selling Author and was recently featured on SpeakUp TV, an Amazon Prime TV series. He stars in over 100 speaking stages, podcasts, and live international summits on an annual basis.

Author's website: *www.JonKovachJr.com*
Book Series Website & Author's Bio: *www.The13StepsToRiches.com*

Amado Hernandez

WITH A HUNGERING FAITH YOU WILL SUCCEED

I asked forgiveness from our creator, committed to hungering in Faith, and started embracing my professional journey, which forever changed my life.

When I attended college, I spoke with many different people, studied various subjects and cultures. One gentleman approached me during these susceptible and malleable moments in my life and told me that Faith was people's opinions. He poisoned my mind with the belief that if there was no faith, philosophical or scientific explanations could still exist and thrive without feeling.

Those times in college were the worst years of my life because my values and beliefs in Faith had been challenged and compromised everything my grandmother and mother had taught me.

It took me a great deal of researching, seeking, reaching, and reading about Faith, before I started seeing that universal truth of hungering Faith again.

Faith is the substance of things not seen and the evidence of reality. Faith is believing and having a vision. Like the wind, we can't see it and we can't touch it, but it's real and powerful.

Faith is an action, and it moves you towards any vision or goal. It's human nature to want to see things before we believe in them. Our Faith is the opposite. Faith is moving into what you think and includes your vision into that space so that your reality can be objective.

For instance, when I first wanted to become a Real Estate Broker, I aspired to lead a group of agents but didn't quite have my broker's license at that time. Although I didn't have any agents yet to steward For instance, when I first wanted to become a Real Estate Broker, I aspired to lead a group of agents but didn't quite have my broker's license at that time. Although I didn't have any agents yet to steward over, I began with my Faith, started building my career, and learned as much as possible.

Faith can save your life and help you make it out alive

It was probably one of the most challenging times for our professionals in Real Estate and my market, when most of the major players went under financially. Through Faith, I believed that meeting a couple of people who had access to distress sales would make a huge difference. I was a guest speaker at a church in Los Angeles. Unbeknownst to me, there was a gentleman in the audience by the name of Tony Evers. He was the CFO of a bank. At the time, I had no idea that this bank had asked me if I wanted to list some of the distressed properties his bank had. The next question he had was "How many can your company handle?" To which I responded, "Let's start with 25." It only took a week for me and I already started getting the assets!

Having Faith in my destination and that my plans would work, I walked up and spoke with Mr. Evers. He was impressed with my proposals and wanted to do business with me. A month passed without hearing from him until one of his subordinates called me and said they wanted to start giving me access to those deals. They asked, "How many can you handle?" I had no idea, but I said, "Why don't we start with 25." Then the deals started pouring into our laps.

Had I given up as most people did in 2008, I wouldn't be here to share this chapter with you because, by Faith, I believed I would meet someone I needed to achieve my desires and aspirations.

I've met some of the most influential people in my life through the principle of Faith, like Erik "Mr. Awesome" Swanson, my mentors, my agents, my teams, and even my family.

Over the past few years, I've been overly busy training people, developing teams, and seeing significant results, but I've always continued my quest of hunger and steadfast Faith in meeting more people who will help me ascend to my goals and dreams.

I'm just a simple kid who grew up in humble beginnings in Mexico, the state of Michoacán, in a small town called Villamar where the soil is so rich that everything you plant grows super-fast. I live with an active Faith. To do business at an entirely different level, you've got to have a hungering faith. My Faith has moved my family into other states, and I have opportunities to travel the world.

Now, Adriana (my lovely fiancé) and I have entirely changed our fates and get to travel to Florida, Colombia, Panama, Cancun, Mexico City, Nashville, TN, and other regions throughout the world. The more you hunger with Faith, the more your world will change. I'm a living testament to that.

I continue to hunger by Faith and become associated with high-energy people, and the only way I can do that is by being like-minded and desire to share that vision and passion with others.

Work towards results, visualize everything possible, and you will have remarkable experiences and a fulfilled life

I come from a humble background; we had chickens and pigs in our backyard, a community water well where we dug the water out. But my paternal grandmother and my mother were the most amazing teachers on Faith. They taught me to work diligently and focus, and intentional connections and our creator will never hold anything back from us.

My visualizations in sales and career have fully outperformed my expectations in over 32 years in business. My grandmother's and mother's principles and lessons on Faith have more than transpired in my results and life as a whole.

My Grandma's words will inspire many for generations to come, "Be grateful, have a good attitude, and you will prosper." We're all destined for greatness if we work for it. Our creator allowed us to define and acquire our excellence.

We need to raise our posterity and future generations on the principle of hungering Faith

I have three boys and one girl. They're all super-achievers like me. I've taught them the importance of having Faith and executing their Faith from a very young age. That means there's no doubt, and you're not going to see the fruits of your labors immediately. You're acting on that Faith and hungering to keep it alive. Naturally, the Law of Reciprocity will reap the benefits promised by my grandma and mother.

When you first plant seeds of Faith within you, dig the hole, cover the seed, water it, nurture and nourish it. You will face obstacles like theoretical birds that will uproot your focus and progress. If you want your Faith to bear fruits like a tree, you will need to be solid and steadfast in your hunger.

I'm proud to share that my children have nurtured their hungering Faith as instructed and have all become very successful in their respective professions with their families. I have grandkids now, and I'm super proud of them. When I'm at the table with my family, I repeat the lessons of hungering Faith to them only to perpetuate my grandma's wisdom.

Faith requires honorability

What's wrong with our culture, society, and general beliefs as humans today, is that we are naturally skeptical, fueling the rivals of Faith. If only everyone were taught the principles and steps of Think And Grow Rich by Napoleon Hill, we'd understand that Faith backed by a burning desire ignites the will to win and grow in prosperity.

Another way to describe hungering Faith is patriotic Faith. We must associate with more things that unite us together rather than divide us. As we connect with like-minded people who have Faith like ours, we become world changers.

Skepticism continues to harm one's Faith. As a whole, when we distrust our intuitions, we weaken our hungering Faith leading us to our aspirations. I never back down from my Faith, and if I couldn't comply, I would explain why. Today, you have so many people that want to make themselves feel good with no substance. If we ground ourselves on the studies and teachings of Napoleon Hill, Earl Nightingale, Jim Rohn, Brian Tracy, Erik Swanson, Jon Kovach Jr., and other great leaders who carry on their promises and the universal truths of success, we will eliminate skepticism in society amongst us.

But you know, we need to share those same principles and have that unbelieving world believe, and we need to share that vision that we were living in the greatest country ever, and everything is possible. Politically, academically, and financially.

Too many people and skeptics feel that it must be an accident to achieve great things because we are either not of the correct color, gender, or social status. Whatever you're looking for is subsequently looking for you also. By Faith, you have to move towards that of which you are searching.

**Build the muscle of Faith to overcome
its rivals every day**

I have an engineering background, and scientifically, a bumblebee cannot fly per its shape, weight, wing size, and body configuration. Despite the odds, a bee does fly, and a bumblebee's flying nature is one of the most abundant life sources to our very earth. You, too, were built to defy odds.

You will still have opportunities amidst your failures as you learn to overcome challenges through Faith. Failure is essential when we're pushing ourselves to break through our ceilings, our self-limitations, our own beliefs. And when you fail, you become open, and you start asking why. And when you discover your why, that's when you become unstoppable.

AMADO HERNANDEZ

About Amado Hernandez: Amado was born in Mexico of humble beginnings and raised in Los Angeles, California. As an avid reader, Amado always focused on self-development. He coaches sales professionals to make six and seven figures in real estate.

Amado believes in a progressive culture, one people-centric where clients' dreams come true and salespeople thrive; at the end of the day, we all want to be respected and pursue our happiness. My goal is to leave a legacy-making a difference in people's lives.

With 33 years of Real Estate experience, Mr. ABC Amado Hernandez successfully operates and grows his Excellence Empire Real Estate Moreno Valley office. Broker/Owner Amado first opened his doors in 1995, and Excellence currently has over 60 offices in Southern California, Las Vegas, Merida Yucatan, Mexico, with over 900 Agents. He is also part owner of a highly successful Mortgage company, Excellence Mortgage, and owner of Empire Escrow Services. Mr. Amado is also involved with his community and currently serves as Director at Inland Valley Association of Realtors and will be the President-Elect for 2021.

Author's Website: *www.ExcellenceEmpireRE.com*
Book Series Website & Author's Bio: *www.The13StepstoRiches.com*

Angelika Ullsperger

FAITH IS THE KNOWLEDGE OF YOUR FUTURE

Few things are assured in life. Glitz and status rub off quickly, and friends may come and go. What we *can* hold close in this tumultuous life is Faith. Faith lives in the depth of the soul. It can be nurtured or rooted out, and it can morph and evolve. The spiritual conceptions we hold dear originate in various ways. Family, friends, and the environment can shape these notions early in life, or they may be formed through learned experiences. Faith is rewarded when events come to pass as you believe they should, and in this way, Faith multiplies.

Faith can be an essential part of one's life or of no concern at all. One can orient their life in the direction of their Faith, or Faith may grow around some pursuit or calling. Regardless of what it means to you, you may wish to consider its worth. This taboo topic is usually avoided at all costs in conversation. Still, I've found that many people are more than willing to share their Faith, provided you assure them that you will listen and question without berating. It may suit you to melt down these spiritual tokens into glistening nuggets of wisdom.

Faith is the knowledge of your future. It is knowing what you desire and having faith in your future. Knowing it is only a matter of time and persistence. It is when you have tried everything but know there is still an answer; when you have lost everything but have enough Faith to know it will be all right and that you will recover.

Faith protects you from any force which pulls on you as you travel on the path towards your dreams. A world in which you have acquired this knowledge is a world in which you can reach your full potential.

Your mindset and thoughts shape your reality. Things will be okay in the end if you believe so, or if you believe that they won't, you will create a reality in which things are NOT OKAY. Your future truly lies in Faith. Create your ideal future by cultivating Faith in yourself. Don't allow thoughts of low self-worth to creep in. Be mindful, and notice when the negative thoughts sneak in. Conquer them. Speak over them until they no longer have the confidence to show themselves.

There were times when I was stuck outside, barefoot, walking around at night, unsure of where I could go for safety. But even then, I kept Faith that everything would be okay. That is Faith— knowing that everything will be OKAY. It's just a matter of time. Every second that passes, you are closer to a better period in your life. Having developed this Faith that everything would be okay helped create a future reality in which that was true. Back in middle school, I created a picture of a hand held sign saying *HOPE*. Everything about that image was genuinely on point and it was shaded just wonderfully. I'll admit, I tend to be overly critical towards myself, but this was different. I created a beautiful hyper-realistic hand holding a large but simple poster. "*HOPE*"

It didn't need to say anything more. To me, Faith is hope. No matter what happens, if you keep hope, you keep going. At the end of every night, before you fall asleep, you are reminded of hope for a new day. To this day, I still have the picture on my wall.

Let Faith be your shield as you push through the trials and tribulations of life. In the end, no matter what you must go through, the knowledge and understanding of Faith are what propel you forward. Have Faith in yourself and your skills. Depending on your beliefs, you may or may not be faithful in a religious sense, but regardless of the belief of a higher power, there can still be Faith.

The strength of the Faith you have will directly correlate to the subconscious mind's ability to transmute your desires into reality. Without Faith, you will unknowingly create lousy luck just as quickly as you could create good fortune for yourself. Many people develop Faith from their environments, but not everyone is that lucky. We are fortunate that, just like desire, Faith is a state of mind that can be cultivated and strengthened.

By delving deeper into Faith and the information around it, genuinely learning, developing into alignment, you will better understand it; the aspects, the history, and every part in which you understand that you can use to strengthen your Faith.

It is written that anyone can develop Faith through the use of auto suggestion. This is important. Throughout life, your brain develops many, many neurological connections. Neurons are the fundamental building blocks of the brain, and we are constantly developing new connections. In addition, neurons get strengthened by recurring actions, events, emotions, and many other things. When we practice auto suggestion, we create new neural connections based on the information we repeat. Every time a phrase is repeated, the connection strengthens, and the neurons with old, opposing viewpoints weaken. This is a simplified explanation of why auto suggestion works. It changes the brain, thus changing the subconscious mind.

There are even more benefits to Faith. Once you develop a strong enough Faith, you will notice how some worries lose strength. They cannot beat the power of your belief in the future.

If you are to build a wealthy life, you will need Faith to support what you are building. Every strong structure needs a sturdy frame. It won't all come together at once, so Faith is set first to hold all the pieces in place.

Once you get along further in your path, you will see how Faith was one of the strongest helping hands when you were lost. The foundation of Faith lets you build upon yourself. If you fall, you get up, knowing it can still be done. Faith fuels resilience in the path to a healthy and wealthy life, for only through the storm does the bright sun shine.

Nothing works immediately. Sometimes you will feel as if you are making no progress, but be faithful. Every day that you practice, every day that you continue, you're further developing these skills. One thing that stuck with me was something Les Brown said. He said, "Once the bamboo is planted, it takes five entire years of daily nurture and care for the bamboo to barely break the surface." Five years to break the soil, but once it does, it takes only five weeks, thirty-five days to grow ninety feet. Just like the bamboo roots, you need to take care of yourself, be patient, and have Faith. Take time to build your foundation. During those five years, there are many days where you don't see the results, but that doesn't mean that there is no progress. If no one had Faith that the bamboo would grow after five weeks, no one would put in the time and care to nurture it. The results exist in the future. You just need the Faith. The Faith in yourself will push you to doeverything you can, never giving up no matter how many times you fail,because you have built up your Faith. The only thing standing between you and your desires is time.

The concept of a "self-fulfilling prophecy" fits neatly with such examples of Faith. A person may have such Faith that their determination leads them to reach their goal. Whether conscientious of the fact or not, they have helped their Faith into reality. What meaning can be found in this endeavor? Personally, I have Faith that my life has a greater purpose than simply chasing whatever I fancy at any given moment. I derive my modus operandi from Faith! In trying times, this knowledge keeps me determined to walk the jagged road. Wherever life may take you, I ask that you let Faith be your ally.

ANGELIKA ULLSPERGER

About Angelika Ullsperger: Angelika is a serial entrepreneur from Baltimore, Maryland. She is a fashion designer, model, artist, photographer, and musician. Angelika has extensive and well rounded professional experience having worked as a business owner, carpenter, chef, graphic designer, manager, event planner, sales and product specialist, marketer, and coach. Angelika is now a #1 Best-Selling Author in the historic book series, The 13 Steps To Riches. She is a lifelong learner with a sincere and genuine interest in all things of the world with a major interest in the formal subject of abnormal psychology, neuroscience, and quantum physics.

Angelika prides herself as someone who has saved lives as a friend, first responder, EMT, and knowledgeable suicide prevention advocate. With a vast knowledge and experience in multiple professions, Angelika is also a proud honorable member of Phi Theta Kappa, The APA, the AAAS, and an FBLA (Future Business Leaders Association) Business Competition Finalist. She is Certified in basic coding and blockchain technology. Amongst the careers and vast experience, Angelika is an adventurer and avid dog lover.

Her ultimate goals and dreams are to make a lasting positive impact in people's lives through her wealth of knowledge and skillsets.

Author's Website: *www.Angelika.world*
Book Series Website & Author's Bio: *www.The13StepstoRiches.com*

Dr. Anthony M. Criniti IV

AS WEALTHY AS YOU BELIEVE

By rereading Chapter 3 in *Think and Grow Rich* by Napoleon Hill, I was quickly reminded of why I decided to become a coauthor to this series of *The 13 Steps to Riches*. Simple knowledge splashed with dashes of genius is what has made this publication so inspiring to generations of readers. This is one of those rare books that deserves deep analysis. In this chapter about Faith, the following quote demonstrates this point: "Riches begin in the form of thought! The amount is limited only by the person in whose mind the thought is put into motion. Faith removes limitations" (Hill, 2011, p. 104)! These few sentences can be said to sum up the whole book and the decades of Hill's conclusions analyzing the most successful people of his time. It seems simple, but there are layers of complex lessons hidden inside.

In essence, this chapter holds some of the biggest clues on how to think and grow rich. Actually, it elaborates indirectly on Hill's famous "secret" that was never directly stated in this book. That is, that "Anything the human mind can believe, the human mind can achieve" (Hill, 2011, p. 13). As the second step to riches is about Faith, it is tied to the hip of the belief system. Having faith in your business ideas is crucial to your success. After all, if you don't believe in it, then who will?

The power of injecting faith into our thought processes can be so strong that even money cannot escape its grip. From Principle 133 of *The Most Important Lessons in Economics and Finance*, "The belief in what money can do is what makes it powerful" (Criniti, 2014, p. 165). It is crucial for the citizens of a country to have faith that the nation's currency is strong. Actually, it is a matter of national security. If the people do not believe that their money has any value, then it immediately could be worthless (i.e., what occurs after extreme hyperinflation). *The form of money is expressed in physical reality, but the foundation of money is expressed in our total belief system that connects mind, body, and soul.* As stated in The Necessity of Finance, "As long as people believe a specific symbol, whether tangible or intangible, is fit to trade for goods or services, it will endure. Without the belief in the quality of the symbol, the monetary system may collapse and be exchanged for another" (Criniti, 2013, p. 29).

Some of the other highlights of Hill's Chapter 3 on Faith will be discussed next. First, he considers faith, love, and sex to be the most powerful of all the major positive emotions. "The mixing, or blending of these three emotions has the effect of opening a direct line of communication between the finite, thinking mind of man, and Infinite Intelligence" (Hill, 2011, p. 79). With deep reflection, the prior statement demonstrates intense consequences if applied correctly. That is, if you really want to be extremely knowledgeable and/or be connected to omniscience, then you must find ways to incorporate a cocktail of the above three positive emotions into your actions.

Ironically, the one main thing that this chapter demonstrated to me was that Napoleon Hill was probably not religious, but more likely a fully-committed scientist. Just by stating the words "Infinite Intelligence" instead of "God" tells us that he is looking at the universe from a different angle. More proof of his scientific outlook on life is when he discusses the miracles of Christianity. "The sum and substance of the teachings and the achievements of Christ, which may have been interpreted as 'miracles', were nothing more nor less than faith. If there are any such phenomena as 'miracles', they are produced only through the state of mind known as faith" (Hill, 2011, p. 91). In other words, he is going against what is typically taught in the Christian religion (especially during his era) by saying that the miracles of Christ are not as spectacular as depicted – they can happen every day by those who believe in their thoughts and actions. *With the right state of mind, anything impossible can happen anytime by anyone.*

Faith can also be interpreted to be very useful for your survival needs if applied properly. If you can deeply believe in what you desire to do or your purpose, then you can help save yourself or your family in life's worst case scenarios. Hill states, "... all thoughts which have been emotionalized, (given feeling) and mixed with faith, begin immediately to translate themselves into their physical equivalent or counterpart" (Hill, 2011, p. 81). Accordingly, if you can believe in your rescue plan in a survival situation, then you increase the likelihood of it occurring.

I found a similar pattern in my extensive research of some of the most famous survival stories for my book *The Survival of the Richest*. Many of the survivors had faith that God wanted them to survive their difficult struggles, which kept them going until the end (i.e., the Uruguayan Rugby team that survived a plane crash in the Andes Mountains) "... many survivors that I studied found relief in spirituality. A belief in a higher power enabled them to be very successful against their struggles" (Criniti, 2016, p. 117). This conclusion led me to list *proper emotional usage* and *spirituality* as secondary mental immediate survival essentials in my survival essentials list (Criniti, 2016, pp. 101–104).

Napoleon Hill continuously mentions various attributes of auto-suggestion. He even lists a mantra to be repeated daily called a Self-Confidence Formula. He discusses how daily repetition of certain positive thoughts can reconstruct your mind and your life. "It is a well-known fact that one comes, finally, to believe whatever one repeats to one's self, whether the statement be true or false" (Hill, 2011, p. 84). Although it is extremely important, you will have to wait for the next book in this series because it is the third step to riches.

Another example of the golden nuggets of wisdom from Hill in Chapter 3 is the quote: "The mind comes, finally, to take on the nature of the influences which dominate it" (Hill, 2011, p. 83). As the old saying goes, "people are a product of their environment." If you hang around toxic people too long and are not strong enough, eventually your mind will also become toxic. There is a transition process that will change people over time to eventually think the same way as those who they spend the most time with. This reinforces the reason why, if you want to be successful, it is important to choose your companions wisely. Being surrounded with positive people will help you to create the right mental framework to deal with the struggles of life properly.

In conclusion, acquiring Napoleon Hill's second step to riches (faith) is crucial to becoming a success. Having faith in what you do can be a powerful driving force, especially if mixed with the proper emotions.

The proof of the power of faith is written all over history, especially in the religious section. One of the best quotes from Napoleon Hill in this chapter elaborates on this point further. "Gandhi has accomplished, through the influence of faith that which the strongest military power on earth could not, and never will accomplish through soldiers and military equipment. He has accomplished the astounding feat of influencing two hundred million minds to coalesce and move in unison, as a single mind" (Hill, 2011, p. 92).

Faith should not be faked though, as it will only have a temporary effect. According to one definition from the Merriam-Webster dictionary, faith is defined as "something that is believed especially with strong conviction." Thus by definition, if you have faith in something, then you must feel so strongly about it that it truly becomes a part of you.

Alternatively, faith can be viewed as a combination of thoughts and actions. *Rather, I think that faith is a combination of strong thoughts and emotions that will produce the most powerful of all actions.* If the faith of the collective of all humanity has helped carry our civilization to the present, imagine the power it can yield to only one person. You can truly be *as wealthy as you believe.*

Bibliography

Criniti, Anthony M., IV. 2013. *The Necessity of Finance: An Overview of the Science of Management of Wealth for an Individual, a Group, or an Organization.* Philadelphia: Criniti Publishing.

Criniti, Anthony M., IV. 2014. *The Most Important Lessons in Economics and Finance: A Comprehensive Collection of Time-Tested Principles of Wealth Management.* Philadelphia: Criniti Publishing.

Criniti, Anthony M., IV. 2016. *The Survival of the Richest: An Analysis of the Relationship between the Sciences of Biology, Economics, Finance, and Survivalism.* Philadelphia: Criniti Publishing.

Hill, Napoleon. 2011. *Think and Grow Rich.* United Kingdom: Capstone Publishing Ltd. Merriam-Webster: https://www.merriam-webster.com/dictionary/desire

DR. ANTHONY M. CRINITI

About Dr. Anthony M. Criniti IV: Dr. Anthony (aka "Dr. Finance®") is the world's leading financial scientist and survivalist. A fifth generation native of Philadelphia, Dr. Criniti is a former finance professor at several universities, a former financial planner, an active investor in diverse marketplaces, an explorer, an international keynote speaker, and has traveled around the world studying various aspects of finance. He is an award winning author of three #1 international best-selling finance books: *The Necessity of Finance* (2013), *The Most Important Lessons in Economics and Finance* (2014), and *The Survival of the Richest* (2016). As a prolific writer, he also frequently contributes articles to *Entrepreneur, Medium,* and *Thrive Global.* Dr. Criniti's work has started a grassroots movement that is changing the way that we think about economics and finance.

Author's website: *www.DrFinance.info*
Book Series Website & Author's Bio: *www.The13StepsToRiches.com*

Barry Bevier

ENCOUNTERING TRUE FAITH

Faith has been a strong and guiding principle in my life since childhood. I was raised in a Christian family where I was exposed as a youth to Faith in God… Faith in the Bible… Faith in a Being that I could not see, touch, or talk with. Faith in a book that was written over a thousand years ago and is the basis for my Christian beliefs. I had to have Faith that it was true and accurate. As a child, I accepted it. I guess it was blind Faith. At an early age, especially in the generation and culture that I grew up in, I rarely questioned my parents' and grandparents' teachings. I've had a saying that has lived on one of my walls for several years. It says, "Faith is not believing that God can. It is knowing that He will!"

Our family business was farming. As a farmer, our life and business was completely based on Faith. Faith that the seed you buy will germinate and grow into crops that produce high yields. Faith that the livestock you're raising will be healthy. We dry-land farmed as we had no irrigation. We lived on Faith for sufficient rain to come at the proper time for our crops to get the moisture needed. We had Faith that the equipment would not break down as we needed it to make it through the year until there was enough money to make major repairs or purchase new equipment.

Faith enters into our lives on a daily basis. Even at small levels I would encounter Faith! When I was kid, I had Faith that my parents would provide for me. Perhaps, unconscious Faith. I didn't even think about it.

I had Faith that this sun was going to rise each and every morning. I had an unconscious Faith that there would be enough food on the table every day, that I would have clothes to wear, that I would have clean air to breathe and water to drink. These were all unconscious Faiths that I really didn't think about on a regular basis. I may have been grateful for them, yet I didn't really think about them. Realizing it now, I had developed Faith as a young child based on my Christian upbringing. By growing up on a farm, I truly encountered the basis of my Faith.

Yet for me, Faith really comes into play when things go wrong. When what I desire, what I hope for, what I am working for, or what I have prayed for does not happen. The fact that sometimes even though we have strong Faith, the outcome we desire, we hope for, or we yearn to see come to fruition does not happen. When that occurs, we must continue growing our Faith. We must become even more "Faithful." A lot of times, when things go wrong in our lives, they are completely out of our control. A disaster occurs. We lose our jobs. A loved one becomes ill or passes. In those cases, our Faith helps us make changes in our lives to accommodate what has occurred.

That is where Faith in ourselves and the resources we have available to get through the tough spots is really important. Having Faith that we are enough is so vital. Faith that we have everything within us and all the resources available to us to get beyond whatever tragedy you are experiencing and break through the grief, sorrow, difficult situations, and whatever has been brought upon us. When unfortunate circumstances occur, we must have Faith that things will change, that things can get better again. Through Faith in ourselves, we can pull through it.

Faith is a factor when we seek to improve ourselves and make ourselves or our situation better. We must have Faith in ourselves that we can grow the skills, the knowledge, the relationships to accomplish our goals. This is where Faith has been the biggest challenge for me: Faith that I can make the change; Faith that I am enough to make this all happen. There's a saying that whatever doesn't kill you, makes you stronger. There is a powerful story about Faith in the Bible — the book of Job. I've read it several times and it provides insight and inspiration to me every time I read it. I highly suggest you read it as well.

I think my real journey with conscious Faith started when I finished my graduate degree in engineering. It was the spring of 1975. The economy was down and jobs for new grads were scarce and I didn't have any job offers. My graduate advisor was consulting on a huge hydroelectric project in Pakistan. He was looking for someone to represent him for a few months at the project site. I didn't have any better options. So, in Faith that it would be a safe place to be and I could accomplish the goals and represent him well, I agreed to the challenge. It was scary to say the least. It was the biggest step in Faith I had ever taken in my life. Other than brief trips to Canada from Michigan, I had never been out of the country. To fly halfway around the globe and live in a third-world country was not only an unbelievable experience, it was unfathomable to me. I remember mustering great Faith that I would be safe, healthy, and able to do the job that my professor had Faith in me to accomplish. In the end, it worked out very well and turned out to be a great launching pad for my career.

Another example of my Faith was in 2010 when my wife, Linda, became very ill. She had been diagnosed 20 years earlier with lupus. She had been treated with pharmaceutical medications since her condition was diagnosed. As most of us recognize today, pharmaceuticals can have severe side effects on our organs and tissues. She was no different than most people and started to develop symptoms of liver, kidney, and other organ distress. Our family had Faith that the doctors and our medical system would be able to cure her. We hoped she would again be the thriving, lively, loving woman that I had married. Yet, sometimes even though we have strong Faith, the outcome we desire does not happen. When that occurs, we must continue our Faith and accept that God has something different in mind for us. Through four months of intensive medical treatment and periodic hospitalizations, we had Faith that that she would recover. We had Faith that God had his hands on the situation and Faith that the doctors treating her would do their very best. We had our continued Faith that the outcome we desired would happen and she would be healthy again.

Unfortunately, that was not the case. She didn't make it. We lost her. My life changed in an instant! I had to believe in my Faith in God's choices to bring me through this time in my life.

Little did I know, the company that I was working with decided to reorganize and chose to eliminate the group I was a leading. I found myself without a job. This may have actually been a blessing because I was becoming a bit weary and frustrated with the profession. It gave me the time to focus on Linda's passing and taking care of the family. It also eventually pointed me in a new, exciting career direction.

After continuing as an engineering consultant for a few years after Linda's death, I decided I had a bigger place in life. I had a bigger mission. God had something more for me. But I wasn't sure what it was. My Faith and persistence to determine what my real purpose in life is led me to where I am today. It has, perhaps, been an unlikely journey becoming a wellness practitioner focusing on brain health and stem cells after spending over 30 years in an engineering career. It was my Faith and persistence that led me to make the changes. After several years of challenges seeking what my mission really is, I've honed in on my new abilities and career to help people with their health naturally and helping them avoid what happened to our family.

Throughout my life, Faith has helped me become stronger. Faith has helped me overcome fear. Faith has helped me discover solutions. Faith has helped me discover my purpose in life. It isn't just a notion that I hold onto in tough times. Faith is an important element to my everyday life.

Faith has helped me to focus on positivity. Our lives are precious yet can also be remarkably difficult. Faith is what helps get me through, illuminating the pathway during dark times, helping to give me strength when I am weak. Faith is also the focused power that breeds abundance. In times of hardship, I tend to move away from positivity. I allow myself to go from a state of abundance to a state of lack. But Faith is a tool that helps me to replenish abundance in my heart and spirit. When I focus on problems, I have difficulty moving past the negative. When I focus on positivity and seek out solutions, I can resolve my problems and move from a state of lack back into a state of abundance. Faith is the pathway for abundance, and I hold it at the forefront of my mind.

> **"Faith is the confirmation of things I do not see and the conviction of the reality, perceiving as real fact that what is not revealed to the senses."**
> **~ Sara Young**

BARRY BEVIER

About Barry Bevier: Barry Bevier is a proud father of two amazing daughters in their mid-twenties, who are pursuing their passions in psychology and architecture in Southern California. He was raised on a family farm near Ann Arbor, Michigan. Growing up, he developed his faith in God, a strong work ethic, a love for nature, and a passion to help others. After completing his master's degree in civil engineering at the University of Michigan, he pursued a career in engineering, which eventually brought him to Southern California.

In 2000, he married the love of his life, Linda. They shared a beautiful life for ten years, until she succumbed to the effects of lupus and 20 years of treatment with prescription medications. Since then, Barry pivoted his career path into educating and helping others. Barry has educated himself

in alternative, natural modalities in wellness and became a Licensed Brain Health Trainer through Amen Clinics. He also works with a new technology in stem cell supplementation that releases your own stem cells.

Author's Website: *www.BRBevier.Stemtech.com*

Book Series Website & Author's Bio: *www.The13StepstoRiches.com*

Brian Schulman

FOLLOWING FAITH

It all started with an app update on my phone in June of 2018. A video icon popped up next to the camera icon and my first thought was, "Oh CR*P!" I was terrified to get in front of a camera and make a video. When I would think about it, I would literally break out in a sweat, my heart would pound and I found it extremely hard to breathe. No joke. All of my fears came out to me. What if my Tourette's came out? What would others say? The fear of not knowing "who I was," the fear of being exposed, and many, many more paralyzing thoughts consumed me! I just couldn't get myself in front of the camera! I would fight with myself… "I am going to do it! I want to. Are you crazy? You are NOT doing this! But, I think this is important. It is leading to something big. Or is it? Okay, I am doing it! Nope, not doing it!" For 5 months, my mind wrestled with itself; not knowing what might happen while knowing all of the things that could happen. I was stuck. Consequently, I did nothing!

I was confident, self-assured and educated, in business, I knew my role. I walked into meetings knowing I was better at my job than most people because of who I was and how I did it. I obsessively prepared. I connected with people. Focused on relationships. I CARED. I would put my suit on and stand at the head of the boardroom table with all eyes on me and I was in my element… I was a superhero - but ask me to record myself on video and I hid. My voice left me.

Making a video meant going back to feeling insecure. Only it wasn't just a feeling, because I really did not know a thing. Physically, emotionally, mentally, technologically etc. Recording a video would be entering into vulnerable space. Think - standing in that same boardroom in the superhero underwear I had as a kid instead of a tailored suit. I went from top of my game to a totally rookie. The fear was paralytic. However, stronger than fear, was my faith.

Faith that, just as I had grown the skills to rock a boardroom or an international stage and make an impact, I was equally capable of growing the skills and learning what I needed to know to start making videos. Faith that everything happens for a reason and the universe always has your back. I saw the power that entering into this vulnerable space would have, not only for me, but for others. Somehow, I knew it, and every time I walked away from making a video, this thought would find me. I knew in my gut it was important to *just* start.

I had to do this. I had already faced a lot in life, both right out of the gates to make it into this world and with many adversities along the way. With love, positivity, faith, and strength surrounding me I conquered the fears that I faced.

I was planning for a business trip that would have me pretty tied up in meetings all day, each day, for 3 days. And I had decided NOW was the time to make not only 1 video, but 5 daily videos, 5 days in a row. What in the world was I thinking!? I had no clue what I was going to talk about!

Keeping the faith throughout the whole process, it happened.

I knew I did not want it to be about business and that was when it hit me. I'm going to tell my personal story, which very few had ever heard. I just need to show up and be me, but do it on video. For the first time in my life, I was truly inspired to get in *front* of the camera.

My bags freshly packed for my trip the next day, sitting in my chair at my home office, I pulled out my phone, and filmed and posted my very first LinkedIn Video - in front of 500 million business professionals!

It went like this...

I'm always asked how are you so positive every-single-day! How do you do it? The answer... it's because I'm not supposed to be alive right now. I was born barely 1.5 pounds in 1975, living in an incubator for months. Fighting for every day with wires attached to me, to make it into this world. I realized, as a kid, that I was 'different.' I was small and had uncontrollable tics and twitches. I did not know what was wrong with me and neither did the doctors. I was finally diagnosed with Tourette's Syndrome when I was in 5th grade. I decided to educate my classmates about TS, which was scary, but I became empowered by my Tourette's Syndrome and knowing I survived what others in the NICU had not. I was resilient.

I hit 'post' on my social media video and then I was paralyzed. TERRIFIED, in fact. What did I just do?! What would people say? I was convinced I would lose my job. I have to delete it! But when I opened the app to hit delete, I saw what others were saying in the comment section and I started to cry. It was as if I had been given permission to let go of every fear I had been holding on to. The overwhelming love, support and encouragement changed my life, forever. Finally, being 'different' didn't feel like a bad thing.

My second video was made from the airport parking lot, still leery, sitting in my car, sweating from the heat (and nerves!), almost missing my flight (as I shot this video 5-7 times). Flight made, full day of meetings, and then immediately thinking. OMG! What do I do for tomorrow's video?! Always reminding myself, "Have faith. I can do this!

I made the next 2 videos around midnight on the same night, knowing I would not have time over the next 2 days to do it any other way. I went as far as to change my clothes so it didn't look like I shot the videos at the same time! I was NOT going to let myself down!

Finally making it home late Friday night, I kissed my wife, two kiddos (aka my Monkeys), and as I laid down, I'm thinking with relief, "Only one more video!" One more and you're done!

After creating videos for years now, I have to tell you… it's never been about 'the numbers.' I have never made a video that was not inspired by something or someone, otherwise it is not genuine and authentic and, therefore, NOT me. If I am inspired, then I have faith and confidence in myself that I can inspire someone else.

Faith has led me to continue creating.

Making those first 5 videos was one of the hardest things I have ever done in my life. It has also been one of the most rewarding. From that fearful start to my journey, I have traveled the world and been given the privilege of being an International Keynote Speaker, a #1 Best-Selling Author, creating two global award-winning weekly live shows and having intimate, vulnerable conversations with people whose lives have changed because we met. And, to be honest, they have changed my life as much as they give me credit for changing theirs. The daily outpouring of messages serve as constant reminders of how my videos have inspired, lifted, given strength, hope and faith to others in a time when they didn't feel they could go on.

I have had the opportunity to collaborate with so many amazing hearts. Inspiring others through my journey of video, to know that by being courageous, getting comfortable being uncomfortable, taking the leap, starting where they are, and despite their fears, they will find their voice to voice their vibe and attract their tribe - just like I did!

Almost 1,500 videos since day one, inspiring others that were just like me at the beginning of my journey, has been a gift. Throughout the process, my fear had me repeatedly asking myself, "What am I doing?" "Where is this going?", but I was asking the wrong questions. It was not about what or where it was going, it was about what we (others who were creating and posting videos) were doing collectively.

It clicked in my head. It was always about showing up, being me, bringing people together and never about business. It was clear to me that I was a part of something that I would look back at and say, "I inspired." I gave people faith in the face of fear and paved the way for others to do the same. I was a part of a movement that would change history. All to be accomplished through faith, facing my fears, starting, having fun, and making videos to support others. I overcame my fear of getting in front of video, and so much more. I found a voice I never knew I had.

BRIAN SCHULMAN

About Brian Schulman: Brian Schulman is known as the Godfather, and Pioneer, of LinkedIn Video and one of the world's premiere live streaming & video marketing experts. He has 20+ years of proven Digital Marketing experience strategizing with IR500 & Fortune500 brands across the globe.

A #1 Best-Selling Author and internationally known Keynote Speaker, Brian founded & is the CEO of Voice Your Vibe, which brings his wealth of knowledge, as an advisor and mentor to Founders & C-Suite Executives by providing workshops and 1-on-1 Mastery Coaching on how to voice their vibe, attract their tribe, and tell a story that people will fall in love with through the power and impact of live & pre-recorded video.

Named "2020 Best LIVE Festive Show of The Year" at the IBM TV Awards, his weekly LIVE shows #ShoutOutSaturday & #WhatsGoodWednesday have aired LIVE for more than 300 consecutive episodes combined and have been featured in Forbes, Thrive Global, Yahoo Finance, an Amazon best-selling book and syndicated on a Smart TV Network. Among his many awards and honors, Brian has been named a 'LinkedIn Top Voice', 'LinkedIn Video Creator Of The Year', one of the 'Top 50 Most Impactful People of LinkedIn' and a 'LinkedIn Global Leader of The Year' for two consecutive years.

Author's Website: *www.VoiceYourVibe.com*
Book Series Website & Author's Bio: *www.The13StepstoRiches.com*

Bryce McKinley

SAVING FAITH

September 28th, 2011, will always be embedded in my mind as it was very evident that I had an extraordinarily little amount of Faith in my life! You see, dripping in sweat, despair, self-pity, and self-demise, I chose to pull my vehicle (in which I had been sleeping in for months at this point) out into the middle of the street. I had written a letter to my mom, and my then 10-month-old son, and hoped for the best for the rest of his life. I had given up! I intended and convinced myself, my human nature, to give in to the auto suggestion that I could no longer push forward. I pulled the trigger!

But I later found that the verse, "Oh ye of little faith," Jesus replied, 'Why are you so afraid?" (Matthew 8:26). This had so much more meaning to me than I had realized!

You see, even the smallest amount of Faith can move mountains, and that desire and hope for a better life for my boy had proven to show God's grace, love, and plan for my life!

In the Bible, Hebrews 11:1 states, "Faith is the assurance of things hoped for, the conviction of knowing things not yet seen."

It wasn't until this moment that I utterly understood the power and magnitude of Faith! The fact that I had been assured of the things I had hoped for and knew, while I may not see them yet in fruition, were on their way!

That evening, after the pistol jammed, I forever assured my Faith. While it may sway, it would not be an element to doubt wholeheartedly! I will never forget the anger, frustration, and yet calmness that came over me.

I stepped back into my car, turned the ignition, and from the back seat of the vehicle, a small still voice said, "Everything's going to be ok!" Wait, did my son just speak at ten months old? No, not a chance! "God? Are you there? Show Up! What do you want from me? Where shall I go? What do you need me to do?" These were the thoughts that ran through my head.

I was scared and yet so overwhelmed with joy! I knew that I knew. He was Real, He showed up, and who am I to doubt the almighty powerful creator that dwells within us all? That night, my Faith was formed and forever strengthened to begin this journey of success, enlightenment, or whatever you would call it. But it was not the beginning. It was just that I had finally come to notice or believe. It was in those moments I began to cultivate the power and understanding of my Faith!

Looking back now, I see the many different feelings of disbelief and shame that held me back from my Faith, and so much more.

In the book "Think & Grow Rich," Hill states, "Faith is a state of mind which may be induced, or created, by affirmation or repeated instructions to the subconscious mind, through the principle of autosuggestion." I would also like to add that Faith can also come by miraculous and divine intervention, especially when you have a mission or purpose you have yet to fulfill on this earth.

So if you are reading my chapter, I would like to encourage you that you, too, have a purpose and if you have ever doubted that, you are not alone. But you do not have to stay there, in that place of uncertainty or confusion.

Some have said, "If you think you can't, you won't. But, if you think you can, you may." I had heard that once and shortly after the incident above, I chose to write some of my affirmations. Listed below are what I have read aloud for the last ten years, daily, and repeatedly for approximately 20 minutes every morning. Feel free to use them and/or tweak them to your liking.

I am a real person of God, I am a capable leader. Today, God comes first. I choose to put His will above my own will. I show others the grace He has shown me, and I love others the way He has loved me. I look for every opportunity to add value to those that cross my path. I see people as my priority and not my distraction. I use my talents, strengths, and time to not simply better my life but also all those who are around me. I am the person God has called me to be.

I am an entrepreneur, a leader, a loving husband and father, a loyal friend, and a positive influence on all who are watching me.

I give when I feel selfish, I am courageous when I am fearful, I will remember when I am tempted, and I will be grateful when I feel I am lacking.

I will walk slowly today, and I will savor the small things.

I will intentionally look for all the little good things that make up my day.

Decision by decision, dollar by dollar, choice by choice, I will build an enduring legacy.

I will not take myself or my day too seriously. I will enjoy a smile, and I will relish a laugh. I will take time to play.

Amidst my work, I am always on the lookout for an adventure.

I will invest my time today. I will not waste it.

By the end of this day, I will be wiser, I will be smarter, I will be richer, and I will be better.

I will be all that I dream of being.

I will think big. I will take risks. I will swing for the fences.

I do not let my critics or the opinions of others dissuade me. I have a purpose, and for me, God has a plan.

I will not do anything to hinder or delay the incredible things God has laid out for me.

I will emulate the consistency and integrity that have been modeled for me.

There are no shortcuts and no small lies.

And so, I pray.

"Dear Lord, the battles I go through today, I pray for a fair chance. A chance to equal my stride. A chance to do or dare. If I should win, let it be by the code with Faith and honor held high. If I should lose, let me stand by the way and cheer as the winners go past. Day by day, get better and better until I can't be beaten, won't be beaten. Day by day, get better and better until I can't be beat, won't be beaten. Amen."

"Your belief, or Faith, is the element which determines the action of your subconscious mind."— Napoleon Hill.

I have come to believe there are four types of Faith:

Dead Faith. In the Bible, James informs us that Faith without works is dead. (James 2:17) In other words, if your Faith is real, you will produce fruit. That is, good works are evidence that your Faith is genuine. I've observed that you don't have to motivate sincere Christians to do what the Holy Spirit is already urging them to do. If your Faith is dead, it will be obvious by a lack of good fruit and an abundance of selfish thoughts, cruel words, and immoral deeds.

Demonic Faith. James also teaches us that even demons believe and shudder at the name of Jesus. (James 2:19) Their "faith" is intellectual. Meaning the demons do not doubt that Jesus is the Son of the living God, but they rebelliously choose to serve a different master. And their master, Satan, is crystal clear on the fact that Jesus died and rose from the dead. Satan's theology is probably better than yours or mine. But knowing all the answers and possessing the right theology doesn't save you.

Vain Faith. Not everyone who says that Jesus is Lord of their lives will enter the kingdom of heaven on the day of His return. Only those who do the will of God will be permitted entry. Responding to an altar call, saying the sinner's prayer, or religiously and generously tithing— these alone will not save you. Please don't be the person who completes all kinds of religious milestones and cries out on the final day, "Lord! Lord!" only to hear the dreadful words "I never knew you; depart from me." (Matthew 7:21-23)

Saving Faith. The message of John 3:16 is so clear. "God loves every one of us, He sent His only begotten Son to live among us, and whoever believes in Jesus will have eternal life." Ephesians 2:8–10 provides us with some additional details: "You are saved by grace through

Faith. Salvation is a gift. You are not saved because of any good works you ever did. But you were made to do good works and point people to Christ. God prepared many good things for you to do. As you live by saving Faith, you will supernaturally produce good fruit, works, and evidence that you are no longer a slave to sin."

I Pray that you find Saving Faith and know, "... if you have faith like a grain of mustard seed, you can say to this mountain, 'Move from here to there', and it will move. Nothing will be impossible for you."

BRYCE MCKINLEY

About Bryce McKinley: Bryce is an International Best-Selling Author and one of the Top 5 Sales Trainers in The World! With over 20 years of working with various Fortune 500 companies including but not limited to the likes of Ford, Nissan, Tyco, and ADT. Helping each of them transform their sales process to focus on better conversations and building better relationships.

Over 8,000 transactions in Real Estate later, Bryce is one of the leading experts in wholesaling houses with his 5 Hour Flip method and has been able to close almost every deal over the phone, only ever walking 5 properties.

Author's Website: *www.5HourFlip.com*
Book Series Website & Author's Bio: *www.The13StepstoRiches.com*

Candace & David Rose

FAITH OVER FEAR

Martin Luther King Jr. said, "Faith is taking the first step, even when you don't see the whole staircase." Faith is unseen, but felt. Faith is strength when we feel we have none. And Faith is hope when all feels lost. It's all about believing - You don't know HOW it will happen, but know it will. It does not make things easy. An effort is required. But it does make things possible. To tap into your Faith, you have to accept what is. Let go of what was. And believe in what will be—believing when it is beyond the power of reason to believe.

Plato said, "We are twice armed when we fight with faith." It doesn't remove pain, but it gets us through the pain. It doesn't diminish the anguish, but it enables us to endure it. When you are pushed to the edge of difficulty, trust fully that one of two things will happen: That you will land safely when you fall, or that you will fly.

When you watch a pendulum swing, you learn that for every action, there is a reaction. This is a universal truth. Faith is trusting that the laws of the universe keep this truth in motion. If you drop an apple, it will fall. If you pull an arrow back, it will propel forward with equal force to the resistance it experienced. If a pendulum swings to the left, it will also swing to the right.

Faith and fear cannot exist together. Faith and fear both demand that you believe in something you cannot see. But I have consistently seen better results when a person chooses Faith.

Fear is depleting. Fear is sabotaging. You've probably heard the saying that "the enemy of my enemy is my friend." That friend is Faith. Fear doesn't get you out of bed. Faith does. Fear doesn't mobilize. Faith does.

Creation of any kind takes Faith. And I believe Elena Cardone puts it best in her book *Build an Empire: How To Have It All*, when she says, "You're either building an empire, or you're destroying one." Faith builds, fear destroys. And you and I are in the mindset of building, not destroying.

Your higher power (I call mine "God") doesn't ask what your budget is when "it" gives you a Dream. It only asks how big your Faith is.

Now, Belief is what I would call "Gateway Faith." But to REALLY get what you want, Belief is magnified if you kick it up a notch into Knowing.

Every time we have been in a situation where our income has significantly decreased, by job loss, for example, I buy one item that I feel pushes our budget. It is an outward representation that I have Faith in a positive outcome. There's something to be said for spending your last dollar on something "frivolous." It signals to the universe that you not only BELIEVE, but KNOW that it will all work out. Never have we been disappointed.

I don't mean to be reckless. I mean, buy the necessities FIRST, but leave a little at the end to do something (or buy something) that makes your day. An analogy I'd like to use is this: When you're packing a box, suitcase, or car, don't pack it to the brim. Leave a spot for something unexpected. If it's full, you can't receive more. Create a place for what you want, so that what you wish for can come to you. Doing so shows that next-level Faith. That Knowing Faith is the assurance of things hoped for and conviction of things unseen. Be convincing, and you will see results.

~ Candace Rose

There are two types of Faith I'd like to explore. The first is Faith in God and the second is Faith in Self.

There was a fisherman who one day went out to sea fishing. The winds came up, and the current swept him further out to sea. He lost his oars and his boat sprung a leak. As a man of Faith, the first thing he did was pray. "God, please help me; I'm stuck and need to get home to my family." As he started bailing out the water, another little boat came by.

"Hey, do you need help?" … came a shout from the other ship.

"No," the fisherman said, "I have faith that God will help me!"

"Alright," came the reply, and the little boat sailed on. A little while later, the man's boat was almost full of water. Again, another boat came by.

"Hey, do you need help?"

"No," replied the fisherman, "God is coming to help me." Now, his boat has completely sunk. A third boat comes by.

"Hey, do you need help?"

"No, God is going to help me," the fisherman said. And he was left. The next thing the fisherman knew, he was standing in front of God. He looked at God. With anger in his voice he asked, "Why didn't you save me?"

God replied, "I tried. I sent you three different boats. You just refused to get aboard any of them."

Growing up, I viewed Faith only as a religious concept. If you need something, ask God, in Faith, believing he will give it to you, and it will be yours, which this story describes just that. The fisherman had such great Faith that God would save him, that he failed to see all the ways God tried. From this story, we can learn that while Faith in God is important, it will only get you so far. Without action, we will be left drowning, which is where Faith in Self comes in.

"I think I can…I think I can." Those are the words the little engine repeated the whole time he was climbing the hill, which is a lesson in Faith in self.

My two daughters desired the freedoms that earning their driver's licenses would provide them. I took them to take the test for their learner's permits. When they came out, I learned that one had passed, but the other had not. We talked about what went wrong. Or which questions she had missed. The ultimate issue she had was her lack of Faith in herself. She kept saying, "I can't pass the test because I don't test well." Her sister, however, passed the test. She said, "I knew I was going to pass it." Notice the difference? My first daughter had filled her mind with doubt and negative thoughts, which feeds fear. Fear is the opposite of Faith. Where fear lives, Faith can't survive. Without Faith and the action it encourages, you will never be able to reach your goals.

So, how do we eliminate fear and break down the barrier it creates? We do that through positive affirmations. Things like, "I think I can!" …"I've got this!" … "That promotion is mine!" … "I will pass that test!" … "Show me the money!" As you repeat these sayings both aloud and internally, you start training your mind and chasing out fear and self-doubt. This develops the Faith needed to accomplish your goals. As your Faith grows, it keeps building on itself like a snowball rolling down a hill.

God helps us gain momentum towards our goals. When you combine your Faith in God with Faith in Self, you start to see the "boats" God puts in your path to help you along the way.

~David Rose

CANDACE & DAVID ROSE

About Candace and David Rose: Candace and David Rose are #1 Best-Selling Authors in the 13 volume book series *The 13 Steps to Riches*. They grew up together and currently live in South Jordan, Utah, with their 6 children, 5 chickens, 4 cats, 2 dogs and a rabbit. They are both Veterans of the U.S. Army. David served as a mechanic and Candace as a Legal NCO. David is currently a Product Release Specialist, delivering liquid oxygen and nitrogen to various manufacturing plants and hospitals throughout Utah, Colorado, Idaho and Nevada. Candace is the owner of Changing Your Box Organization, where she specializes in helping people organize their space, both physically and mentally, with the ultimate goal to help you change your box and find more joy in your life. Both Candace and David are proud members of the elite Champion Circle Networking Association in Salt Lake City, UT., founded by one of our Coauthors of *The 13 Steps to Riches* book series and the Habitude Warrior Mastermind Senior Team Leader, Jon Kovach Jr.

Author's Website: *www.ChangeYourBox.com*
Book Series Website & Author's Bio: *www.The13StepstoRiches.com*

Collier Landry

FINDING FAITH IN THE NADIR

Collier, are you sure you want to do this?"

… asks the gentleman seated directly before me, across what can only be described as a behemoth of a cherry wood legal desk. I hear his voice, and I'm pretty sure he thinks I'm listening to him, staring intently while I let the gravity of his words settle in.

But I'm not.

What I am staring at are the countless rows of legal books that adorn the wall behind him. It looks as though they are lined up in chronological order. I notice a few missing in various spots, but for the most part, the shelves are full.

"You know that you don't have to do this, son," says another gentleman seated directly to my right.

I continue to pay their words no mind as I wonder, does one really have to read all of those books to become an attorney? I mean, I love to read, but those books are probably pretty boring, especially to a twelve-year-old boy.

I can remember the previous summer on a trip to Washington, D.C. when my mother mused that I should learn to play the piano so I could "put myself through law school by playing piano for customers at Nordstrom." When we returned back home, I was promptly enrolled in piano lessons with the local teacher.

The lessons lasted up until six months prior to when my world was flipped completely upside down; before phrases like 'foster care' and 'premeditated murder' became part of my lexicon.

"Collier, we do have other witnesses," the second man's voice chimes in again.

Suddenly my daydreaming is cut short, and I'm snapped back into reality. "No, I'm testifying," I respond emphatically, "… no matter what."

They both nod in what appears to be a moment of relief. Did they possibly think I was going to chicken out?

Reassuringly I continue:

"I know what I heard. I know what I saw. I know what he did, and he's not going to get away with it!"

After months spent in what can only be described as complete isolation, apart from my time spent in school, I felt like Manette sequestered in *A Tale of Two Cities*. It seemed like my address was not in Mansfield, Ohio, but rather 105 North Tower in the Bastille. As both Manette and Collier are French names, the irony is hard to ignore. Apparently, God does have a sense of humor, after all.

The men continue:

"Your foster mother will bring you to the courthouse in the morning around seven-thirty tomorrow. We'll have some snacks, donuts, etc., for you, and then you will wait for me to come and get you with the bailiff," they explain.

I nod in compliance, still in a foggy daze.

That night I hardly slept a wink, my mind racing at what was about to happen that next morning. The last six months had obliterated any Faith I had in God whatsoever. After all, if there was a God, why would they take my mother from me? Why would it be done in such an evil and insidious way? Why would they allow my family to turn their backs on me? Why is this happening?!

The fear had begun to set in that there was a very real possibility that the man who planned and executed the murder of my mother could actually be acquitted. After all, he had a legal team of 3 lawyers - which was a lot for small Ohio town.

I already knew how violent this man was. I knew his temper was capable of anything. My mother and I had experienced the brunt of it my entire life. If my father were to be acquitted, he would resume custody of me until I became of age. I was quite certain that every day would be a replay of this nightmare, stuck in repetitive insanity.

My father's side of the family had denounced me as a turncoat, pointing the finger at a twelve-year-old boy for doing the right thing.

My mother's family wanted nothing to do with me either, casting me off as the boy who will "be just like his father."

What if everything I have done in the last six months, my solo crusade to not let my mother's murder go unpunished, was all for naught?

I was alone, and I was terrified. I had officially touched the nadir. That morning as I make my way into the witness box, I notice the courtroom is packed. I see people I hadn't seen in six months. I see people I had never seen.

TV cameras are everywhere. This was one of the first televised murder trials in Ohio history. I may look calm, but inside I am terrified.

This is the most difficult thing I had ever done in my life.

I place my hand on the Bible before me and raise the other. The bailiff's voice fades as I slowly begin to tune out again. I look at the Bible, which up until this moment, had always been a symbol of Faith. My gaze shifts to my father, seated amongst his posse of lawyers, surrounding him with stacks of briefs and notepads, all sitting there taking notes as nonchalant as if they were at home reading the Sunday newspaper. Make no mistake, however, behind that façade, my father and his legal team are indignant, apoplectic even.

Suddenly, a wave of overwhelming serenity assuages my fears. I realize how sad it was that my father chose this path in life. After all, he was a doctor; outside looking in, life was pretty good for our family these last few years by normal societal standards. Why commit such a senseless and selfish act? The subsequent devastation affected not only my family but our community as a whole.

However, it is all about me at that moment, and I become reassured of what I always knew to be true: I am doing the right thing. I found that Faith in myself, my words, and my voice is all I really needed. I had successfully stared into the abyss, refused to let it engulf me and insisted that it was not going to deter my character or soften my resolve.

For the first time in six months, I feel Faith inside of me. I am solid.

Over the next two days of grueling testimony, I was unfettered, holding up under cross-examination like I had done this 100 times before. My attention to detail - dates, times, people, places, things - shattered the narrative the defense had been building.

I walk out of that courtroom with my head held high and my heart full, not because of what I said but because of what I did.

The following ten days seem like an eternity as the trial begins to wind down into closing arguments and then jury deliberation. Having already testified, I am able to resume a sort of normal life, playing tennis and hanging with friends I hadn't been allowed to see outside of school the last six months.

I finish hitting tennis balls around and come upstairs into the facility to a crowd of players and people surrounding a TV, glued to it.

The facility manager swiftly approaches me and says, "Collier, you have a phone call; let's take it in my office."

It was Lieutenant David Messmore, the detective who had listened to the word of a then eleven-year-old boy that his mother was not simply a "missing person," but had been murdered at the hands of his own father.

I picked up the receiver. The only thing I heard was, "Guilty. Guilty on all counts."

My eyes began welling up with tears. I was speechless. The seemingly insurmountable task of pushing the colossal boulder, one that had been sinking into my chest for the last six months, had finally reached the summit.

"We did it, Collier. Your mother would be so proud." "Thank you, Lieutenant Messmore," I replied.

I hung up the receiver and sobbed, caught in an undertow of sadness and utter relief. On one hand, my belief in myself and my conviction to do the right thing was finally validated. I felt vindicated. On the other hand, I knew that my old life was unceremoniously gone forever and the future lay bare with complex uncertainty.

At that moment, I truly knew the real meaning of Faith. Faith was not found in some ancient text or captured inside a specific religion - Faith was inside of me.

And I finally came to realize its true power.

COLLIER LANDRY

About Collier Landry: As a formally trained musician and photographer, Collier Landry segued into filmmaking as a means to creatively express and deal with his own traumatic story—that of the premeditated murder of his mother by his own father.

Subsequently, Collier is the creator and subject of Investigation Discovery's 'A Murder in Mansfield', a documentary directed by two-time Oscar winning director Barbara Kopple. In the film, Collier, who witnessed the murder and at age 12 became the chief witness for the prosecution, returns to Ohio seeking to retrace his past and confront his father, who remains incarcerated and in denial of his guilt.

The film explores not only the collateral damage of violence and its traumatic repercussions, but the beauty of human strength and resilience through seemingly insurmountable odds.

Collier has been featured in *Variety, The New York Times, The Hollywood Reporter, Esquire, USA Today*, is a TEDx Speaker, and a guest on the *Dr. Phil* show. Collier is the host of the 'Moving Past Murder' podcast. He resides in Santa Monica, California.

Author's Website: *www.CollierLandry.com*
Book Series Website & Author's Bio: *www.The13StepstoRiches.com*

Corey Poirier

YOU GOTTA HAVE FAITH

I thought affirmations were cheesy for much of my life.

I remember watching *Saturday Night Live*, and there was this character whose name was Stuart Smalley (played by actor, politician Al Franken). He did this daily affirmation sketch where he ended with words along the lines of, "I'm good enough, I'm smart enough, and Dog-Gonnit, people like me," while staring in a mirror at himself.

At the time, maybe age 16, I thought it was something they made up for the sketch. I didn't even know that affirmations were a real thing. I thought, "Wow, those writers, they are so creative." They came up with this character and these things called daily affirmations.

Now keep in mind, I didn't read my first book until age 27. That book was Dale Carnegie's *How to Win Friends and Influence People*. The second book I read? *Think and Grow Rich* by Napoleon Hill.

So the first time I realized these things called affirmations were an actual thing was when I read *Think and Grow Rich* for the first time, also at age 27.

I was completely oblivious until that point, and suddenly, it was like I woken up to a whole new world. I was like, "those affirmation things were real? Was that character based on an actual practice?" Of course, you eventually discover that almost all great characters are based on some real elements.

I say all this to note that I wasn't very comfortable doing affirmations at first as I was still stuck around this idea that they were these cheesy lines from a Saturday Night Live sketch.

For me personally, it just didn't feel natural to repeat stuff as a way of affirming something. That is perhaps why once I discovered they were a real thing, and I discovered them in a book that was already changing my life, I still didn't do any affirming or affirmations.

I started a mastermind. I tried the vision board thing, tapped further into my desire, and created a statement of desire. I practiced most of what I was learning in *Think and Grow Rich*, but not affirmations.

Then *The Secret* came along, and it gave a further window into the idea of affirming what you desired.

People in my life who I never envisioned practicing affirmations were practicing affirmations and attempting to manifest. They were doing things I never, ever thought I would see them doing, all in the hope of attracting abundance, and here I was, feeling like I was farther down the path than they were, coaching some of them, and I still wasn't practicing affirmations.

At the time, I was starting to interview Influencers and slowly beginning to acknowledge that many of them were also practicing affirmations. I had to accept that there must be something special about this finally, and the only way I would know for sure was to give it a try myself.

At this point, I had been reading 3-5 books a month for almost five years, and *The Secret* had been out for a year, but it was the fact that I was interviewing Influencers to learn what they did differently than others that finally got me to take action on this thing called Affirmations.

Now, you may be wondering why I have been writing a chapter on Faith without using the word Faith once up until now and instead, using the word affirmations repeatedly.

The reason is this: I didn't practice affirmations because I didn't have Faith that they would yield any results.

But now, faced with the fact that so many Influencers I was interviewing believed in affirmations and clearly experienced results, I had to accept that maybe it was just me and that perhaps I had to start practicing a bit of Faith. And so I started.

I had a business launch coming up, and I aimed to have a statement of desire backed by repeated affirmations about what would be true due to the launch. I had a specific result I wanted to affirm. I recalled Napoleon Hill saying that you had to be very specific in bringing to life what you desired. So I read my statement aloud each day and then affirmed what the result would be.

I repeated things every day for weeks and weeks. Then we did the launch, and there were crickets, no responses. I didn't achieve my goal, not by a long shot, despite having felt the goal was very achievable. To salvage the launch at the time, I had to go one by one to the people who expressed a bit of interest to answer their questions and ultimately enroll them in our program.

I was perplexed because I followed what I believed to be the steps in setting my intentions, reaffirming them daily, and I believed I had absolute Faith it would come to pass. I also had a plan in place; I followed a program that yielded similar results for thousands to what I had been aiming to manifest.

This played a big number in both my Faith and belief in affirmations. I mean, I had to either accept that I was doing something wrong, or I didn't have what those others did who had been successful in doing exactly what I couldn't do in this case. I was all but ready to give up on affirmations. I mean, I was enjoying success in so many areas and truly manifesting much of what I had set out to, but when I tried to have Faith in repeating what I wanted to experience, it had failed me. Or had it?

It wasn't until I interviewed an influencer and asked him directly about whether affirmations always work that I began to see things differently.

He explained that they always work, BUT the Universe may deliver something different than you think you need. He detailed how he set affirmations around the success and abundance he desired with a specific business, and when it failed, he thought, "I wonder what I did wrong."

It wasn't until sometime later he met someone he wouldn't have met had that business succeeded, and they became a power couple and launched a business that allowed them to impact many more than he would have had the original business succeeded as he hoped. That business 'failure' was necessary for the bigger success and impact to take place.

It led me to think about how Steve Jobs was in charge of Apple and hired a guy who ultimately fired Jobs. I'm sure had he been setting affirmations, they wouldn't have included him getting fired from the company he built. Still, that firing led him to start another computer company which became Pixar, which led to him becoming the biggest shareholder of Disney while impacting more lives, and ultimately Apple recruiting him back and seeing more value in him than ever before; which led to him inventing products that have changed our lives forever, like the iPhone, iPad, and so on.

Whether you are a fan of Jobs or Apple or not, it's safe to say that the Universe took him on a path that was likely initially against his will to bring him to a bigger and better place ultimately.

At this point, the interviewee who had shared this with me noted that he realized even though he didn't get exactly what he wanted, the Universe instead gave him something better, much like what happened with Jobs. That is when the light-bulb went off for me. I didn't get exactly what 'I' wanted from the launch, but it did result in something better as well.

And that is the moment I truly found Faith in setting affirmations. It was also at this moment that I realized while I needed to be specific about what I was wanting to manifest, I also had to add in the words, "or something better," and not be so tied in the exact result I could envision. I had to have some Faith.

Those three words, "or something better," changed everything for me, and my Faith in affirmations and manifestation became absolute.

It sounds crazy that after all that time and doubt, this is what it took to establish Faith for me.

From that day forward, though, when I repeated affirmations, I always added, and still do, "or something better," and came to realize that the Universe wants me to ask for what I want, and to be specific BUT also to be open to the idea that the Universe may deliver something better overall.

Admittedly, since then, my life hasn't played out exactly as I planned. I have always been given what I asked for OR something better.

I guess it turns out in the end, **You Gotta Have Faith.**

COREY POIRIER

About Corey Poirier: Corey is a multiple-time TEDx Speaker. He is also the host of the top-rated Let's Do Influencing radio show, founder of The Speaking Program, founder of bLU Talks, and has been featured in multiple television specials. He is also a Barnes & Noble, Amazon, Apple Books, and Kobo Bestselling Author and the co-author of the *Wall Street Journal* and *USA Today* bestseller, *Quitless*.

A columnist with *Entrepreneur* and *Forbes* magazine, he has been featured in/on various mediums and is one of the few leaders featured twice on the popular *Entrepreneur on Fire* show.

Also appearing on the popular Evan Carmichael YouTube Channel, he is a New Media Summit Icon of Influence, was recently listed as the # 5 influencer in entrepreneurship by Thinkers 360, and he is an Entrepreneur of the Year Nominee—and, to demonstrate his versatility, a Rock Recording of the Year nominee who has performed stand-up comedy more than 700 times, including an appearance at the famed Second City.

Author's Website: *www.TheInfluencerVault.com*
Book Series Website & Author's Bio: *www.The13StepstoRiches.com*

Deb Scott

FEED YOUR FAITH

Why does Napoleon Hill put "Faith" as the second key ingredient to *Think and Grow Rich*? What is Faith? How do I get it? Why is it important to me in creating tangibly what I desire?

Faith is created in your heart and mind, which creates a high vibration, like love, which must express itself outward in a tangible way to the desire you have directed your Faith towards— positively or negatively.

Consider you are watching a horror movie. You are in a theater, surrounded by many people. You know the images on the screen are not real; you understand you are watching actors following a script. You are smart. You know this to be true in your mind as soon as you purchase the movie ticket in the lobby.

Why, then, when the plot changes to a scary, unexpected, and horrifying scene do you scream? Why do you have an emotional reaction of fear when you know in your mind that none of what you are watching is real? Why does your emotional self react as if it were true, despite your understanding it absolutely is not?

The key to my story is to prove that your mind cannot separate what is real from unreal. Your mind reacts to what you see, hear, say, or what you are surrounded by. You can't unsee it. You can't unhear it. You can't un-feel it.

Faith is like the reaction of watching that scary movie.

Faith is a positive high frequency that automatically forces your emotion to manifest a specific result of equal value. Positive Faith must create a positive desire, which then must create a positive result accordingly. Negative Faith, or fear, also creates a negative equivalent result.

Can you have Faith that your desire is possible? If you believe this, then you will fuel your Faith with positive words of affirmation, surround yourself with positive people that have already done what you desire, and turn away from negative energy as fast as you can. You will protect your Faith as the true treasure to your soul's desire.

"Fear is useless; what is needed is trust," Jesus said.

I often say this when I have a moment of doubt because I have to train myself to maintain Faith that "all things are possible with God."

I can't wait to perform when the performance time has arrived; I must train in advance, knowing there will be falls and setbacks, and have an immediate antidote ready at hand to squash and shorten that negative short-term obstacle. My Faith must stay strong because it is the key to success.

Every single great success in my life has always been met with impossibility. It's always impossible until it's done, right? Nothing worth achieving will come without resistance, which is why you must feed your Faith with positive words your own mouth speaks, your own ears can hear, your own hands write. Surround yourself with Faith-filled people, and like a sweet perfume, Faith will automatically fall upon you.

I had a goal at the beginning of this year to sell 10 million dollars in real estate. Did I know for sure I could do it? No. I think other people believed in me more than I did. But I had Faith that anything was possible, and if I did the right thing in the right way for the right reason to genuinely help people, I knew God would bless me and send me the people I needed to help make that goal come true. Easy? No. Possible? Yes.

Not even eight months into the year, and I have just about reached my goal. By year's end, I will have well surpassed my outrageous goal! Besides receiving one of the top sales awards at EXP Realty, the ICON status, I might be one of the newest realtors to receive such an award in only my second full year of real estate. All because a bit of Faith to manifest any desire always guarantees a big result.

I surrounded myself with people who had done what I wanted to do. I trusted and prayed and listened and learned. I made a plan, and I worked hard to follow that plan. Quite honestly, money was not my number one motivation. Helping people have a positive experience was my motivation. I desired to change that paradigm because I had such bad experiences with bad realtors in the past. Receiving 5-star reviews was my biggest motivation because I enjoy helping people and doing my best to create positive energy for the people God places on my path wherever I am, whatever I am doing. This byproduct is absolutely earning a lot of money, a nice award, and some shares in company stock. My Faith and desire created a result automatically, just like 2 + 2 = 4.

Napoleon Hill states, "All thoughts which have been emotionalized, (given feeling) and mixed with Faith, begin immediately to translate themselves into their physical equivalent or counterpart."

This is why studies show when you see a picture of a good deed or see a good deed being done in front of you, it will create the same endorphin response in your physical body because your mind can't distinguish between the picture and the real event. Your mind receives what it sees and responds accordingly.

If you add Faith to this equation, your mind will translate that Faith into a positive. If you add fear to the equation, your mind will translate that into a negative. This is why it is critical that you focus on Faith-building images, Faith-building affirmations, write down Faith-building goals, and surround yourself with Faith-building people and events. You attract what you are, and you must become Faith to attract more of it.

I remember in college having a desire (described in the prior volume in this series) to make the original college swim team at Regis College in Weston, MA. The problem was, I had no prior official competitive experience—the only one trying out for the team in this situation, to be precise. But I had always loved swimming and being part of a team, and I had Faith that just because it hadn't been done before did not mean it couldn't be done now.

So I prayed, and I practiced. Because our pool was not completed yet, I had to walk from Regis to Wellesley College to practice extra on my own because I did not have a car to get there. I practiced and prayed and fed my Faith. I worked hard to do my best with what I had. The result? I was the only member who made the team without prior competitive experience, made Most Improved Player, and was elected by my peers as Co-Captain my senior year. That was Faith.

Fake It Until You Make It

"Conduct yourself just as you would if you were already in possession of the material thing which you are demanding," According to *Think and Grow Rich*. This leads Faith to believe the world we touch comes after the world we create in spirit where Faith lives. First a thought, then an action.

I don't know if you are reading this book because you desire more money, more joy, more peace, or a way to start your own business. I know that anything you want to create must first have a desire and then Faith that it is possible.

Show me anyone who didn't start from nothing. We all come into the world as naked babies who can't even walk or talk. We are dependent on our parents for everything. Yet, innocent babies all grew into great men and women who changed the world for better or worse through thousands of years. Each had a desire and believed through Faith that their visions would become reality.

Faith does not exempt you from obstacles. I believe the closer you are over the target to your life purpose, the more you will be attacked. This should encourage you, not discourage you. Nothing great happens without some resistance, but the individuals who succeed never give up on their Faith, never stop believing, never stop learning how to feed their Faith, and starve their fear.

Write down five ways you can feed your Faith today.

DEB SCOTT

About Deb Scott: Deb Scott, BA, CPC, and Realtor was a high honors biology major at Regis College in Weston, Massachusetts, and spent over two decades as an award-winning cardio-thoracic sales specialist in the New England area. She is a best-selling author of *The Sky is Green & The Grass is Blue: Turning Your Upside Down World Right Side Up*. She is an award-winning podcaster of The Best People We Know Show. Following in her family's footsteps, she is a third generation Realtor in Venice, Florida. As a certified life coach, Deb speaks and teaches on how to turn bad situations into positive, successful results. As a top sales specialist, she enjoys teaching people "sales without selling," believing that integrity, good communication, and respect are the winning equation to all outstanding success and happiness in life.

Author's Website: *www.DebScott.com*
Book Series Website & Author's Bio: *www.The13StepstoRiches.com*

Dori Ray

FIND YOUR FAITH

Delaware was officially behind me, as was my last job, and most of my hope. As we drove up the highway back to Philadelphia, I started setting my mind towards the West Coast. "California, here we come," was ringing in my ears!

I had enough energy left to tie up all my loose ends in Philadelphia. I had one goal in mind as I set my sails toward the Pacific Ocean—starting over and "getting it right!" I had become a professional at starting over but had not "gotten it right" yet. That was the part that really needed work!

After all the well wishes and going-away parties, I headed to the airport with a little over $700 in my pocket, a food stamp card, and a laptop. I didn't know at the time that the laptop was the most important thing in my hands other than my daughter, whose sadness I pretended not to see.

I was sad enough without thinking about how I was ripping her high school experience to shreds. I knew this was hard for her, but I had run out of options on the East Coast, or so I thought. My child would just have to roll with the punches, and I would try my best to make it up to her. Making it up later turned into over-compensating, which she would pay the price for much later in her adult life.

My daughter's tears were dripping as the plane took off. She pleaded with me to change my mind and stay in Philadelphia, but there was no turning back. We were already up in the air. We had to make this work.

On the plane, I continued to read the paper I had written on in the apartment in Delaware. Over the past several weeks, I focused on getting better and getting things back on track. I had learned so much from my Mentors and Business Partners. I knew I had to speak the things I wanted into my life.

After getting myself and my child settled in the plane, I took out my little note and my brand new "starting over" journal, and wrote out a few affirmations that I would commit to speaking out loud for ten minutes every day, so that I could keep myself moving in the right direction. In my profession of network marketing, I had heard hundreds, if not thousands of stories, and witnessed some with my very eyes, where people claimed to have used words and affirmations to turn their whole lives around. However, up until that point, it had never worked for me.

The truth is, I was never consistent.

The one common thread among all the successful people who used affirmations to turn their lives around was *consistency*. All of them agreed that it takes at least twenty-one days to make or break a habit. Most of us, myself included, are not consistent for a week and still expect major miracles!

I wrote these affirmations in my journal:

I am Happy. I am Healthy. I am Strong. I am a great Mother. I am a Great Businesswoman. I am Fearfully and Wonderfully Made. I am Great with my Finances. I am an Excellent Speaker. I am Successful. I am Financially Sound. I am a GreatWife. I

am a Great Friend. I am a Great Daughter. I am Happy. I am Healthy. I am Wealthy. I am Strong!

I taped my little note to the inside of the book and committed to using these two as loaded weapons to take down anything and anyone who tried to stand in between me and my BIG COMEBACK! Who would have known that the first place I would have to use the weapons was the home where I was being hosted?

The truth is, I was embarrassed. I silenced myself because I was embarrassed. I had convinced myself that people did not want to hear from a mentally ill woman who could not sustain her own life. How dare I have the nerve to stand on stage and tell people how to transform their minds, bodies, and bank accounts! I felt like a fraud every time the microphone was in my hand, I was speaking on a leadership call or doing any activity where people looked for instruction. All of my partners were gracious because I was talented. I was a strong team member when I wasn't sick. However, it was customary for me to "go missing" for months, and there were no questions because everyone already knew, **Dori Was Depressed!**

My plan, which I had discussed with my friend who would be hosting us in California, was to leave everything in the past. I would forget about all the things causing the stress and depression and "start over." I would take advantage of the change of scenery, the pleasant climate, and new people to become "the woman" I was destined to be. As I pulled open the laptop, I took one last look at the business I decided to leave behind, and focused on reinventing myself. I wrapped my arm around my still crying daughter, closed my eyes, and prayed that the mustard seed of Faith I was clinging to was enough for both of us. I kept a little to send back to my other daughter, who I left behind. When we arrived on the West Coast, we were greeted by my "friend," our hostess, who my daughter immediately sensed had an agenda. That added another layer of issues in trying to adjust to our new lives.

There were a few things that gave me life. I looked forward to calling back home, talking to my family, and staying connected to my business partners. After being treated like unwanted house guests with bad weave hair by our hostess, God sent us two Angels disguised as business partners. They made us feel right at home in La Puente, California, until our Faith had been tested enough to prove us worthy of a trip back home to Philadelphia.

In California, I was under the impression that everyone knew that I had fallen on my face and had "lost it" and was starting over again. This had become a pattern that people begun to expect and accept from me.

I knew I could not let that dominate my thoughts. When those thoughts tried to creep in, I had to quickly refocus and turn my sights back to the present and the future.

I became clearer in California, and was able to help my daughter navigate her way through eleventh grade through homeschooling. Some days, we cried more over physics than we did over missing home. But little miracles kept showing up every day as we clung to that mustard seed of Faith that continued to move us toward our goals which were becoming clearer for me every day. With the help of my Angels, my sidekick and I started to enjoy California. We experienced Runyon Canyon, awesome church services with our friends, a video shoot with a famous recording artist from Philly, all kinds of ethnic foods, including real sushi and authentic Mexican food from a Queen! I even got a chance to hook up with a great friend from Philadelphia who invited me to serve on Skid Row with her. That experience helped me to put my situation into perspective. I began to see the hand of God all over this move and was starting to get my mojo back. There was only one problem. My daughter wanted to go home. We were still strangers in someone else's home. I had run out of money. All I had left was my food stamp card. I had not found a job, and the business that I was starting to rebuild would not generate quickly enough to sustain us living on our own in California. Although I had started looking for my place, deep down inside, I wanted to go home. And guess what? I added it to my list of things I thought of and said every day.

After adding the line to my affirmations, I started to tell my daughter we were going home *every day*. Every time she asked me when we were going home, I would say to her, "Next week." One day, I received a call from a cousin who was unaware we had moved to California. He was calling to purchase the product I was selling at the time. When he learned we wanted to come home but had no money, he immediately gave me his credit card and told me to buy the tickets **now**. I don't know how many steps I skipped up to get to my daughter. All I remember was jumping on her small frame with tears flowing, saying, "Pack your bags, baby! We are going home!" She said, in her you said that yesterday voice, "When, Mom?" I looked her in her face with joy levels I had not felt in a long time and said, "TOMORROW!"

The journey continues in *Volume III: Auto Suggestion*.

DORI RAY

About Dori Ray: Dori "On Purpose" Ray is a native Philadelphian. As a Business Woman her mission is to help people transform their minds, bodies, and bank accounts!

Dori was educated in the Philadelphia Public School System. She graduated from the Philadelphia High School for Girls in 1982 and Howard University School of Business in 1986 with a BBA in Marketing. Dori is a member of Delta Sigma Pi Business Fraternity and Delta Sigma Theta Sorority, Inc.

Dori leads teams around the world. She is a sought-after Speaker and Trainer within her industry and beyond. She is an experienced Re-Entry Coach as she has helped hundreds of Returning Citizens get back on track after incarceration.

Having suffered from depression for 20 years, she always reaches back to share her story and help break the cycle of silence. Her audience loves her authenticity!

Book Dori for speaking engagements www.linktr.ee/dorionpurpose

Author's Website: *www.linktr.ee/DoriOnPurpose*
Book Series Website & Author's Bio: *www.The13StepstoRiches.com*

Elaine Sugimura

EXPECTING THE UNEXPECTED

If FAITH is believing that anything is possible with consistent and committed action, then I can speak to this with relative ease. I can recollect from the time of my youth that I had bigger dreams than those around me.

My desire to succeed at anything I put my mind to was paramount to just living life comfortably. I was "trained" at a young age to assess all that was presented to me and to figure out how to manifest the WINs that would, in turn, create the MAGIC for which I was searching. To be the best student, daughter, wife, mom, and executive meant having a clear vision of what my path would look like if I made certain choices. At that point in time, life was moving along quite nicely and exactly how my parents envisioned it would be for their young, brash teenage daughter, and then something rocked our world.

In the previous chapter, I spoke of my desire to be with someone I became attracted to, who soon became my life partner, friend, husband, and father to my children.

Faith played a huge part in my young adult life. Like any other relationship prior, I thought my parents would embrace the person I brought home for them to meet and get acquainted with. Soon I realized that was not the case. Too much history to share here but let's just say the cards were stacked against us. Tears were shed daily until I chose to shift my thinking. I knew this was what I wanted, and if I stayed committed to our vision of LIFE together, I knew we could create MAGIC. We fought to be together for over three years, and the Faith I placed into our vision is what brought two humans together who love each other fiercely. What could shake our world now?

When you face a life-threatening disease, knowing that your family (a husband, and two small children) may need to navigate life without you, you challenge yourself to dig deep to find the magic pill that will kill the disease so you can go back to living LIFE the way it was. That, obviously, did not happen quite as I had hoped. As the days progressed, I realized that I had to take control of my mindset based on what I was being told, educate myself on what was about to happen to my body, and generate the FAITH to see that there would be a light at the end of a very dark tunnel. Most would have said, "Why Me?" That never entered my mind. I closed my eyes and asked myself who I get to *be* to create the environment to overcome this illness. The belief that I could draw upon those around me to support my journey to recovery was key to healing both my body and my mind. At that moment, with two kids under the age of five, I knew I needed to create a community to rally in front of me, behind me, and every day till Sunday! I thought once was enough. Years passed by, and I successfully put this scare behind me.

I held on to my Faith that this disease would take a back seat if I kept my mindset positive and spoke out loud without blame, shame, fault, or guilt. I kept my Faith alive throughout the entire treatment process and did not allow anything or anyone to stop me from believing there was ONLY ONE WAY!

To beat this deadly disease by killing it with kindness, joy, love, and inspiring others to be a voice and stand for others going through the same process. Sharing in the misery of both mental and physical pain was daunting, but through Faith, I was able to regain my composure, if you will, and willed myself to a healing state of mind and body. Life was finally back on track, or so I thought.

Have you ever had a moment where your life flashes in front of you? Mine came when I remembered that vision I had years ago to witness both my son's graduation from high school. That day actually arrived, and that was the moment that I said, "I beat Cancer down, and it does not get to rule my life any longer!" Celebrations all around, and I was asked to create a new goal of my successful challenge against this lethal disease. I chose, and the new goal I set was to witness both my son's weddings. This was a huge wish of mine because that gift meant I would gain two new family members—daughters-in-law. I was beyond excited for the future and to witness both boys in their glory. I went about my life, and as a jet-setting fashion executive, I was traveling in Asia when I had an opportunity to meet a famous fortune-teller from Taiwan. A trusted friend, a manufacturer who created accessories for the brand I was then working with, treated my team and me to a beautiful dinner at the Mandarin Oriental Hotel in Hong Kong. A few things happened before we took the ferry over from the Kowloon side to the Hong Kong side of the island. I had just received a FedEx just before we left for dinner. I threw the package on the bed and took off for our dinner engagement.

We arrived at dinner, and the Madam Fortune Teller was intrigued by my presence and asked to do a reading for me in front of the team. I was an open book, so I was fine with the exercise, thinking what she could say that would ROCK my WORLD? Her mysterious way of being was captivating the audience of nine. She lit a cigarette and asked a few questions, and proceeded to look up a few things in her black book. She then came back and said, "You just received an important document, follow through with the contents immediately!" Chills ran down my spine as the FedEx I spoke about earlier was our living trust that my husband, Hiro, sent to me for review during my 18-hour flight home from Hong Kong to New York. I chose to stay neutral and hushed what I was thinking and listened intently to her following words. She continued and said, "Either you or your husband has a life-threatening disease; when you arrive home, go to the doctors, the both of you, and ensure every part of your system is checked!" I felt more chills down my spine. Her last comment to me was, "Stop worrying about your older son, worry about the youngest as I see motorcycles, accidents, best to keep him away from this."

This was another moment of, "WOW!" My youngest son is still an avid two-wheel lover. He has no fear, and this rang so true for me that he chose not to invest in a motorcycle once I shared this story. Crisis averted. I left dinner that night feeling overwhelmed, to say the least, and chose to fall back on my Faith that the spiritual gods were on my side, and that this, too, shall pass.

I arrived home, spoke with Hiro, and we both scheduled doctor's appointments to ensure we were healthy and life would be "normal" as it had been for the past ten years.

Well, you guessed it, life took a wild turn. Of course, as my doctors always stated to me, you are in the 3% group that has unique issues. They found another pea-size lump on my right breast, and I was sent to radiology to have it checked out. The females reading this know that once we are examined, we get to sit and wait to be excused if the scans look good. After five ladies were excused and I was waiting for my release, I was asked to stay and view the scans with the radiologist. It did not look good.

Everything moved quickly after that, and I was in and out of doctors' offices and hospitals. I had one moment of truth; will I survive it this time?

Breast cancer was alive in my body, and it was a different, very aggressive cancer. There was no time to wait. I chose to be aggressive with a mastectomy and to embark upon a major 18-hour reconstruction surgery, finally. Talk about FAITH—I needed it, big time.

I chose to stay in consistent, committed action, knowing that if I believed I could win this battle again, I had to be versed on what was available to me from doctors, surgeries, recovery, and whatever else they told me to do in preparation for what was about to happen.

I closed my eyes, prayed, created the space to open my mindset to all possibilities, and it carried me through to where I am today. I am ALIVE. I am HEALED. I just received a 100% cure diagnosis from my oncologist. FAITH carried me through many dark moments, and today, I feel free, full of joy, love, and inspiration!

ELAINE SUGIMURA

About Elaine R. Sugimura: Elaine is an accomplished fashion executive turned entrepreneur who has a passion to create leaders amongst leaders. Currently, she owns several businesses and as CEO, she runs a franchise food and beverage organization that requires both strategy and execution. Fun fact: she is an adrenaline junkie—the higher, the faster, the better. Her love for adventure has led her to travel to many parts of the world by plane and automobile. She and her husband, Hiro, share their home in Northern California. They have raised two extraordinary sons and have added two beautiful daughters-in-law to their growing family.

Author's Website: *www.ElaineRSugimura.com*
Book Series Website & Author's Bio: *www.The13StepstoRiches.com*

Elizabeth Walker

FAITH GIVES RISE TO THOUGHT

Over the last twelve years, she held onto her Faith as though her life depended on it. She relied on her Faith in the sanctity of marriage, Faith that it would get easier, Faith that she would be able to change it, and Faith that all of those things were possible. She believed with an unwavering Faith that in the end, everything would be OK.

A wise man named Ben once gifted her a mantra, "In the end, everything is OK, and if it's not OK, it's not the end." She based her Faith on that. And she held onto that mantra for many years.

She had held onto Faith that this perfect place would be the answer to all her problems, and yet over the past eight months, things had only become worse.

There was some reprieve on the days she spent lying in the sun at a beautiful pool on top of the hill overlooking a plethora of nearby islands. And there was certainly joy found in home-schooling her two children, excitedly watching them discover curiosity. The way they would gleefully wait on the jetty for their learning package that would come via post and then via a boat was a pleasure to behold.

Three days earlier, she had decided that either some things would need to get better or she was going to leave. She knew, deep down, that the prospect of them getting better was very slim. She was holding onto hope, bargaining with the universe to keep together that which she had worked so hard for.

It was a warm and balmy night, the palm trees gently swaying in the breeze and the ocean caressing the coral shore in and out, in and out. For most people, this sounds like the start to a perfect evening, and for many, it was. The music was playing, the children were dancing, and lovers on the beach were kissing. It was perfect for everyone except her.

Amidst this beautiful scene, there was only confusion in her mind. What did it mean? What would happen next? Was it time? And if it were, how would she know?

This was not the first time she had had these questions; however, it was the first time she was willing to do anything about them.

Despite the confusion, there was a strength inside her, a knowing in her body. Her mind was racing and creating all sorts of disastrous scenarios. Her body had a strange sense of calm. Something that, although it was familiar to her, she had not felt in an exceptionally long time. She put the children to bed and rang a friend who worked in the bar just below her room in the resort. She said she needed something to put her mind at rest, and a new Ben came to the rescue. The irony of the Latin meaning of the name Ben was not lost on her. It means being blessed.

A martini glass with a bright lime drink in it was swiftly delivered to her door. He had before and told her again that it would be alright. He hugged her and told her he believed in her. He said to her that perhaps the best solution was to leave and create something new over time. And the girl who never drank downed the glass in less than thirty seconds. It instantly calmed her mind as she felt the warmth of its spirit surge through her body. She was about to embark on the biggest journey of her life, and at this point, even she did not know it.

That night she prayed, and as she did, she felt the guilt of having drunk alcohol instead of relying on Faith, and she cut her prayers short as the guilt became overwhelming. What would her children think? What would her parents think? Could she be the first person in her entire family tree to do this?

As she gently cried herself to sleep, embraced in guilt and the warmth of the tropical air, she felt something inside burning. She believed in herself, and something more significant was reawakened.

She remembered who she was; she came from a long line of successful men and women. All of them had suffered their forms of adversity. The one thing they had all taught her was that Faith in something bigger than herself and in the spirit itself was essential to be successful in life. And as she lay there feeling guilty and broken, this burning inside grew and grew. She became stronger as she connected to a Faith instilled in her from an incredibly young age.

You see, Faith is holding unfailingly, a belief in the mind that describes the future in detail, despite all current evidence to the contrary.

What she had been experiencing over the past thirteen years gave her enough evidence to let go of all her Faith, or so she thought. This burning feeling inside of her, not just in her body but her mind as well, reminded her of everything she could believe. Her Faith was restored! And with this, her language changed. She started saying to herself that she could and started saying it was possible, she started saying it was worth it, and most importantly, she started saying she was worth it.

It is important to remember that the language we use to ourselves, both verbally and inside our own head, determines our external projection. In other words, what you see from the outside is exactly what has been created over time due to our Faith and internal dialogue. Faith gives rise to thought. It is Faith that transforms something from the spirit world into reality.

It was Faith that allowed her to see the possibility of success as the very next day. She stepped into the great unknown.

It was a memory of Faith, which by the way, is Faith, that allowed her to know that the unknown was only unknown until she took a step in its direction. It was Faith that reminded her just how powerful she was. Faith allowed the voice in her head to stop believing she was not good enough and start believing that she was in exactly the right place at exactly the right time.

Remember, it is Faith that allows a direct connection through vibration between the mind and the spirit. Faith is the only way to communicate between the brain and the spiritual realm directly.

She knew that she'd been taught this burning in the body, the Faith in herself, and the Faith in spirit (which is far more abundant and expansive than her), and that very next day, she stepped into the great unknown by way of a helicopter.

As the blades were spinning and pounding air down on to the ground, she took the hands of her two children and all climbed aboard. As the chopper lifted off the ground, she felt her Faith grow stronger and stronger. She had finally done it! She had left! And she realized at that moment that she had held onto her Faith the whole time. Through thirteen years of pain, shame and blame, she had held on to Faith. With each kilometer she flew away from her island home, that Faith grew stronger and stronger.

As the days went on from there, she noticed that if she maintained a high vibration and frequency, her Faith in herself and the natural rhythm of the universe increased. She had full Faith in the universe and understood what the word meant. UniVerse = One Song. Her Faith allowed her to remain connected through the darkest days of her life to this song, the one we all sing. The one that is available to all of us when we tune into the spiritual realms.

The Faith that she continued to hold as her journey unfolded over the next ten years surprisingly was not unwavering. Every time she felt disconnected, though, she could return to her Faith in the universe. In these times of detachment, she would remove herself from all distractions and sit quietly in nature. Be it at the beach, a mountain, the bush, or a river; she would sit or sometimes lay and reconnect to Faith. The Faith that she could do it, the Faith that she was worth it, the Faith that she was a miracle, the Faith that riches would come, the Faith that while she lay there through mere vibration, she could be one with the spiritual realms.

It was simple, really, and she had realized as she looked back, that every time she felt lonely, unworthy, unwanted, rejected, not good enough, fearful, angry, guilty, or sad, it was merely her disconnecting from Faith and removing herself from the one song. The time she spent alone was a beautiful reminder of how Faith never leaves her. She only ever leaves her Faith.

I am glad she held onto Faith all those years. And I am glad she sings with the universe and encourages others to do the same.

She is me.

ELIZABETH WALKER

About Elizabeth Walker: Elizabeth is Australia's leading Female Integrated NLP Trainer, an international speaker with Real Success, and the host of Success Resources' (Australia's largest and most successful events promoter, including speakers such as Tony Robbins and Sir Richard Branson) inaugural Australian Women's Program "The Seed." Elizabeth has guided many people to achieve complete personal breakthroughs and phenomenal personal and business growth. With over 25 years of experience transforming the lives of hundreds of thousands of people, Elizabeth's goal is to assist leaders to create the reality they choose to live, impacting millions on a global scale.

A thought leader who has worked alongside people like Gary Vaynerchuck, Kerwin Rae, Jeffery Slayter, and Kate Gray, Elizabeth has an outstanding method of delivering heart with business.

As a former lecturer in medicine at the University of Sydney and lecturer in nursing at Western Sydney University, Elizabeth was instrumental in the research and development of the stillbirth and neonatal death pathways, ensuring each family in Australia went home knowing what happened to their child, and felt understood, heard, and seen.

A former Australian Champion in Trampolining and Australian Dancesport, Elizabeth has always been passionate about the mindset and skills required to create the results you are seeking.

Author's website: *www.ElizabethAnneWalker.com*
Book Series Website & Author's Bio: *www.The13StepsToRiches.com*

Erin Ley

EMPOWERED BY FAITH

In *Think and Grow Rich*, Napoleon Hill beautifully states, "Faith is the head chemist of the mind. When Faith blends with the vibration of thought, the subconscious mind instantly picks up the vibration, translates it into its spiritual equivalent, and transmits it to Infinite Intelligence, as in the case of prayer."

Faith is the deepest part of my being, connecting me fully with God. It's a state of mind, a state of beingness, whereby I release all worldly worry and rely fully on God's will.

One example of this was when I was diagnosed with cancer in 1991 at age twenty-five. Doctors introduced me to topics such as, "If the chemo doesn't work as fast as the tumor is growing, you'll be dead in a month," or, "As a result of this surgery you may end up blind," and even, "Please get your things in order, you will not make it out of the hospital. I'm sorry."

Non-Hodgkins Lymphoblastic Lymphoma is a rare, deadly pediatric cancer. In 1991, very few people survived that diagnosis. It was a grueling two-and-a-half-year protocol with a harsh prognosis; however, I credit my Faith in God, myself, and my doctors for my defying the odds every time and going on to thrive.

At the beginning of the protocol, I went deep within and began to understand Faith on a more powerful level than anything I had learned in the all-girls Catholic school and Sunday Mass. God and I instantly became best friends. I prayed, meditated, and stayed connected to Him, feeling His presence within, and bringing calm to my storms. We all have this gift. Some tap into it, and some do not.

Just three months into treatments, the veins in my arms collapsed due to the toxic chemotherapy. The surgical team had to place a port in my chest, with a catheter going into the vein in my neck, whereby doctors and nurses extracted blood for testing and injected chemotherapy for treatment. At the same time, the spinal taps stopped working. The doctors treated my brain with chemotherapy prophylactically. My spine built up fatty tissues as a defense mechanism based on the significant amount of spinal taps I received. The doctor needed to extract cerebrospinal fluid to biopsy and inject chemotherapy, just in case the cancer spread to the brain. They could not continue performing spinal taps, so instead, the doctors told me I had to have an Ommaya reservoir placed in my brain. The surgeon sat with my mother and me and told us he would cut open my scalp, drill a hole in my skull, and implant the reservoir by inserting the catheter into a ventricle in my brain. There were many risks involved that he acquainted us with, the least of which was blindness. As he continued to speak, he went on to sound like Charlie Brown's teacher. I tuned out.

During this time, as surgery after surgery was happening, never planned, just one surprise after the next, I knew it was up to me to optimize my mental, emotional, physical, and spiritual health. I did not have a choice. I had done the personal development work on myself to know that everything I needed to get through all of it unscathed was within me. I knew negative outcomes would result if I focused on fear. As the fear came through, I acknowledged it and released it quickly, having Faith that I'd regain my excellent health.

I'll never forget this line from Napoleon Hill's book, *Think and Grow Rich*: "ALL THOUGHTS WHICH HAVE BEEN EMOTIONALIZED (given feeling) AND MIXED WITH FAITH, begin immediately to translate themselves into their physical equivalent or counterpart."

I developed "Manifesting UPO vs. UNO 101":

1. Positive Thoughts + Positive Actions

   = Unstoppable Positive Outcomes (UPO)

2. Negative Thoughts + Negative Actions

   = Unstoppable Negative Outcomes (UNO)

After the initial shock and tears, I knew I had to release the worry. I became intentional about meditating, visualizing myself in the palm of God's hand. I had Faith He would carry me through all of it. My Faith in God, Jesus, the Holy Spirit, and the Blessed Mother transcended all worry and concern. I knew what I had to do, and that was to stay focused on what was right with my life as opposed to what was wrong with it, focused on attaining excellent health right then and there.

I wrote out a crystal-clear vision for my life regarding where I wanted to be in two-and-a-half years when the protocol was over. Based on my readings and my intuition, I knew that this crystal-clear vision had to be brought to life at that very moment. I could not wait years to experience the inner peace and joy excellent health provides. I prayed and meditated, visualizing the loving bright white light cleansing my body, healing my scars, as I began finding the blessings in it all. My Faith is what I believe ignited my desire to be become focused, fearless, and excited about life.

We cannot be in Faith and fear at the same time. It is impossible. I knew I had a decision to make. Which of the two did I want to entertain? I chose Faith. Not only did I heal from the surgeries and the cancer altogether, but I also went on to have three beautiful, healthy children the doctors swore would never happen.

My Faith is so strong that I can create exactly what I want, and so can you. The only time in life I derail is when I allow myself to introduce fear and doubt. Fear and doubt are dream-crushers. When you replace fear and doubt with Faith and confidence, you are unstoppable. I had to have the Faith and the courage to keep going, never to give up, because confidence comes as we continue to focus on what we want and have the courage and Faith to step into the uncomfortableness that life serves us from time to time. It is through the valleys that we stretch and grow. Our greatest lessons are learned there; therefore, each new peak is greater than the last.

Trust yourself. Trust your Higher Power. Embrace, acknowledge, accept, and celebrate change while walking enveloped in Faith.

I always say, "Celebrate life, and you'll have a life worth celebrating." The miracles keep happening, and the blessings are abundant. We all have God-given-gifts that we are meant to utilize during our lifetime. I listen to my gut, and my intuition, to tap into those gifts. I know I live on purpose when it feels right, when it lights me up, and when it feels effortless. From this place, I love to create, in Faith, knowing my life is on track.

Our soul knows what direction our life is supposed to take and what track we are on. When we experience depression, anxiety, fear, lack, or scarcity, I honestly believe our soul cries out, letting us know we are off purpose. We can always course-correct in the present moment at any time.

How many of you put 1000% Faith in others before you even put 10% Faith in yourself? Stop allowing yourself to trust other people before permitting yourself to trust yourself. Prior to my cancer diagnosis, I looked to the outer world for validation for everything—who I was, how pretty I was, how smart I was, how successful I could be, everything. Then, post-diagnosis at age twenty-five, I learned about this whole inner world, and, at that point, I had an instant awakening. I got into the driver's seat of my own life. I did not allow others, or even life, to drive me, my thoughts, decisions, feelings, or actions any longer. I developed complete Faith in myself.

Having fully aligned with who I truly am, I have not struggled with any (what people refer to nowadays as) imposter syndrome. Since 1991, I have felt the strong desire to share the hard-earned wisdom I have embraced with the world. I want to scream it from the rooftops and have everyone in the world know what I know. The love, joy, and inner peace that comes about, as a result, are magnificent.

As a lifelong student in this class called life, I love moving onward and upward in Faith, always learning and growing. I will continue to be a student of life until I take my last breath; moreover, I will continue to teach what I have learned, what many refer to as 'the secret.' When family and friends talk about retirement, I cringe. I love what I do and never want to stop. I feel truly blessed.

Set a crystal-clear vision for *your* life and have Faith that it will become *your* reality. All things are possible if you are open to the possibilities, in Faith.

ERIN LEY

About Erin Ley: As Founder and CEO of Onward Productions, Inc., Erin Ley has spent the last 30 years as an Author, Professional Speaker, Personal and Professional Empowerment and Success Coach predominantly around mindset, Vision and Decision. Founder of many influential summits, including "Life On Track," Erin is also the host of the upcoming online streaming T.V. Show *"Life On Track with Erin Ley,"* which is all about helping you get into the driver's seat of your own life.

They call Erin "The Miracle Maker!" As a cancer survivor at age twenty-five, single mom of three at age forty-seven, successful Entrepreneur at age fifty, Erin has shown thousands upon thousands across the globe how to become victorious by being focused, fearless, and excited about life and your future! Erin says, "Celebrate life and you'll have a life worth celebrating!"

To see more about Erin and the release of her 4th book *"WorkLuv: A Love Story"* along with her "Life On Track" Course & Coaching Programs, please visit her website.

Author's website: *www.ErinLey.com*
Book Series Website & Author's Bio: *www.The13StepsToRiches.com*

Fatima Hurd

FAITH IS MY COMPASS

Faith is knowing all that you desire will come to fruition when surrendering all to God. It's knowing that what you want with your heart's desire will show up because God has your back!

I woke up one morning and sat on my bed. I felt an overwhelming grace of gratitude for the little guy next to me laying sound asleep in his crib. My heart was filled with pure love as I recognized that I now had another beautiful person to live for. Having him beside me inspired me to be the best version of myself. I got up, got dressed, and kissed my little guy before heading off to work.

That day started like any other workday. I walked in and checked my emails. I felt off, almost like I couldn't breathe. I called home to see if the baby was okay—he was. I went back to checking my emails when my manager came in and asked me to follow him. I was surprised, but I followed anyway.

I had just gotten back from my days off, so I figured maybe they just wanted to get me caught up with something I had missed while I was away. I was led to the director's office and asked to take a seat. It was nerve-racking at this point. I noticed that my director wouldn't look at me at first. Then she began. All I heard was, "This is the part of my job I dislike the most." She proceeded to tell me that due to the recession, the company decided to cut back, and staff reductions were inevitable. She lost me at that point, I knew what was coming. I was trying to process what she was telling me but couldn't focus. I have never been laid off in all my years. I had managed to overcome two major layoffs—one in 2001 after 9/11 and the second one when the company was sold. I was in disbelief and was struggling to process. She kept emphasizing that it was nothing, that I had done wrong, and it was a staff reduction, but it was all the same to me. It just meant I didn't have a job!

I went home feeling defeated and afraid. I wasn't sure what to do. I was given a small severance package, and once that ran out, I had to apply for unemployment.

I was a single mom with a four-month-old who needed me. This is not the life I dreamed for myself at twenty-nine years old, living at home with my mom.

The first week was hard. I felt like I had no purpose, and it was difficult finding a job in the middle of the recession. I stopped watching the news as I could no longer bear the bad news of the financial collapse. I continued to apply for jobs, but I never got a call as staff reductions were happening in all casinos due to the recession. I also worked through the emotions that came with defeat. I gave myself grace and allowed myself a pity party. It almost felt like another breakup. I was sad, angry, and confused. Weirdly enough, I almost felt a sense of relief, because even though I did not know it then, my time there was over. The truth was that I was miserable with my job, but I was afraid to quit on my own, so God helped by laying me off. There were bigger and better things in store for me; I just had to get out of my way.

I envisioned being able to provide the best life for my son and me. I held on to Faith that this was all happening for a reason. Even though I had lost my job, we had food on the table, and my son had all that he needed and then some. When my attitude became about gratitude for spending this time with my son and my mindset shifted to a positive one, things began to turn around for me. I took advantage of this time to enjoy my son and to learn more about myself. I had Faith that all was going to be okay. Instead of wasting my energy thinking about what I was going to do, I shifted my attention to what I wanted to do.

I pulled up my sleeves and began the work. I continued to put in job applications but kept my Faith that God guided me in the right direction. I picked up my first book by Jack Canfield, *The Success Principles*. I read it from cover to cover, and my journey began to transform my life. I promised myself and my son that I would never give my power away again, and the day they let me go was the last time I was going to allow someone to tell me my worth. This is what gave birth to my entrepreneurial spirit. I was ready to create and design the life that I wanted. Who do I want to be, how do I want to show up? I was ready to manifest and have it all come to fruition. I started to visualize the life I wanted.

I created a vision board and got very clear on what I wanted for every aspect of my life. I began to use affirmations and got really honest with myself. I remember thinking about falling in love again because I deserved it with someone who loved my son and me. I began to write down everything I loved about this man and everything that he loved about me and described his love for my son. I wanted him to be the father figure my son needed and deserved in his life. I quickly realized that even though I thought I was done with love after being hurt, that love was not done with me.

On December 23, 2008, I went and bought, collected, and borrowed supplies I needed for my vision board. I put all my love and Faith and surrendered to God the vision that I had in my heart for my life. I wrote every word by hand, cut out every picture, and pasted it into the board with love, hope, and Faith. I visualized every picture with my son, me, and the mystery man in it. I couldn't see his face, but I could feel his heart. I felt so much love, and it felt so real that it almost felt like a memory. I yearned for someone in my life that I could feel comfortable with in my own skin and to be myself. Being honest with myself lead to putting it on the vision board to design the life I wanted.

I wanted to be an entrepreneur and create my income and my hours. I poured my heart, soul, and Faith into setting my intention for those opportunities to show up because I was ready to receive. I put the intention on New Year's Eve with the certainty that the new year would be the best one yet for my son.

One day I signed up for a dating app. I was initially reluctant, but there was a driving desire inside me to do it as though being guided, so I did. A few days later, I met my now-husband. We talked every day. It felt so natural, as if I'd known him forever; I knew he was the one. Three years later, we were married and welcomed two more children. As a mother, my biggest desire for my son was for him to have a dad that loved him unconditionally, someone that was supportive, and caring. His relationship with my son is amazing! Anyone can be a father, but my husband chose to be a dad to my son, and their bond is strong!

My life experiences groomed my true purpose as I released the shackles that held me back. I grew up with limiting beliefs, but I chose not to stay a prisoner of them. Working on myself has been key to shifting my mindset; however, desire and Faith have been the power driving things to fruition. The power of Faith is one of the secret ingredients to designing the life you want. I know now that my life reflects my beliefs, and when I change my beliefs, I change my life.

I have created my best life so far. I live in California with a heart full of gratitude for the long days on the beach with my little family and continue to create opportunities that lead to success in all areas of my life. Gratitude is my way of life, and Faith is my compass through life!

FATIMA HURD

About Fatima Hurd: Fatima is a personal brand photographer and was featured in the special edition of Beauty & Lifestyle's mommy magazine. Fatima specializes in personal branding photographs dedicated to helping influencers and entrepreneurs expand their reach online with strategic, creative, inspiring, and visual content. Owner of a digital consulting agency, Social Branding Digital Solutions, Fatima helps professionals with all their digital needs.

Fatima holds ten years of photography experience. An expert in her field, she helps teach photography to middle school students and she hosts workshops to teach anyone who wants to learn how to use and improve their skills with DSLR and on manual mode. Hurd is also a mother of three, wife, certified Reiki master, and certified crystal healer. She loves being out in nature, enjoys taking road trips with her family, and loves meditation and yoga on the beach.

Author's website: *www.FatimaHurd.com*
Book Series Website & Author's Bio: *www.The13StepsToRiches.com*

Frankie Fegurgur

IS YOUR SUCCESS INEVITABLE?

Life has a way of making sure you really want what you say you want. For example, you had hoped that by identifying your burning desire, the clouds would part, all the stoplights would turn green in front of you, and you'd reach your goal without breaking a sweat. But I bet as soon as you declared your definiteness of purpose, life got in the way.

Suddenly, someone went out sick at work and all that free time for finally starting your side business was quickly filled with building someone else's dream. And the money you wanted to invest got devoured by surprise car repairs. And the running shoes you bought to shed those pandemic pounds gave you blisters and then shin splints. The list went on and on until you ended up more discouraged than you started! What's up with all of that?

I've known that pain all too well. When I left the certainty of a military paycheck to start a business, it was like deploying to another galaxy. I went from knowing where to be, what to do, and how to dress 24/7 to having no schedule, no idea how to market or sell, and no clue how to afford my obscene dry-cleaning bills. Sure, as a Sergeant in the Marine Corps, I didn't get paid well. Yet, I had earned that uniform with blood, sweat, and tears, whereas wearing a cheap suit in an office felt more like playing dress-up at high-school career day.

I often struggled with feeling too young, not educated enough, and not financially successful enough for anyone to take me seriously.

After buying a modest-looking book entitled *The Think & Grow Rich Action Pack*, this feeling of lack began to shift for me. This copy still sits on my desk, complete with my last name written across the tail, as 15 bucks was no small expenditure for me just 15 years ago. Today, recognizing the power of its pages, I'd gladly pay substantially more. This is in large part because of the principle of faith.

Of the 13 principles for success presented by Napoleon Hill, the concept of faith is what I struggled with the most. Intellectually, I understood that I needed to 'be positive.' I couldn't discern a deeper meaning behind the nature of faith and how it related to self-confidence.

That makes co-creating this series of 13 books a total act of applied faith. Nothing obvious stood out as qualifying me to write about principles I didn't entirely understand. I was introduced to this project *seemingly by accident* and was full of doubt whether I had something worthwhile to contribute. Learning about the guest authors was almost the final blow; how could my name share the same pages alongside such titans?

Then something inside of me seemed to offer a different narrative: "I can run with the greats." It was almost a whisper, not even louder than the click of my mouse as I began to shut down my computer. But the voice persisted, and soon I imagined standing on the same stage as these titans. Not only was I thanking them for their influence on my life, but I was there to give my signature speech. Now, I have no idea if it was faith that grabbed me or just plain old sleep deprivation playing tricks on me, but I committed that night to see this opportunity through. At that moment, I demanded something greater in my life and established a much deeper appreciation of faith.

To share my recent realization, I'll describe both sides of the same coin: faith and self-confidence. Faith is knowing that all around us is the abundance of an infinite intelligence. Self-confidence is embodying that same creative energy also found within each of us. When you combine this awareness with love, it's like rolling out the red-carpet superhighway from your subconscious straight to your desire. This is critical to understand because, without faith, it's very unlikely that the remaining principles will be of much use to you. If you are skeptical or have been in a rut, read on to learn simple ways to develop faith and confidence.

Lately, many people have struggled with self-doubt and low self-esteem. Before we discuss how to build confidence, we need to address this feeling of disconnection from our personal strengths. Did you choose this life, or did you end up with what you were willing to accept? If you've allowed the "it's too late" seed to sprout in your mind, then I need you to hear me, friend:

It's time to dream again. It's time to suspend your disbelief about what is possible for you. It's time to acknowledge the greatness inside of you. It's time to take action with the tenacity that only comes from knowing you are unbreakable AND unstoppable.

You now know that our subconscious isn't concerned whether we are feeding it lies or truths. By choosing to feed it love and faith consistently, you utilize the power of autosuggestion. It may seem odd to be so committed to receiving your desire when there is a lack of evidence in front of you. Many people can't handle not seeing and instead focus on the opposite of faith.

The opposite of faith is a certainty. Certainty is needing guarantees. It's wanting all those stoplights to be green. It was me wanting the safety of a military paycheck, despite claiming to desire a much more significant income. We cling to the safety of the side of the swimming pool when all the fun is diving in the deep end!

And yet, countless people are settling for something less than they are capable of achieving. They are forcing and fighting, trying to willpower their way through the daily grind. Certainty is having to know exactly how it all works out before we decide it's worth it to take action. Stop telling the universe that you won't give until you receive! You might be asking how you can possibly give what you don't have. While it's true that you can't offer what you don't possess, I'd challenge you to look again. See what you are and what surrounds you with a fresh set of eyes.

Instead of blaming our circumstances or our associations for why we lack what we desire, we can build evidence to the contrary. You can generate the momentum to be ready for your next big speech, or that next tough conversation, or when you need a reminder that all the obstacles you are encountering are happening for you to get what you said you wanted. With a big belief in faith, big wealth in all areas of your life is possible. We don't get what we hope for; we get what we expect.

When you bargain with life, demand your desire *and then some*. More and more people are enjoying the success they previously believed impossible. Why not you?

To tune into faith whenever we feel disconnected, begin the process by focusing on what is, not what we want or don't want. When we sit still, it does not matter how close or far we are from our desire. The point is to observe what is real.

Unfortunately, just as I described, most of our desires are not our own (please refer to the volume on Desire, the first book in our series). For most people, their sense of confidence comes from external validation. When we buy or achieve something, we are applauded by those around us, emphasizing the belief that we need to be having and achieving to maintain self-worth constantly. This limiting belief is not only flat-out wrong but also highly contagious.

Fortunately, beliefs are solidified through the combination of repetition and emotion. You must begin to keep small commitments to yourself to provide evidence for your subconscious that this new desire should be obtained without resistance. To do this is simple; multiple times a day, visualize your desire. Secondly, experience it as if you already have it. Lastly, embody the behaviors of someone who has what you desire. To gauge if you have acted from faith, look at your daily life for clues. When something big or small doesn't go your way, does it wear you down or build you up? The average individual is beat down by adversity. The champion is elevated!

As our discussion comes to its natural interlude, we are reminded that source energy surrounds us. We must also acknowledge source energy is within us. Not only is everything possible, but it's already created—we must simply be present in our experience. Abundance is meant to be our default. Faith is aligning with this truth.

What do you have faith in? What steps have you taken to experience your desire in the present moment? How are you living consciously and on purpose? Send me a message; I'd love to hear more about your journey!

FRANKIE FEGURGUR

About Frankie Fegurgur: Frankie's "burning desire" is helping people retire with dignity. Frankie distills the lessons he has learned over the last 15 years and empowers our youth to make better financial decisions than the generation before them. This is a deeply personal mission for him—he was born to high-school-aged parents, and money was always a struggle. Frankie learned that hard work, alone, wasn't the key to financial freedom and sought a more fulfilling path. Now, he serves as the COO of a nonprofit financial association based in the San Francisco Bay Area, teaching money mindfulness. He, his wife, and their two children can be found exploring, volunteering, and building throughout their community.

Author's website: *www.FrankMoneyTalk.com*
Book Series Website & Author's Bio: *www.The13StepsToRiches.com*

Freeman Witherspoon

FAITH, THE KEY TO AN ABUNDANT LIFE

Faith is defined as "a trust or confidence in the intentions or abilities of a person, object, or ideal from empirical evidence." Faith is also defined as, "the process of forming or understanding abstractions, ideas, beliefs, without empirical evidence, experience, or observation." The concept of Faith is oftentimes misunderstood. Because of this misunderstanding, most people are not able to experience the fruit of Faith. Faith has inherent energies and vibrations that can cause one to excel or fulfill their dreams in life irrespective of who you are or where you come from.

"Now faith is the substance of things hoped for, the evidence of things not seen. For by it, the elders obtained a good report. Through faith, we understand that the worlds were framed by the word of God so that things which are seen were not made of things which do appear. By faith, Abel offered unto God a more excellent sacrifice than Cain, by which he obtained witness that he was righteous, God tesDfying of his giEs: and by it, he being dead yet speaketh. By faith, Enoch was translated that he should not see death; and was not found because God had translated him: for before his translaDon, he had this tesDmony, that he pleased God. But without faith [it is] impossible to please [him]: for he that cometh to God must believe that he is, and [that] he is a rewarder of them that diligently seek him."
(Hebrews 11:1–6)

This text unravels the concept of Faith and how it applies to everyday life. Faith is having a certainty of something before it becomes tangible. In walking in that unseen reality, we can begin to take the proper action to bring our dreams into reality. Success is possible for anyone, and it can be achieved through Faith. Faith induces commitment, discipline, and hard work towards the desired outcome. The moment someone sets their mind to achieve a dream, they will take the appropriate steps to make that dream a reality. Anatole France asserts that, "To accomplish great things, we must not only act but also dream; not only plan but also believe." Faith is an integral part of living a successful life.

Everything in this world is governed by Faith. God framed the world through Faith. Thus, He spoke things into being when there was no reality.

Without Faith, there is no way one can receive anything from the Lord. It is very interesting to note that God is not going to be pleased by the house we live in, the car we drive, or the clothes we wear. The only way to please Him is through our Faith. It is important to understand that Faith is a living thing with the ability to grow. Therefore, to strengthen your Faith and produce results that will usher you to a place of abundance, wealth, fortunes, and even fame, then you have to keep nourishing your Faith.

My initial introduction to the power of Faith came at the age of six when I had the opportunity to live with my grandparents following a tragic loss.

I oftentimes found my young mind wondering how can a good God let bad things happen. My grandmother, the richest woman in the world, (rich not in money, but rich in God's Spirit) touched my life tremendously. Her riches were not of the treasures of this world but the divine. She believed in God and walked in the realities of virtues that hold the universe. She imparted these virtues in me and taught me to lean on my Faith and never give up.

The person that I am today is a result of those encounters with my grandmother.

Her nurturing and guidance was so impactful. She taught me to be strong and never focus on the challenges of life. She encouraged me to always look up to God—who sustains all things. She made me understand that God is the only one to change things for me and that it was necessary to trust Him for myself. She cautioned that, every time, everything in this world is going to fail, and we, therefore, needed to keep our Faith in God, and that is how we are going to survive.

Indeed, I watched these words manifest. Whenever things went wrong, and I found myself in strange lands, God was there for me. If we can dare to believe God, He is never going to fail or disappoint us.

Later in life, my Faith currency was required once again. I was bedridden due to an infection in my spinal column. It came on suddenly, and I went from being in perfect health to being in a hospital bed all in a single day. The first few weeks, my medical team's only solution was pain management. They probed and prodded, performed test after test, all in the course of trying to find a remedy. Finally, after several biopsies, antibiotics were tried, and presto—my breakthrough. The whole ordeal lasted over two months, providing lots of quiet time, especially at the midnight hour.

Little did I know that God was using that experience to reach out to me. God allowed me to endure that "valley experience" because He wanted a relationship with me. As everything seemed to be falling apart, people started giving up on me. That was when I began to nourish that seed planted in me long ago—my Faith. All along, I had this seed in me, but I wasn't nourishing it. At the moment where it seemed all hope was lost, I started to communicate with God. As I kept whispering my pain and agony to Him, He listened.

As time went by, God spoke to me and changed my life. I increased my Faith in Him, and things started to change. Paul wrote to the people in Rome and made them understand that Faith comes by hearing, and hearing the Word of God. (Romans 10:17) As I was meditating and ruminating on the word, something came alive in me—Faith. It was during these times I noticed my situation beginning to change.

My body began to heal, and all of my internal systems began to rejuvenate. That is how I got better. Faith helped me realize there is power in Faith. Faith is the greatest force in life.

Faith can heal, deliver, restore, and even propel you into greatness.

Faith is our link to the divine. I call it the bridge of access. Without it, no one can receive anything from God.

It is human nature to believe in something greater than self. As I placed my trust in God, He has come through for me in many ways. He protected me, and He provided for me. He sustained me and, above all, and He directed me each day on how to go about life. In life, you need to exercise Faith in God.

You also need to have a genuine belief in yourself and your dream, as well. God will sustain you during the tough times, and Faith in yourself and your dream will motivate you to take the appropriate action steps to reach your goals.

Whatever you have set out to become, it is possible. Whatever dream you are carrying, that dream is possible, and you must believe in it. Life is full of possibilities. So there is no need to lose Faith in your dreams. Dreams come true every day for those that have Faith and put in the work. We often give up on our dreams too easily, which is why we never see the beauty of the dreams. If we can believe and hold ourselves accountable, we can see the manifestation of our dreams. Today, whatever dream you are carrying, you have to dare to believe in it, and that is how you can manifest that dream.

I am a benefactor of Faith. Faith has brought me so much more reward than anything in this life. Faith has connected me to incredible people all over the world, and these relationships are steadily thriving and growing each day. Faith has transformed me into a person of purpose. This can happen to anyone who will dare to believe. If we can believe it, we can achieve it. We capture God's attention when we begin to walk in Faith.

This unravels why Paul gave that assertion that without Faith, it is impossible to please God. Without Faith, no one can please God or can have their dreams manifest. It is as simple as that.

Take Faith seriously if you want to manifest your dreams. Eleanor Roosevelt stated, "The future belongs to those who believe in the beauty of their dreams." Faith creates the future of success. There are hidden energies in Faith. These energies and vibrations are only unleashed when we believe. Believe in yourself and your dream and then you can experience the glory of it.

FREEMAN WITHERSPOON

About Freeman Witherspoon: Freeman is a professional network marketer that manages several online businesses. He considers himself a late bloomer to network marketing. Prior to partnering with network marketing organizations, he served for over 20 years in the military. He has incorporated his many life experiences into managing successful business models.

Military service afforded him the opportunity to travel throughout the world. He has lived in Heidelberg, Germany, Seoul, South Korea, and many places throughout the United States. Freeman currently lives in Texas with his wife and three dogs; a Dachshund named Dutchess, a Yorkie named Boosie and a Pomchi (Pomeranian-Chihuahua mix) named Caesar.

Author's website: *www.FWitherspoonJr.com*
Book Series Website & Author's Bio: *www.The13StepsToRiches.com*

Gina Bacalski

WHERE FAITH CAN LEAD YOU

It was always a goal of mine to be single and thirty. But at twenty-eight, when my two-year engagement ended, I was devastated, and really angry. Although I was the one to ultimately end things with my fiancé, it left me feeling severely heavy and broken. I didn't want to get married in the first place, and it took an incredible amount of Faith in what I believed was a "broken" institution, for me to be able to even say yes. And then to have it all break apart anyway, before it had even begun, left me depressed, lonely, and seething.

It never ceases to amaze me how God places the right people in your life, just as you need them. There were the obvious players, like my mother, who made me all the comfort foods that I ate as a child growing up; my long-time best friend Ryan, who literally stayed at my house for a few days until I stopped crying; and Corey, someone that I desperately needed that I didn't even see coming.

Corey came into my life in the most unexpected way. When the smoke had cleared, I decided to throw a masquerade party with all the things I was going to use for my wedding. And I did. It was magnificent. I rented an old mansion and all my friends came dressed up. I looked and felt like a million bucks in my new, short, spunky haircut, red sheath dress, and sparkly heels.

In walks in this cocky, much too good-looking jock that I didn't know. He nonchalantly followed me to the kitchen where I refilled a bowl of snacks.

"Are you Gina?" he asked me.

"Yeah," I answered a bit warily, my fake smile faltering a bit. Why is this punk at my party and why is he talking to me?

"I heard you threw this party with all the things you were going to use for your wedding."

Now I was angry. Who the hell was this kid, and who invited him? My eyes narrowed and my heart beat faster as adrenaline filled my system. "Yeah," I said in a rush.

He paused and looked at the ground. When he looked back at me, his eyes were soft, which confused me at first. "Mine left me at the church."

I was not expecting that. "Oh," was all I could say. But then we shared a look between us, and I knew, and he knew, that we were the only two people in that entire house that knew what pain we were both going through.

We were like peas and carrots after that moment. He showed me the formula for getting over a near spouse, which was to get involved in a show, or a book series, or something that would take up all of your brain space.

Although this was working, Corey also didn't let me wallow in my sadness for very long. He forced me to go clubbing with him, he cried with me when I needed it, and he deleted my ex from my phone and blocked him from all my social media.

The next two people came sort of all at once. My amazing therapist, who Corey encouraged me to seek out, and my new roommate Christina, who is still one of my closest friends to this day.

Christina answered my Craigslist roommate-wanted ad on a whim. She had just moved to Utah from Georgia and didn't really know why she was in Utah to begin with. We became fast friends and she joined Corey and me on my "mandatory Corey adventures".

I was making some great progress with my therapist, and I was educating myself with the tools and books she was giving me. I found out that Tony, my ex, was all wrong for me in all the worst ways—from psychological manipulation and abuse, to his physical appearance. This was all very frustrating for me. My therapist additionally challenged me to date outside of my "box," and to try new things and experiences, to be open to new possibilities and opportunities.

Then, one night after meditating at the LDS San Diego Temple, I made a choice that my therapist applauded me for. The choice was really a deal I made with God, and it went something like this:

"Okay God, I tried it. I tried to find someone, I tried to get married and obviously, I failed epically. So, I'm done. If YOU want me to get married, YOU put him in my path. I'll go to all the singles events and church but I am not seeking ANYONE out. If you want me to meet someone, you have to put him in my path, 'cause I am DONE."

Although I had tried at something and failed, I was still willing to have the Faith to try again. I didn't leave it all up to God or the universe or what have you, I knew I still had to take action and do my part (hence the applause from my therapist). I had the Faith to put myself in situations where I could meet someone and be vulnerable again.

When I got back from my lovely, self-reflection trip to San Diego, Christina sat me down for a talk. "Gina, I have to tell you something but you're probably gonna kill me once I tell you."

"Okkkaaaaayyy, out with it." I looked at her and waited.

"I'm moving to San Diego. I know I've only been here for a month, but I am just not loving it and I really feel like I need to move to San Diego to be closer to my auntie and cousins. I'm sorry!" She paused and looked at me. "You should come with me!"

Although she said it as a joke, I really let that suggestion sink in. I had just gotten back from there for the first time in my life (SeaWorld when I was three didn't count) and had instantly loved it. I surprised even myself when I responded with "Okay! Let's go."

"Wait, are you serious?"

That was all the thinking on it I needed. "Yeah, I am. Let's move to San Diego!"

Three weeks later, I was in San Diego with a new job, new house, with new roommates, and making new friends. I loved everything about my choice. Corey practically kicked me out of the state of Utah, and even my dear friend, Haroon, who lives in England, was instrumental in my dramatic and sudden change of job and residence.

Being a member of the Church of Jesus Christ of Latter Day Saints (or Mormon, as it is better known), we have many different kinds of social events and opportunities to interact as singles, and somehow there are always copious amounts of food. Wednesday nights were the nights where there were classes and dinner, so my roommates and I all got dressed to the nines and went to the Wednesday night activities.

I make friends fairly easily, and by my third Wednesday, I had pretty much met everyone. Although I met a lot of fun people, there was no one I was really drawn to, which I was totally fine with. I half decided and half felt pulled to go to a new class that night and that's when I saw him.

I didn't know him. He had big green-brown eyes, and shoulders for days. I pulled Christina over and we sat down behind him. After the class ended, a few of us were chatting but he hadn't turned around yet. So I tapped him on the shoulder. He turned around.

"Hi! My name's Gina, what's yours?"

He cocked a half smile at me and I forgot to breathe. "Jay."

I then did something I'd never done before in my life. "Let's talk! You should take me on a date sometime!" As I heard myself say this, I wrote my number on a piece of note paper and gave it to him. He accepted it and then our teacher announced that dinner was ready downstairs and away I went.

Two days later, he called and took me on the best first date I had ever been on. Four months after that, we were in a committed relationship and last April, we celebrated our 8th wedding anniversary.

Jay is my soulmate, the other half of me, and the center of my happiness. He has completed me in ways that I didn't know I needed, but can't live without. Having the Faith to try again and taking the steps to put that Faith into action led me to a marriage I honestly never thought could exist. Where will your active Faith lead you?

GINA BACALSKI

About Gina Bacalski: Gina is a Real Estate Agent, licensed since June 2018. Her background is in Early Childhood Education where she received her Child Development Associate from the state of Utah and has an AS from BYU-Idaho. For the past seventeen years, Gina has thoroughly enjoyed her experience in the service industry helping families in the gifted community.

In 2019, Gina helped Jon Kovach Jr. launch Champion Circle and is now CEO of the organization. She brings her genuine love for people, high attention to detail, and strives to exceed client's expectations to the Real Estate industry and to Champion Circle.

Gina married the man of her dreams, Jay Bacalski, in San Diego, in 2013. The Bacalskis love entertaining friends and family, going on hikes, and attending movies and plays. When Gina isn't helping her clients navigate the real estate world, she will most often be found dancing and listening to BTS, watching KDramas and writing fantasy, sci-fi and romance novels.

Author's Website: *www.MyChampionCircle.com/Gina-Bacalski*
Book Series Website & Author's Bio: *www.The13StepstoRiches.com*

Griselda Beck

LEAD, LOVE, LIVE WITH UNSHAKEABLE FAITH

Faith: Unshakeable belief in the absence of evidence. Faith gives us release and surrender, to be bold and courageous, the patience and serenity to love ourselves and others, and the confidence to take risks in the process of creating extraordinary outcomes.

Six years ago, I did the bravest thing I'd done up until then. I quit my corporate job to pursue my desire for entrepreneurship. Talk about unshakeable Faith! I had so many fears:

- Fear of failure
- Fear of judgment
- Fear of my network watching and analyzing every step I made
- Fear of not being able to generate an income consistently

These fears are typical of any person looking to make the employee to entrepreneur transition. I overcame that fear by implementing several of the following concepts and tips.

Deep down, I knew I was capable. I knew I would be ok no matter how it worked out (or didn't), and I wasn't quite sure exactly what I was leaping towards, but I knew staying where I was out of comfort was not the answer.

Faith in God

Believing in something or someone greater than yourself gives you a direction to surrender everything outside of your control. Some may refer to this as the source, universe, or higher power. For me, I believe in God, even though I cannot see Him.

I believe He is my source of a higher power in the universe. I have experienced Him and His power through unexpected opportunities and what some may call "coincidences." Believing in something greater lightens the weight of the world on my shoulders.

Faith in Possibility

Faith is also believing in the possibility that something can occur even though I have not yet experienced it. Having Faith allows you to take risks. The bigger your Faith, the greater the risks you are willing to take. People who have great Faith create great things! Six months ago, I declared I would be a bestselling author by August.

I thought I was going to have my own book and could picture the cover so clearly! That book is still in the process of being written and is slated for next year. An unexpected opportunity was presented for me to co-write a book with many of my close friends, which has proven to be an amazing experience! Here we are! I was committed to my vision and unattached to what it would look like. *The 13 Steps To Riches, Volume 1 Desire, Featuring Denis Waitley* (the first volume of this book series) hit the bestseller list! My vision came through because I had Faith in the possibility that I would be a bestselling author by August 2021.

Faith in People

Faith gives us the strength to hang in there when we're not sure how things will turn out. That is commitment. Faith provides us with the ability to release and surrender. In the absence of evidence and certainty, it gives us peace. Faith allows us to stay committed to people by seeing them beyond the hurt they've caused or their current behavior or actions. Instead, see them for who they are as you know them to be. Faith gives us the ability to love unconditionally.

Faith in Myself

Most recently, Faith has taken on a whole new experience for me. Having Faith is an unshakeable belief in myself as an entrepreneur and a loving partner. Entrepreneurship, especially for the brand new, is a roller coaster ride of ups and downs as you navigate expansion, stabilization, and growth. At each stage of your journey, you get to face yourself in new ways which require you to have unshakeable, maniacal Faith in yourself to carry you above the self-doubt, self-criticism, unworthiness, and limiting beliefs that hold you back, hold you small, and would otherwise keep you from living your best life and going for your dreams. Dating and relationships are very similar in that journey as they, too, present an opportunity to face yourself and all of the beliefs that hold you back from leaning in with love, trust, intimacy, and connection.

Faith is a critical ingredient needed to move your vision forward. A lack of Faith leads to a lack of permission to dream. Without Faith, all we have are wishes and plans. Faith gives us the confidence to take that leap and take the risk to take action. Without Faith, we cannot lead or inspire people. The more Faith you have in yourself, the more Faith you will inspire in others, whether your clients, your team, your relationships, your significant other, your friends, family, or the entire world in a movement you've created and inspired.

So how do we build Faith?

Look for the Evidence

Part A) Make a list of thirty accomplishments that you're most proud of in yourself. Think of times when you got to lean into something fully and remained committed without evidence.

Part B) Make a list of thirty things, moments, or people you're grateful for and have been blessed with. I encourage you to spend some time on this one and choose those blessings that required something outside of you—God, Source, Universe, Higher Power. Perhaps it was a time when an opportunity presented itself at just the right time, perhaps a time when you thought something was going to be hard. Magically, it was resolved with ease or even before you addressed it! Look for MAGIC!

Create New Evidence

Acknowledge yourself daily. When you acknowledge yourself daily for what you created that day, you begin to build a new library of evidence in your subconscious mind that, in time and with repetition, it will begin to believe.

When you experience uncertainty in the future, you will be able to reference this evidence and trust yourself that you will be able to lean in, in Faith, and trust that you will land safely on the other side.

Attitude Self-Adjustment

Notice the negative language inside your head that is running on repeat like that horrible song you can't get out of your head. Powerfully and intentionally interrupt it with a new statement that lights you up on fire!!!! The problem with most affirmations is that they are usually generic statements we've heard or seen before in a book, on a blog post, or social media.

Instead, I invite you to get creative and be that disruptor your thoughts need. Make it fun. Make it outrageous!

Letting Go and Getting Curious!

If you're like most of my clients, you'd like to know what will happen so that you can plan for it. This desire to feel a sense of control is your way of keeping yourself safe. You feel safe because you are operating within what you know. While this may make you *feel* safe, it also keeps you from allowing and exploring a new possibility for your life. If you're not allowing for the possibility that another outcome is possible, then it cannot exist. Read that again—If *you're* not allowing space for a new possibility, a new possibility *cannot* occur. Essentially, you deny its existence. The message you are sending out into the world/universe and to God is, "I don't want it."

Not with me? Let me put it like this:

If someone offered you a million dollars right now, and all you had to do to collect it would be to say "thank you" and flash a smile, would you accept it? I "hear" some of you saying "YES!" What if I asked you in a different language than you understand?

Would you take it then? Consider for a moment that you didn't understand a word I said. I may as well have said, "You *owe* me a million dollars?" How often in your life are you missing out on possible opportunities simply because you didn't recognize them?

Another example: Have you ever encountered someone who buys a new car that you've never noticed before? Then all of a sudden, you see it everywhere? This is an excellent example of "looking for" and "being open" to possibilities. We can only truly be *open* to possibility when we let go of control and surrender to what may come as a result of having *Faith* that *anything* is possible at any given moment.

Having Faith is necessary to lead with your heart. When we lead with our hearts, we create big change. We create transformation. Not only do we create that transformation in ourselves, but we also create that and inspire it in others. "Have a little Faith," they said. They were right!

GRISELDA BECK

About Griselda Beck: Griselda Beck, M.B.A. is a powerhouse motivational speaker and coach who combines her executive expertise with transformational leadership, mindset, life coaching, and heart-centered divine feminine energy principles. Griselda empowers women across the globe to step into their power, authenticity, hearts, and sensuality, to create incredible success in their business and freedom in their lives. She creates confident CEOs.

Griselda's clients have experienced success in quitting their 9-5 jobs, tripling their rates, getting their first clients, launching their first products, and growing their businesses in a way that allows them to live the lifestyles and freedoms they want. She has been featured as a top expert on *FOX, ABC, NBC, CBS, MarketWatch, Telemundo*, and named on the Top 10 Business Coaches list by *Disrupt Magazine*.

Griselda is an executive with over 15 years of corporate experience, founder of Latina Boss Coach and Beck Consulting Group, and serves as president for the nonprofit organization MANA de North County San Diego. She also volunteers her time teaching empowerment mindset at her local homeless shelter, Operation Hope-North County.

Author's Website: *www.LatinaBossCoach.com*
Book Series Website & Author's Bio: *www.The13StepstoRiches.com*

Jason Curtis

FAITH BUILDS FAMILIES

What is Faith?

The Apostle Paul taught that, "Faith is the assurance of things hoped for, the evidence of things not seen." The prophet, Alma (Book of Mormon scripture), made a similar statement: "If ye have Faith ye hope for things which are not seen, which are true."

Faith is a principle of action and power. When you work toward a worthy goal, you exercise Faith. You show your hope for something that you cannot yet see.

Whenever I've worked toward a worthy goal, I've exercised my Faith. Faith is something you can hold your hope in for something that you cannot yet see.

Faith Helps You Win

There have been numerous times in my life when Faith has helped me win. I wouldn't be alive if it weren't for my mother's Faith to seek out President Spencer W. Kimball, the President of the Church of Jesus Christ of Latter-Day Saints, during the time when I was fighting for my life in the hospital. President Kimball came to Primary Children's Medical Center where I was staying due to a deathly illness. He put his hands on my head and gave me a blessing, like a direct prayer to God through him to me. I believe I wouldn't be alive without that blessing as I didn't see any signs of healing until that apostolic blessing and encounter from a church leader. My Faith helped me believe I would overcome that illness because I had Godly blessings on my side.

Another time Faith helped me was after going through nasty divorces. I knew there was more to my life than broken hearts and emptiness. I wasn't going to live my life alone. I carried my Faith that I would meet someone who would make me happier beyond belief and understand me. When I began to date my wife, Brianna, it was quickly known, through the power of Faith, that we were meant to be together. The Faith Brianna and I share is the reason we have two beautiful daughters in our lives.

My Mentors of Faith

There are a few shining examples of Faith for me. I've mentioned my mother already. She was very instrumental in my beginning years teaching me this principle. To this day, she is still one of my greatest inspirations.

As I grew into my teenage years, I met an individual named Les Maxfield. I really looked up to Les. He took me under his wing and taught me the principles of Faith through action and his knowledge of the scriptures and Gospel. He was a friend, mentor, and a sort of father figure to me. Les Maxfield has always been like a second father to me. He always made me feel like one of his sons, who were some of my friends and cousins.

If it weren't for my mentors of Faith, I may not have grown up to understand this lifesaving truth and foundational principle.

Teaching Faith To My Posterity

Now that my wife and I have two daughters, I've had plenty of time and opportunities to teach them about Faith. Here are the main principles of Faith I hope to perpetuate:

Faith in the Lord, Jesus Christ. Having Faith in Jesus Christ means relying completely on Him, trusting in His infinite power, intelligence, and love. It includes believing His teachings. It means believing that, even though you do not understand all things.

Living by Faith. Faith is how you show the Lord how you live your life. The Savior promised, "If ye will have faith in me ye shall have the power to do whatsoever thing is expedient in me."

Increasing your Faith. Faith is a gift from God. You must nurture your Faith to keep it strong, just like any muscle in your body. If you exercise it, it grows strong. If you put it in a sling and leave it there, it becomes weak.

The Adversary of Faith

Naturally, the answer I think most people would say here is the Devil, Lucifer. In my opinion, my number one adversary is myself. In my Faith, there's a Parable of the Natural Man.

"A person who chooses to be influenced by the passions, desires, appetites, and senses of the flesh rather than by the promptings of the Holy Spirit... Such a person can comprehend physical things but not spiritual things. All people are carnal or mortal because of the Fall of Adam and Eve. Each person must be born again through the Atonement of Jesus Christ to cease being a natural man."

I have noticed, on several occasions, that when I've allowed the Natural Man in my life, how I've been weak in my Faith. Having the Holy Spirit in my life is my compass and guide. I cannot imagine living my life without Faith.

Exercising Faith

The most memorable time I had to exercise Faith was when my wife and I decided to have our daughters. We had to go through so many obstacles. Procedure after procedure, and setback after setback, but it all paled in comparison to the outcome of having these two precious girls. Without having and exercising Faith, we wouldn't have our family today.

We overcame this by having a rock-solid belief and Faith in our Lord, Jesus Christ. No matter how hard or time-consuming it was to bring our daughters into our life, we knew our family was meant to be.

JASON CURTIS

About Jason Curits: Jason has been a serial entrepreneur for fifteen years and has enjoyed serving and helping his fellow entrepreneurs build their businesses and win in this game of life—on purpose! Jason created On Purpose Coaching because he knew, through his life experiences, that he could create an impact in others. He focuses on helping his clients create better relationships with their customers. This fosters trust and rapport while generating customer loyalty.

Jason is a Navy veteran of six years. He has sailed the seas and oceans in serving his God and country. Curtis and his wife, Brianna, have been married for eight years, and they have two children.

Author's Website: *www.JasonLaneCurtis.com*
Book Series Website & Author's Bio: *www.The13StepstoRiches.com*

Jeffrey Levine

PUBLIC SPEAKING: FEAR OR FAITH?

I did very little speaking in front of people in high school, college, and law school. For some reason, it just didn't happen. However, when I first started a tax law practice with a partner, I needed to learn how to speak to get business. Neither my partner nor I had any public speaking experience, but because we had a large overhead and no clients, I needed to learn how to speak in front of people. Since I was very shy, this endeavor presented a challenge for me. My partner and I decided that I should sign up for a Dale Carnegie course on public speaking.

In my first class, we were tasked with presenting a two-minute speech. When it came to my turn to speak, I stood up, opened my mouth, and nothing came out. I froze with fear of being criticized. And that led to embarrassment about the situation. I was ready to quit the class. "I can't do this," I reasoned, fully knowing that my partner and my business relied on my ability to conquer this fear and feel comfortable speaking in front of people. I decided to remain in the class.

During my second week in class, I was again armed to give my presentation. And again, the same thing happened: I froze. That time, I was ready to give in to my fear. I was so embarrassed by my repeat performance that I decided to quit. I didn't show up for the next class.

After missing that third week of classes, I received a call from the instructor. He said he would spend time with me outside of class to help me become a better speaker. All he wanted from me was the Faith that I could do it and to show up to all the private mentoring sessions and regular classes. He told me if I did that, I could be a good speaker. I agreed.

Each week, with his mentoring, I became more relaxed and confident. Before too long, when I stood up in front of the class, words finally came out of my mouth. I was thrilled. By the eighth week, I felt comfortable in front of the class and started enjoying my speeches.

By the end of that course, I had desired to improve and loved speaking in front of the class. At graduation, I was shocked that I earned the most improved speaker award. I saw that, with Faith that you can do it, anything is possible. I never imagined that I would finish the course or get an award, so I was thrilled. But I had a more significant challenge coming up.

A local radio announcer asked me to appear on her show. Since I had never appeared on the radio, a slow dread started to overwhelm me. The night before I was to appear on the radio show, I couldn't sleep. The fear of the unknown showed up loud and clear. What if I couldn't answer the questions? What if I froze and couldn't speak? And what if I gave the wrong answers?

Thankfully, along with the fear, Faith showed up as well. *If I could conquer public speaking, I could do a radio show*, I reasoned.

However, with a lack of good sleep prior to my radio premiere, I was tired and didn't show up as I might have hoped. Due to my lack of energy and clarity, the show went just okay. As I was leaving, the radio show host told me something I've never forgotten. She said, "You don't know how powerful this radio show is. It reaches thousands and thousands of people."

I was shocked. I hadn't thought about the other side of the broadcast; I'd been too immersed in my own thoughts. With that realization, I knew that I would need to be a guest on more shows since that would be an excellent way to help people and get my name out there.

Even though that particular host never asked me to appear again, I called another radio announcer with my renewed Faith and asked if I could appear on his show. Because I had important money issues to discuss, he said yes. I knew I could do this!

That show went really well, and he asked me back every week for the following ten years. I was thrilled because I became the go-to guest for financial advice.

In addition, the radio announcer had a good friend who was the general manager at a local TV station. He told me to call him. Before long, that general manager asked me to be a guest on his 12 pm daily news show.

Even though being on TV represented a new challenge, for some reason, I felt different. Since I had conquered public speaking, radio, and now had the Faith I could do TV, it seemed easier. I had a sense that TV was for me. Because of this Faith, I was invited back for many years and was also included in their 6 pm segments.

Unbelievably, another TV station called me to do a financial segment on their morning news. I was on TV four to five times a week between the two stations, and I loved every minute.

After selling my business in New York and moving to Arizona, I had become so well known that I was asked to do a documentary. That was another big challenge for me. However, I was ready for it and had Faith that this new project would be just an extension of TV.

Unfortunately, I oversimplified the leap from TV to documentary. The latter was more like being in Hollywood. Every time I hesitated or mispronounced a word, I started over. That continued seventeen times. Since I was sweating profusely because of the hot lights and feeling very drained, I called for a timeout. After changing my shirt and walking around the building for five minutes, I felt a lot better. I came back with a new Faith that I could conquer the documentary without hesitating or mispronouncing a word or stuttering.

Take number eighteen was a charm. With my newfound Faith, the whole process seemed much easier, and the rest of the filming was very successful.

Because I was becoming a better conversationalist, I suggested to the producer that we do a question-and-answer documentary the next time. Since I had done hundreds of TV and radio interviews that way, I had Faith that such an approach would work better for me.

After doing three more documentaries in the next six months with a question-and-answer format—successfully—I thought I was ready for the big time.

In 2019, I was informed that there would be a sequel to the film The Secret. Since nothing came about in March, April, or May, my mind was constantly thinking of it and I was excited to see the sequel. But nothing was created. On June 1, when I woke up, I saw the words "Beyond The Secret" on the screen of my mind. As soon as that happened, I called Don Boyer, who had done documentaries before, and I told him what had happened. He liked the name and said, "Let's start filming."

Before long, he was filming people in the original *Secret* movie, along with new entrepreneurs who were very successful. Since I was the executive producer as well as a cast member, I was excited.

As a cast member, I had to fly to California to be filmed. Again, that was a challenging experience. Because the documentary could be a big success, I felt the pressure to do a great interview. After all, this experience could potentially change my whole world. However, because I put so much pressure on myself, it didn't go well, and I had to go back and do it again.

The next time, I had Faith that I could do it. As I arrived at the studio, in my imagination, I saw the interview going extremely well and the producer with a smile on his face. I started to get very relaxed, and the filming went just as I imagined.

With Faith, you can have anything you desire. It is such a strong vibration. By using your imagination, you can see from the end what you want to happen. Also, by acting "as if" in seeing what you want already done, that is when the magic happens.

On the other side, if you let fear dominate your thoughts, you will be held back by the negative whispers of your mind. You'll agree that you're not up for the challenge and choose comfort over trying something new.

Every day, you have a choice to either let fear dominate your mind (like most people do) or choose Faith and let the magic start. It is your choice. Choose Faith and have what you want, or choose fear and stay stuck in the mud.

I suggest that the best medicine for turning fear into Faith is living a life you could only compare to your dreams. Go for it and have an exciting life. Remember, since we live in an abundant world, start enjoying the Faith and the fruits of abundance that are all around us. Your job is to stand up and grab it; it's yours for the taking!

JEFFREY LEVINE

About Jeffrey Levine: Jeffrey is a highly skilled tax planner and business strategist, as well as a published author and sought-after speaker. He's been featured in national magazines, on the cover of *Influential People Magazine*, and is a frequent featured expert on radio, talk shows, and documentaries. Jeffrey attended the prestigious Albany Academy for high school and then went on to University of Hartford at Connecticut, University of Mississippi Law School, Boston University School of Law, and earned an L.L.M. in taxation. His accolades include features in *Kiplinger* and *Family Circle Magazine,* as well as a dedicated commentator for Channel 6 and 13 news shows, a contributor for the *Albany Business Review*, and an announcer for WGY Radio.

Jeffrey has accumulated more than 30 years of experience as a tax attorney and certified financial planner and has given in excess of 500 speeches nationally. Levine is the executive producer and cast member in the documentary *Beyond the Secret: The Awakening.*

Levine's most current work, *Consistent Profitable Growth Map,* is a step-by-step workbook outlining easy-to-follow steps to convert consistent revenue growth to any business platform.

Author's Website: *www.JeffreyLevine.Solutions*
Book Series Website & Author's Bio: *www.The13StepstoRiches.com*

Lacey & Adam Platt

FAITH IN BEING & DEVELOP INSPIRED FAITH

Faith In Being

I remember as a kid hearing the phrase, "Faith is a belief in things you cannot see." As an infrequent churchgoing kid, I didn't really have a firm understanding of what Faith meant. I was a teenager before we really even started going to church so I didn't have an idea of what religion truly looked like.

I had lived my life up to that point without too much guidance or direction from anything or anyone other than my parents. I do believe that my parents had Faith in something, but they just weren't really great about communicating what that was. We struggled as I was growing up because we were constantly moving. I needed to develop my own understanding of Faith. As I started to attend church, I learned from the adults who were teaching the lessons what Faith meant to them. I heard a lot of opinions and variations, but nothing really made sense to me.

When I was in college, I attended a class on religion and I remember the teacher saying, "If you want to truly KNOW anything for yourself, pray and ask." It was at that point I realized I didn't really KNOW anything for myself. I had all of these outside voices and opinions swirling around in my head, but nothing I actually KNEW for myself.

At that point, I began to ask myself some very tough questions. *Who am I? Why am I here? What is my purpose in this life?*

I wish I could say that I knew all the answers, but I didn't. What I have learned is that there are levels of learning. And just when I thought I KNEW something, I was taught another level. I used to get frustrated by this because I felt like I didn't really understand anything. Now I know that if I were given everything all at once, I would simply drown. I now resolve to receive what I need, when I need it.

Nowadays, my definition of Faith is the knowledge that there is a *Being* out there who is more powerful than me and who has a plan for me. He can see the bigger picture even when I can't. He is understanding and knows how I fit into it all. I know that this *Being* has my best interest at heart. He is a *Being* who knows me so well. He knows exactly what to say, do, and causes me to take action. He puts people in my life at the exact times when I need them and for the precise reasons. He challenges me in ways that only He can. He loves me unconditionally and wants me to be happy and successful. He is my heavenly Father!

My job from this point forward is to listen and take inspired action steps. When I do, things work out. I have learned this through repeated attempts to control my own life and not do things that I feel prompted to do, only to watch things fall apart and go sideways. How many times can we watch things crumble to the ground? How many times can we say, "Next time it will all work out," only to repeat the same process expecting a different result? I had to let go of perfectionism and control. I had to let go of the thoughts that I know it all and that I am in control of my life, and surrender to the idea that there is a force out there stronger than me. When I am successful at this, things turn out amazingly well. When I struggle, they don't. It really is that simple.

Years ago, I had a coach who told me that "struggle is a choice." At first, I thought she was crazy, but as I continued to struggle, I saw the light in choosing not to. I simply shifted my thoughts to come up with a solution rather than sitting in the problem, struggling. It has saved me a lot of time and headaches. I'm not saying that we will never struggle, and I am not saying that sometimes we don't need to honor the struggle and learn from it. What I am saying is that we need to identify in the moment whether we can create a solution and move on, or if there is more to it. Awareness is the key!

~ Lacey Platt

Develop Inspired Faith

I believe Faith is one of the most important powers we can harness in this universe. Faith allows us to tap into our subconscious mind and harness the powers of the universe in a powerful and profound way. Faith allows us to turn our desire into something tangible and removes limitations. We must have Faith in ourselves, what we can accomplish, and in God. If you are not religious, then either the universe or merely a great idea—A power that moves us to achieve amazing things in our lives will support our Faith.

Faith is also one of the most misunderstood principles in the world. Many people harness parts of its power but do not fully harness all of its potential power. You see, Faith is a verb. It is an action. There are those out there who think that all you have to do is believe and it will happen.

That's part of it, but not all of it. You have to take action with the belief that things will work out the way they are supposed to. Remember that life is happing for you, not to you. You need to take action on the inspired action steps that you receive, and then have Faith that things will work out the way they are supposed to.

The times in my life when I have seen things happen and materialize were when I have had a deep desire for something, put a plan in motion to achieve it, and then have Faith it will be what I want or need in my life.

I was on a zoom mastermind meeting with the amazing #1 *N.Y. Times* Best-Selling Author, Sharon Lechter, who is the Featured Author in this book. Sharon shared some insight into Faith. She said that she doesn't like the phrase "taking a leap of Faith." She said she prefers to say, "take a leap with Faith." That little shift of words from "of" to "with" may not sound very big. But think about it. If you take a leap *of* Faith, you are just hoping that something will work out. Alternatively, when you take a leap *with* Faith, you take action with confidence towards your goals and dreams, knowing that it will work out the way it is supposed to for you at this time.

Let me share a story of when I had to exercise Faith. When I was getting my master's degree in Business Administration, my MBA, I really struggled in finance. I took the class because it was a required class to graduate. In order to pass the class, I had to get a C or better. Well, I didn't do very well on the final and got a C-, and didn't pass. I was so discouraged with myself. I was never very confident in school because I had a learning disability when I was younger and never did very well. This was a struggle for me and I was not sure I could finish my degree and get my MBA. In order to get the degree, I had to take the class again. This meant paying for it a second time and hoping I did well enough to pass. Notice I used the word 'hope.'

After talking it over with my wife, she said she had Faith in me and persuaded me to never give up. So I created a plan to talk to the professor about taking the class again. He let me review my exam to see what I had missed. We also worked out a plan for me not have to do the actual workbook exercises again, as I did well on them the first time, and he would simply transfer my scores to the new class. This way, I could focus on what I really needed to work on. Thanks to my wife, I had Faith that I truly could pass this time. I created the plan, took action, and ended up passing with an A-! I went on to graduate with my master's degree and was the first person in my family to do so.

So my suggestion to you is to create a plan. Take a leap *with* Faith. Work the plan. And know that the world, God, and the universe all want you to succeed. You have to be willing to put forth the effort. That doesn't mean that the plan is going to be perfect every time. You will undoubtedly have to make adjustments from time to time. As you take the leap with Faith, follow inspired action and adjust as you go. You now have a recipe to achieve anything you desire in life!

~ Adam Platt

LACEY & ADAM PLATT

About Lacey Platt: Lacey is an energetic, fun loving, super mom of five! She is an Achievement Coach, Speaker and new Bestselling Author who enjoys helping everyone she can by getting to know what their needs are and then loving on them in every way that she can. Her ripple effect and impact has touched the lives of so many and continues to reach more lives every single day. Allow Lacey to help you achieve your goals with proven techniques she has created and perfected over years of coaching. Lacey and her husband have built an amazing coaching business called Arise to Connect serving people all around the world.

About Adam Platt: Adam is an Achievement Coach, Speaker, Trainer, Podcast Host and now a Bestselling Author. Adam loves to help people overcome the things stopping them from having the life they really want. Adam owns and operates Arise to Connect. Adam believes that connection with yourself, others, and your higher power are the keys to achievement and greater success in life. He is impacting thousands of people's lives with his message and coaching. He lives in Utah with his wife, five daughters, and their dog, Max.

Author's Website: *www.AriseToConnect.com*
Book Series Website & Author's Bio: *www.The13StepstoRiches.com*

Louisa Jovanovich

FAITH IS ONLY THE BEGINNING

Faith is evidence of things not seen but hoped for. When I surrender to the unknown, it gives me peace. We often get in our own way of feeling the need to control every situation, but that does not leave space for peace. What do we want to be right about? Do we want to be right about not trusting in Faith because we can't see, feel, touch or taste it? Or do we want to be right about how Faith brings peace and gently guides us? I will choose the one that lights me up and brings me joy.

Faith, along with desire, is the foundation of creating a life I love. Desire lights a fire and creates that burning sensation that lets me dream big. Faith lets me know I get to trust the process. As long as I choose to keep showing up, my purpose will continue to unfold. I know I have been led my entire life. I have always had powerful feelings that pull me forward. Faith, to me, is trusting in something greater than myself.

When I was seventeen years old, I met a beautiful soul whose name was Melissa. She brought so much light into every room she entered. I remember meeting her family and knowing how much they loved her. I was drawn to her energy. She had something incredibly special, and I found it captivating. Sadly, Melissa couldn't see this in herself. Even though she impacted every life she touched, she shared with me that she was sad and felt alone. Those emotions haunted her. They also haunted me because I couldn't understand how that was possible. Faith is knowing you may feel sad, overwhelmed, or alone, but those feelings don't last forever. There is trust that there is something more than this moment, believing that things are happening for us and not to us.

I'm heartbroken to share that Melissa passed away from an accidental overdose at the age of seventeen. I was able to see the light inside her, but she couldn't see it herself. Most of us do not see ourselves as others see us. If only she could have appreciated her beauty, her light and love, and that beautiful spirit—because her presence could have changed the world. I live my life remembering her and the impact she had on my life. I now know that when I show up authentically, I can see how people relate to me. I get to experience the power that my own energy carries. I learned to participate in life. I don't pretend that I don't matter or that I don't make a difference. This may sound arrogant to some. When I make a difference when I'm confident gives me the courage to show up, and as a result, inspires others to do the same. I get to know that I matter so I can help others see how much they matter.

I believe that people are put into our lives as lessons, and Melissa was not the only person that left an imprint on me. When I was a little girl, I remember my dad telling me to pay attention to those around me and watch how they were doing things. I interpreted that to mean I was not good enough or I was not doing it right. I felt very self-conscious and uncomfortable. I let those words and statements hold me back from experiencing my full self-expression. I held onto that for my entire life and spoke words unconsciously to myself. I now choose to see it differently. I am so grateful that now I show up for my life, and I'm open to the messages in inspiring books, such as *Think and Grow Rich;* I learn from world leaders and others on my same path. What my dad was sharing with me was a profound statement and not something limiting or hurtful. Where in our lives do we misinterpret what is being said? How do we shift in our listening to use them as powerful statements and not limiting beliefs?

Opening my mind has given me the opportunity to grow and take on new challenges I would have never dreamed possible. I have Faith and trust in myself and my journey. I know that I am capable and that I am always ok. I have embraced that I may fail, look bad, or feel embarrassed, and all of that is also ok. It's human. I get to show up and live a fully self-expressed life. Some argue that they don't have Faith because they can't explain it, yet they hurt and are in pain. I choose to believe in something I feel and can't explain because it offers me peace and freedom. We all wake up each day because we didn't die the night before. Is that living? Or just surviving this life? I don't want to get through it, I want to channel my God-given energy and prosper, and I want to lead others to do the same by example.

Even though Melissa is no longer with us, I am here. The fact that you are reading this means you are, too. The world is full of beautiful people who also carry that light. We are all here with our light to share. We matter, and people love us. I have Faith that sharing my story will help others. We do not see ourselves for who we are, but we need to understand that we make a difference by choosing to know we matter. About a year ago, I was riding my bike and listening to Eckhart Tolle interview Oprah. He asked her, "What do you like to do?" She answered, "I love to learn, and I love to teach." My brain popped in with, "Yes, me too!" Then that little small voice said, "Who do you think you are?"

A year later, I did a "find your purpose" meditation and as I was being guided through it, out jumped the thoughts "I am a world leader!" This time, my brain instantly enjoyed that thought and said YES! As Napoleon Hill shares in his chapter on Faith autosuggestion, I have been able to shift out of repeating to myself, "Who do I think I am? I don't matter."

I'm so grateful and I know I would not be grouped with these remarkable authors and opportunities if I didn't realize who I am and the difference I get to make. Small shifts daily and doing things that showed me I can do it. I get to be someone who loves people with my entire heart. I get to let you know that you matter. My Faith gives me knowledge that there is a more significant force than myself. I believe we don't get what we want in life, and we get what we believe. Looking at my core beliefs has helped me see areas where I have blind spots, and I get to look at those. I have Faith that this is still just the beginning. I am just starting this process. It's a beautiful journey.

LOUISA JOVANOVICH

About Louisa Jovanovich: Louisa is the founder of Connect with Source. She is a mindfulness and emotional intelligence coach. She enjoys helping others identify blind spots and create new beliefs which empower her clients to access a life they have never dreamed possible. She has completed 20 years of personal and transformational growth including Land-mark Forum, Gratitude Training, and is a Clarity Catalyst Certified trainer. She works with entrepreneurs who seek clarity and want to up-level their lives.

Her life experiences and school of hard knocks are what make her a knowledgeable and compassionate leader and enable her to help guide others through the process of looking for answers within in order to find success and breakthrough their limiting beliefs. Her unique coaching techniques help her clients see the truth behind the stories that are keeping them stuck in the reality they created.

Louisa is a single mother of two teenagers living in LA. Her love and compassion towards others are her superpowers, helping others reclaim their confidence, find their voice, and know their worth.

Author's Website: *ConnectWithSource.com*
Book Series Website & Author's Bio: *www.The13StepstoRiches.com*

Lynda Sunshine West

FAITH OVER FEAR WINS EVERY TIME

Faith
Erases
Anxious
Reactions

This is my acronym for FEAR.

You see, when your fear is strong, your faith is weak. When your faith is strong, your fear is weak.

In 2015 I embarked on a journey like no other, a journey that would test my faith daily, one that would unfold things about me that I didn't know and would put me on a path of growth, courage, strength, perseverance, desire, passion, drive, and so many more words. I woke up on January 1, 2015, and had an epiphany. "I have so many fears. I'm going to do something different this year. I'm going to face a fear every day. Every morning when I wake up, the first thing I'm going to do before my feet hit the floor is ask myself one question, 'What scares me?' and then I'll wait for the answer. I won't get out of bed until an answer comes. The first fear that pops into my head is the fear I am COMMITTED to facing that day."

When I made that declaration to myself, I had no idea what the next 365 days would hold for me and how tapped into my faith it would bring me.

"Why would someone decide to face a fear every day for a year?" "Did you really have that many fears?" "What kind of fears did you face?" "What was it like?" These are a few of the questions I hear when I talk about The Year of Fears. I'll answer a few of them here and, as I share my story, you'll see how faith played a HUGE part in breaking through fear every day and how it changed my life.

I grew up in an extremely volatile, abusive alcoholic household. The abuse caused a lot of pain, heartache, fear, and, worst of all, I became a people-pleaser. While I carried all of that pain around for decades, being a people-pleaser was my worst attribute. I used to pride myself on being "a chameleon." I could blend into any situation, and everyone liked me. That was my survival mechanism. Be quiet. Blend in. Don't make a raucous. Sit in the corner. Don't bother anyone. Don't make a scene. As a people-pleaser, I never knew who Lynda was. Since I wanted everyone to like me, I did and said what I "thought" you wanted me to do so you would like me.

This was one of the things I discovered while facing a fear every day.

Part of my fear-facing was learning who I am, speaking up for myself, saying yes when I wanted to say yes, and learning how to say no. Boy!! That was the scariest, saying no to people. While I knew it was going to be hard, I did it BECAUSE I was scared. "Do it BECAUSE you're scared" became my new mantra.

My faith was tested daily. Faith of God. Faith of others. Faith of self. The faithfulness of God and others was easy, but faith of self? I had to learn how to believe in myself to have faith that I could conquer the challenges before me, the 365 fears.

Growing up in an abusive environment where the people I'm supposed to be able to trust daily said things like "you're stupid," "you're ignorant," "people are only nice to you because they feel sorry for you" really did a number on my mindset. I was bound and determined to change this mindset once and for all, no matter how hard it was.

On a random morning, the answer to my daily question, "What scares me?" was extremely specific: approach and talk to a stranger in Starbucks. I had used Starbucks as a remote office like many entrepreneurs. I would immediately pull out my laptop, start working, and not make eye contact with anyone. While it may seem like a small, even silly, fear, it was a crippling fear. Fear is fear. My decision to face a fear every day for a year was a commitment to myself for growth. And, boy, how I grew!

Back at Starbucks, I was standing in a corner, watching people come in, place their orders, and leave with their coffee. One man came in, placed his order, and then he sat down. My victim! My target was a person sitting alone so I could have a conversation with them. And there he was: alone, sitting, waiting for his coffee. I was finally going to face this fear. I stood there, staring at him, desperately trying to develop my opening line of the conversation.

After he picked up his coffee and returned to his table, I slowly walked over to him, knees trembling, throat locked up, palms and forehead sweaty, stomach all knotted up. Praying my voice would not fail me, I managed to say, "Hi, sir. I'm facing a fear every day this year. And today's fear is to talk to a stranger in Starbucks." He responded suspiciously good-humored, "Okay!?"

So far, so good. I got the words out of my mouth in a coherent manner, and he responded. "Do you mind if I have a seat?"

"Sure. Please have a seat."

I chatted with him for about five minutes, stood up, and said, "Thank you for your time. You helped me break through this fear. I appreciate it." I turned and walked out of Starbucks. I felt like throwing up. But I didn't.

I did it. I tapped into my faith in self. I broke through that fear, the fear of judgment.

God was always there to help me, but I needed to do the work. I just hadn't been ready until 2015, at age 51. It's all good, though, because it's part of my journey, my story. I know now that all of the things I went through are what created who I am today. I, for the first time in my life, love myself FOR WHO I AM. I have always had faith in God, but I finally have faith in me.

While faith in God will carry us far, faith in ourselves will carry us further because we're willing to take more risks and put ourselves out there more.

They say, "Turn your pain into your purpose." One of the greatest blessings I received from facing 365 fears is discovering my purpose and then living "on purpose" rather than "on accident" (like I had the first 51 years of my life).

Once I started believing in myself and raising my hand to share my voice with the world, I was met with praise. That's when I discovered I am not stupid and ignorant like they told me I was. Rather, I am brilliant, and people actually like me because I'm a nice person, not because they feel sorry for me. This was a huge part of my journey because others started doing the same when I started raising my hand and speaking my truth. They saw what I was doing, and it gave them FAITH that they, too, could do it. They started walking their path and speaking up for themselves.

When we share our story with the world, it gives others confidence and courage to do the same thing, the confidence and courage to stand up for themselves and tap into their faith in God, faith of others, and, most importantly, faith in self. When we have faith in ourselves, there's nothing stopping us. Sometimes it takes an outsider to guide us onto that path. Who is that person for you? Reach out to them right now. Don't wait another day. They will help you tap into your faith so you can start living your life "on purpose."

Faith is felt, not seen. It's such an interesting concept because, while it's not tangible to the touch, it is tangible in the heart. If we don't understand something, it's hard to believe in it; therefore, we believe based on facts or faith. Sometimes faith is all we have to guide us.

How strong is your faith?

LYNDA SUNSHINE WEST

About Lynda Sunshine West: Known as The Queen of Collaboration, Lynda Sunshine West ran away from home at 5 years old and was gone an entire week. She came home with her head bent down, riddled with fear, and wouldn't look people in the eyes for decades to come. At the age of 51, she decided to stop letting fear rule her life and went on a journey of facing one fear every day for a year, 365 days in a row. In doing so, she gained an exorbitant amount of confidence and developed her Simple 7-Step Process to Help Others Break Through Fear.

Lynda Sunshine is a Speaker, 11 times Bestselling Author, Executive Film Producer, Red Carpet Interviewer, and the Founder of Women Action Takers. Women Action Takers' mission is to empower women to write, publish, and market their book and get them on stages to AMPLIFY their voices. She believes in cooperation and collaboration and loves connecting with like- minded people.

Author's Website: *www.WomenActionTakers.com*
Book Series Website & Author's Bio: *www.The13StepstoRiches.com*

Maris Segal & Ken Ashby

FAITH EATS OBSTACLES FOR BREAKFAST

As a couple from diverse backgrounds, together over eighteen years, we are no strangers to formal religion. Ken is the son of a Southern Baptist preacher and Maris was raised with traditional Jewish roots as taught in a private Hebrew school. We both believe that *faith* exists beyond the structures of religion. *Faith* has no walls, no age; *faith* has no gender, color, or class; *faith* is infinite and unconditional; *faith* is not solely limited to any religious belief.

How often have we heard about people who persevered in spite of seemingly insurmountable odds? Along with billions of people worldwide, we are both awed by the space program and remember back to our childhood when Apollo 13 ran into potentially fatal challenges. Gathered at the television with our families, we watched, waited, and prayed, *faith*fully trusting the astronauts would return successfully back to earth. We imagined that the astronauts had a powerful *faith* in their team and training, and they trusted them to find a workable solution that ensured their safe return from space. Their "successful failure," on what seemed like a routine flight at that time, made history. In a biblical context, many of us learned the story of Noah's Ark from the Old Testament. The story of a man who was told by God of impending global destruction due to the wicked in the world. Noah was instructed to build an ark large enough for his family and include a male and female from every creature on earth. Based on *faith*, Noah acted! We have also heard the story of the human courage exhibited by a mom who, with Herculean strength, lifted a wrecked vehicle to free her children trapped beneath it; stories from natural disasters where people survived after being buried in rubble far beyond life expectancy. These stories are great examples of *faith* and power derived from a belief and a trust in possibilities.

Faith is defined as "complete trust or confidence in someone or something." For millions on our planet, *faith* is steeped in religious structures, dogma, and doctrine that form a life road map with guidelines and lessons.

Perhaps for you it is God Almighty, Jesus Christ, Mohammed, Buddha, or another being? In practical terms, it does not matter which "someone or something" we profess as the basis for our *faith*. These revered beings become lifelong depictions, the painting, the embodiment of truth. They grow to be religious icons for the less conscious (that would be all of us) to guide our mortal existence. When we as human beings don't know where to turn for strength, we look to those highly evolved and immortalized models as ultimate trusted sources. Their lives modeled for us what pure consciousness looks like, with teachings and lessons of love versus hate, growth versus destruction, rising and stumbling, life and death, and ultimately hope. The structure alone, labels, rules, practices, and norms can often exclude others who are not aligned or believe differently. Interestingly, our understanding of the core of most religions is consistent with Genesis 1:27, "So God created man in his own image, in the image of God he created him; male and female he created them."

Joseph Campbell, the American professor of literature, spent his life working in comparative mythology and comparative religion. Campbell pointed out that the idea of a savior is not unique in Christianity. He says, "The interesting thing is that when you read the life of the saviors—Jain saviors, Buddhist saviors, Hindu saviors, the Christ—the same motifs are there, time and time again."

The communities of faith *built* around religion offer stories that explain the unexplainable. These stories become the go-to support and what many count on in times of urgency or crisis. Is *faith* that definable, or could *faith* be even more significant than we can imagine or immortalize from a resonating story? From a place of curiosity, consider that these stories may be a mythical reminder that opens us up to the innate source that resides in each of us. What matters is our ability to let go of a difficult circumstance we may be encountering and reframe our unwelcomed predicament as an opportunity to reach within, allowing the divine power inside us to break through.

Faith lives and breathes on a higher plane than our recorded history or any specific point of view, which is the product of our nature and nurture. *Faith* is a daily choice as we lead in our personal and professional lives. We choose to carry *faith* into our family, our friendships, and our work. In all cases, our *faith* creates wholeness and the basis on which trust is built. Even with our political and religious leaders, we most often have faith that ultimately they will do their best to serve with integrity. When trust is broken in any part of our lives, we choose to have faith that things will turn out OK. What happens when we lose faith?

Maris: I was married 11 months when the Northridge, CA earthquake ripped apart my apartment. In a moment, as my then-husband and I clung to each other, hearing the piercing screams come from the depths of our being, we said, "I love you," certain in that moment that it would be our last. Oddly, my life did not flash before me as often people say it does when faced with death. The gas lines were hissing and spreading gas aroma in the air; our apartment building sunk into the newly liquified earth, crushed our cars and our neighbor's apartment beneath us. As we lifted him to safety and all made our way to the street, we realized there would be more tomorrows. From that moment, I lived life differently, from a place of inner *faith*, knowing that I was not done on this earth and that mine was a life meant for using my gifts to impact others. Years later, as I navigated my then husband's affairs, my *faith* was broken, shaken to the core and everything I believed in regarding commitment and marriage was tested. The corner turner for me was my mom's words, "Breathe and have faith that what you need is inside of you."

There is no question that the ritual repetition and daily practice of a deep grounding in the inclusive principle of *faith*-constructs a firm foundation for our lives. The constant reiteration of wisdom teachings, empowering thoughts and words will formulate our guiding principles and values, which becomes the GPS for our *faith*.

Ken: There was one specific point in my life when I felt I had lost my faith in everything. I was like a boat without a rudder. My mind was drowning in the past, stories of worthlessness and self-beat-up. I was driving through the Rocky Mountains on a road with a steep cliff hugging the highway. My self-doubts were careening me toward just giving up and heading my vehicle toward the abyss, which could end everything. One thought seeped into my awareness. If I did take that drastic action, I could endanger others in the oncoming traffic. The thought awakened something in me, and I decided to pull off into a rest stop, a pull-out. I eased into the small parking lot, turned off the engine, and closed my eyes. At that moment, sitting in a calm space, I pulled myself out of the old recurring stories echoing in my head and embraced the present. I listened to the divine within and let *faith* surround me; I chose life. I had *faith* that I was here for a reason and that my past was not my present. At that moment, I exercised one of the true pillars of *faith*; I simply surrendered. With no evidence, with no proof, I had *faith* and trusted that I was held by the universe and meant for more.

Faith, in the most common usage, is always waiting behind the door of trust. When we both look at what could have ended our lives in each moment described above, we are grateful for that moment that brings us here today, standing in gratitude and responsibility, knowing that we are co-creating with each other our families, our clients, and the universe for a greater purpose."

If we can accept that *faith* is not exclusive or proprietary to any specific organized religious community, then the possibilities of *faith* connections expand beyond our wildest imaginations. The recognition that *faith* lives and breathes in all expressions may lead us toward human healing. This acknowledgment, built on the respect of the divinity in us all, is the powerful surrender to success beyond accomplishment, a richness that transcends monetary accumulation, and a will to thrive not just survive. The natural power within us is the anchor for a *faith* that can lift us to our higher purpose.

This cellular, circulatory flow of trust and surrender to the unknowing brings the peace and power to see obstacles as possibilities, to see circumstance as transitory. This type of resident and powerful *faith* + belief + trust "eats obstacles for breakfast."

Reflection:

- What role does *faith* play in your everyday life?
- When in your life have you chosen to surrender to *faith?*
- If you did this once, what is stopping you from doing it now?

MARIS SEGAL
& KEN ASHBY

About Maris Segal and Ken Ashby: Maris Segal and Ken Ashby have been bringing a creative collaborative voice to issues, causes and brands for over forty years. As strategists, producers, coaches, authors, speakers and trainers, their work with the public and private sectors unites diverse populations across a wide spectrum of business, policy, and social issues in the U.S. and abroad. Their leadership expertise in Business Relationship Marketing, Organizational Change & Cultural Inclusion, Personal Growth, Project Management, Public Affairs, Corporate Social Responsibility and Philanthropy Strategies has been called on to support a range of clients from classrooms and boardrooms to the world stage including; Olympic organizers, Super Bowls, Harvard Kennedy School, Papal visits, the White House, consumer brands, and celebrities across the arts and entertainment, sports and culinary genres.

Ken Ashby and Maris Segal recently launched Segal Leadership Global—a community of collaborative strategists, coaches and trainers creating global connections and possibilities in times of change and One Song—a creative music and song writing leadership workshop series designed as a collaboration team building tool.

Often referred to by their clients as "the connection couple," their philosophy is "our shared humanity unites us and when we lead with our hearts, our heads will follow."

Author's Website: *www.SegalLeadershipGlobal.com*
Book Series Website & Author's Bio: *www.The13StepstoRiches.com*

Mel Mason

REMOVING THE INTERFERENCE AND FINDING FAITH

People must think I'm crazy when they see me walking on a trail, talking loudly to my best friend, God. I'm not a "pray to yourself type," silently petting a pine tree and asking for my life to get better. I do my best to accept every little thing that happens to me, but I find my Faith being tested more often than I'd wish.

I have a very personal relationship with God. I literally treat Him like my best friend. So when I'm struggling with my Faith and circumstances aren't going the way I want, I'm blunt with my friend. To be honest, I have been known to scream and yell and swear at God. I will yell out loud.

"God, why is this happening?" I scream, shaking the leaves off the trees. People stray far away from me on the hiking trail, but whatever! There's nothing my best friend God can't see. There's nothing to hide. And so I flat out scream at Him, "Why did you put this in my life and then not let me have it?" and I argue, "Why does it have to be like this? Why?"

And then, in the next breath, I say, "I know that your vision is way bigger than mine, and I trust you." And that's the end of it. I choose Faith over fear because every time my Faith is being tested (and it's tested a lot), I believe I have a choice. We have a choice. We can choose Faith, or we can choose fear.

We all have our problems. I had a horrific childhood, messed up with abuse and trauma. I feel like I'm always being tested, but less intensely now because I've had some practice. I learned a little trick on how to keep Faith when you're feeling stretched, and I want to share it with you.

As the Clutter Expert, I help people remove the interference that keeps them from being one with God. I walk my clients through the process of decluttering their homes, minds, and souls because their clutter is always deeper than just the ugly boxes piled up in the garage, or the junk heaped high in the attic. External clutter is a sign of internal clutter. And a cluttered mind can prevent us from fully experiencing God.

I clear my own clutter regularly. When I make an error, God catches it and fixes it for me. One of my clients needed to move an appointment the other day, and I realized I'd screwed up and placed their appointment in the wrong spot. Yet, lo and behold, that turned out to be just the spot they wanted. I had to laugh. I just looked up and said (out loud, of course, to my friend, God), "Thank you. I love you." I believe that even my gaffes in life are meant to be.

I didn't always have Faith as I do now. When I was young, I had a vision of a very important truth. It didn't appear to me in a burst of light and magic. Mine was more of a palm-to-the- forehead moment. I was about eight years old. My parents were divorcing, and suddenly Faith just hit me and stuck with me.

I found Christianity and eventually became a recruiter for God's army— until my brother committed suicide and a church lady told me God had damned him to eternal Hell. Wow, thanks! I left that church and spent years exploring Buddhism, Taoism, Hinduism, and even the spiritual worlds of metaphysics, yoga, and energy healing—I read everything. After some time, though, I found myself knee-deep in internal clutter. I was in recovery from drug addiction.

My bad situation led me to the book I really needed in the treatment center: *The Miracle of Mindfulness* by Thich Nhat Hanh. It turned my life into what it is now, and it came at the time it was meant to come, and not a moment sooner. I learned that I could use every hard lesson I'd experienced to help others.

My never-ending search for meaning took me all over the place, but along the way, I still knew that my life was guided by this all-encompassing source of energy called God.

I needed to find something to make myself whole. Then along the way, I realized I was already whole the entire time. Everything I needed was within me. I wanted nothing more than to be one with God. I just needed to clear the clutter.

My vision for my life is minuscule compared to God's. His vision is HUGE, so if I imagine what I want, I'm putting a limit on God. By having Faith and trusting God's plan for me, I can have a much happier life. If it weren't for this trust, I certainly wouldn't have a TV show. That was never part of my plan.

Sounds easy, almost like a cop-out, right? *Just leave it up to God? What if God wants me to suffer, and grovel, and live a poor, lousy, bummer of a life?* Don't fall for that baloney. All that stuff is emotional clutter: the call that never came, the job you never got, the money you never made. That's interference, and you need to remove it so God's plan can flow through you—so that you can see the evidence and believe, "Well gosh, there is a plan for me, and it's a good one!"

Thankfully, there's an easy way to clear your emotional clutter without taking any time out of your busy life. It's a super-simple process called habit stacking.

We all have many habits that we complete throughout a typical day. Just a few of yours might be making the bed, brewing coffee, frying an egg, toasting a bagel, brushing your teeth, getting dressed, and heading to work.

We could all benefit from spending some dedicated time each day clearing the muck in our lives to make way for our light to shine through. Ideally, we should be meditating or praying for a few hours each day. But who has time for that?

This is where habit stacking comes in.

Instead of sitting silently in a lotus pose and chanting, "Om," or attending church services every night, you can clear your clutter and deepen your Faith while completing your other habits. Practical, isn't it? You don't even need tight yoga pants or church clothes to do it.

To habit stack, choose an activity you do every day for five minutes, like brushing your teeth. From now on, whenever you do this habit, you're going to add another habit on top of it. You're going to turn your attention toward yourself and be present. That's it. While brushing your teeth, acknowledge, without judgment, all the things that are holding you down and keeping you from the joy God wants for you. Then release those things.

You might say to yourself, "Hi, sadness, I see you. There you are." Or, "Oh, there's some resentment. Isn't that interesting."

By acknowledging your clutter and releasing it, you'll make more space for God's abundance to flow. You'll open yourself to receive it.

Remove the interference. Trust that God's love can and will flow through you. Once you take away the blockages, you can see the evidence you need to have Faith. If you keep that clutter in the front of your mind every day, all you will see is what you lack in your life. You'll be stuck in a negative feedback loop of "What if...?" and regret.

With habit stacking, you can use the daily routines that already exist in your life to remove clutter, so you can start to trust that God has it all planned out for you. The food is going to be provided. The rent is going to be paid. Having Faith is about allowing the awareness of God's abundance to enter your life and provide for your needs. You can either resist or allow and have Faith. Resistance mode is when you are fearful, worried, uncomfortable, and anxious. You are bowing down to interference. This is an unnatural state. But when you make space within yourself and allow room for Faith, you are in your natural state. Remove the interference and live the way your life was meant to be.

Things often seem to go wrong, but it's all supposed to happen. Know that you will be given everything you need to handle these experiences. Accept that you are enough, and you will be at ease. Remove the interference and enjoy the warm embrace of God's love. Faith is that easy.

MEL MASON

About Mel Mason: International Best-Selling Author Mel Mason is The Clutter Expert, and as a sexual abuse survivor, she grew up depressed, suicidal, and surrounded by clutter. What she realized after coming back from the brink of despair and getting through her own chaos was that the outside is just a mirror of the inside, and if you only address the outside without changing the inside, the clutter keeps coming back.

That set her on a mission to empower people around the world to get free from clutter inside and out, so they can experience happiness and abundance in every area of their lives.

She is the author of *Freedom from Clutter: The Guaranteed, Foolproof, Step-by-Step Process to Remove the Stuff That's Weighing You Down*

Author's website: *www.FreeGiftFromMel.com*
Book Series Website & Author's Bio: *www.The13StepsToRiches.com*

Miatta Hampton

FAITH IT UNTIL YOU MAKE IT

If you are tired of living a basic life, it is time to activate your Faith. If you are tired of seeing other people win, it is time to activate your Faith. If you want more but feel held back by fear, it is time to activate your Faith. Here is what I want you to know about fear, it extinguishes your desires and crushes your Faith. It is fear that prevents you from becoming the person you dream of becoming, earning the money you want to earn, and meeting the people you want to serve. Fear is the thing that prevents you from starting the business, writing the book, going back to school, creating the online course, and so much more. There is an answer for fear, and it is Faith. Faith is believing in something when you do not have any proof that it exists. Faith is the ingredient to the feeling that what we want we can have, and the proof of things not seen with the physical eye. Do you have Faith in yourself or confidence in yourself to get to your next level?

I remember being pregnant with my fourth daughter and having to be hospitalized. It was a scary time for my family and me. We had just come home from a beach vacation, and I was extremely fatigued and noticed I had dropped eleven pounds in weight. The weight loss was unexplained and unintentional. I assumed it was due to traveling and being pregnant. By day three of these symptoms, I knew something was wrong. I visited my OB/GYN and had an ultrasound and some blood work drawn. I remember on day four being so fatigued, I could not get out of bed. I could barely stand to take a shower, and I was starting to lose feeling in my legs. Later that day, I got a call from my doctor's office stating my blood work had returned, and I needed to get to the hospital immediately. After arriving at the hospital and getting checked in, the nurse revealed that my blood sugar was over 600 and I was in diabetic ketoacidosis, and that I should be in a coma. I was admitted into ICU and placed on an insulin drip. After being in the hospital for five days, the physicians could not determine why this had happened, but I was diagnosed with gestational diabetes.

The hospital bills started to flood in, $100 here, $200 there. Every bill that came in was larger than the one before it. The largest bill came in at $28,000, after insurance had paid its part. I took the invoice, placed it back into the envelope, and tucked it away out of sight. It sat there for eight months until I finally decided not to allow scarcity and the fear of not enough to rule my mindset. If I wanted to be debt-free, there were things I would have to do, and I needed to start with that $28,000 plus I owed in medical bills. I pinned the invoice to my wall in a place I would have to pass by daily, and I prayed for an answer. I had Faith that I would get the strategy for my next action plan to get rid of this debt. My Faith required action. I called my insurance carrier to discuss how to pay the hospital bill, but instead, I filed an appeal. My Faith led me to intentions and action. Much to my surprise, I received a notice that all debt had been forgiven, and the insurance company would pay 100% of the money owed. I knew I could either get the debt reduced or 100% paid, but it took Faith.

It is important to know that your Faith alone is not enough. Faith without works is dead. Faith without any action is just wishful thinking. There are three things you can do to boost your Faith: set your intentions daily, execute, and believe in your ability to make it happen.

Set Your Intentions

Setting your intentions is the process where you state what you intend on executing. This is the thing that will help you maintain focus and get clear about what direction you are headed in. It will serve as a compass to your three w's: who, what, and why. Who do you serve, what do you do, and why do you serve? Set your intentions first thing in the morning. This will help you stay focused on your goals.

Execute

Take action. Whatever you say you will do, do it. The number one reason some people are successful and others are not is because they take action. Take some time, plan out what your following action is, and write it down on your calendar. I knew that I had a huge hospital bill and that it needed to be paid. I had to take the next action step, which involved calling the insurance company and making arrangements to get it paid. I had to face my fears and allow my Faith to take control.

Believe in Your Ability to Make it Happen

It is about your perspective and how your view yourself. You have been equipped with everything you need to succeed. You need to believe that you can do whatever you set your mind to do. Maintain a positive attitude. For every negative thought that you have about yourself and your situation, speak a positive word. Believing in yourself is the key to getting you to the next level. Do not allow fear of failing to be the deciding factor for going after your dreams. Fail forward. Your desires are on the other side; you need a little Faith to get there. Faith it until you make it.

Take some time to reflect on these three questions.

1.   What fears do I need to release?

2.   What do I want to create or build in my life?

3.   What is the next action I need to take, and how will I execute it?

It took Faith to start a business while working a 9 to 5 job. It took Faith to become a speaker, author, and coach. I told myself all the reasons why I should not do it, "I am a wife, a mother, and I don't have the time." Notice I said *should not*; it was not that I could not do it. I had reached a level of comfort in my life, and I was settled, but felt a tug. A tug that I needed to move in another direction, a tug that I needed to level up in life and in business, and that the thing that I was being called to was greater than me, and was going to take Faith to pull it off. Faith in myself, Faith in my hopes, dreams, and vision. Faith that God was going to see me through every endeavor. I put aside my fears, and I started DrMiattaSpeakes. com. This was new for me, so I knew I needed help. I entered a group coaching program because I needed to be around like-minded people, and I needed support. Out of that program, I leveled up again and started my group coaching program for women called Next Level Woman of Worth (nextlevelwow.com). I took the small leap of Faith and put fear behind me. I understood that my purpose was too great to allow fear to keep me paralyzed.

Know that your Faith will lead you to your wealthy place, and when you give birth to greatness, things will come against you and try to get you to change your mind, but be steadfast and firm in your purpose, firm in your Faith, and immoveable—not being influenced by your feeling, emotions, or the opinions of others.

DR. MIATTA HAMPTON

About Dr. Miatta Hampton: Dr. Miatta Hampton is a nurse leader, #1 Best-Selling Author, speaker, coach, and minister. Miatta impacts others with her powerful, relatable messages of pursing purpose, and she empowers her audiences to live life on purpose and according to their dreams. She coaches and inspires women to turn chaos into cozy, pivot to prosperity, and how to profit in adversity. Miatta provides tools and resources for personal, professional, and financial growth.

Author's website: *www.DrMiattaSpeaks.com*
Book Series Website & Author's Bio: *www.The13StepsToRiches.com*

Michael D. Butler

FAITH CAN BE RESTORED

"Now Faith is the substance of things hoped for the evidence of things not seen." (Hebrews 11:6)

We were born with Faith. We have Faith that someone will feed us when we cry. We have Faith that someone will pick us up after school. We have Faith that what others tell us, they will follow through on.

What is Faith

Faith is belief. But Faith is more than mere believing. Faith motivates us to take action. You can believe a hurricane is coming but having Faith in that fact will motivate you to prepare.

Faith motivates people to take action. Faith can be quiet, Faith can be loud, Faith moves us in the direction of our belief. When we believe something, our Faith creates action and motivates us to move.

Head Faith vs. Heart Faith

Some try to grasp Faith with the mind and miss it every time. They do the religious things of reciting, memorizing, going to church and practicing their religion but I think Faith is deeper than that. You can travel to the most remote village on the planet and visit the most untouched tribe on any continent, and you will quickly learn that every person born on this planet has a deep spiritual connection to God, to the Universe, to their Creator. This Faith is expressed in many different ways, but the truth is every person has an innate desire to worship something. To show honor to a deity, to express worship, and to connect with God. For billions of people, this is more than just a mental acknowledgment of God. It is a passionate pursuit of the divine that they confess they were born with and it is deeply important to them.

Living Requires Faith

We have Faith our employer will pay us for the work we put in on the job. We have Faith that the banks will protect and warehouse our money until we need to withdraw it. We have Faith that our college degree will open doors for a quality job. We use our Faith on a daily basis at a subconscious level without even thinking about it.

Faith in God

Faith in God was natural for me growing up on a farm in Oklahoma. From seeing a butterfly come from a cocoon to seeing horses and cows be born, grow and prosper. It would have been harder for me to deny God than to believe in Him.

Faith in Our Parents, Faith in Our Teachers, Faith in Others Can Be Lost

When we're young, we have no choice but to have Faith in others. We depend on the adults in our lives to feed us, clothe us, change us and care for us. But as we grow, humans let us down, they disappoint us, and lie to us. Maybe not intentionally, but they do. We get hurt, offended and abused. And those violations affect our trust; they affect our Faith.

Our early Faith in others was shattered by disappointment and when promises made were not kept. Words spoken were not followed through on. School teachers let us down, parents disappointed us and siblings did not keep their word. When this happens, it causes trust to erode from an early age. When we are young, we have to assign blame and build walls of protection around our heart to protect ourselves from being hurt again. This act of defense, intended to protect, becomes walls of isolation that insulate us from others who can help us, nurture us and cause us to grow.

Faith Can Be Restored

Forgiveness is a gift and a choice. The healing power of forgiveness will reignite the power of Faith in every person's life who chooses to use it. Faith comes alive and is born again when forgiveness is embraced. Healing happens when Faith is utilized.

Faith has changed our world, from believing the world is flat to chartering ships with our life savings, enduring hardships, overcoming adversity, flying to the moon and soon, landing on mars. Without Faith, none of this would be possible.

Faith is Not Blind

Faith, real Faith, is based on research, data and discovery. Faith is a decision based on careful research and knowledge that is gained by interviewing experts on your topic, as well as gut instinct.

Faith Believes Someone Created the Stars

Faith Believes in the Greatness of Others

Faith Believes What Can't Be Seen

Faith Inspires Others

Faith is Not Always About Taking Action

Faith is Also About Letting Go

Faith moves us forward on our journey, Faith is the journey.

Never lose Faith.

My Personal Journey of Faith

Growing up on the farm taught me many things about life and Faith. When I was young, my dad would often remind me that walking in the dark with a flashlight is the same as having Faith.

While you cannot see a mile ahead, you can see far enough to take the next few steps. And when you get there, you can see even farther.

Faith is Not Mere Optimism

While it's great to be optimistic, Faith is not mere optimism or positive mental attitude. Faith does not come from the head—it's a deep knowing in the heart. Faith is Eternal and Believes the Truth

Your Faith will take you places if you will trust it, learn to listen to it, and honor it. Your Faith will give the boldness and confidence to step into any situation and bring peace to everyone involved. And Faith will safely navigate you into eternity as you take your last breath on this planet. Faith will lead the way, Faith will bring you peace and Faith will give you rest.

"For we walk by faith, not by sight." (II Corinthians 5:7)

MICHAEL D. BUTLER

About Michael D. Butler: Michael Butler has been a guest on *Fox News* and *USA Today* and has gotten his clients onto *CNN, Dr. Phil, TMZ, TLC, Rolling Stone, Entrepreneur Magazine, Inc500, TBN, TruTV, Fox Business* and many others.

His Podcast, *The Publisher Podcast* is heard by thousands globally and features guests from Hollywood and the Literary Industry.

He has published 4 of his own International best-selling books in multiple languages: *The Single Dad's Survival Guide, Best-Seller Status – Becoming a Best-Selling Author in the Digital Age, The Speaker's Edge – Turning Your Part-Time Passion into Your Full-Time Speaking Career* and *It's Complicated – When Finding Love was a Matter of Letting Go.*

He founded and runs 1040Impact.org that rescues kids in human trafficking, educates them and teaches them trade skills to equip them for life in Asia in places like Pakistan.

He is the CEO of Beyond Publishing with authors in 20 countries and over 400 titles by end of 2021.

Author's Website: *www.MichaelDButler.com*
Book Series Website & Author's Bio: *www.The13StepstoRiches.com*

Michelle Cameron Coulter & Al Coulter

THE BIRTH OF
INSPIRING POSSIBILITIES

I know there have been times in all our lives when we have been challenged more than ever expected. Getting through the hard times somehow builds resiliency, strength, and something inside us we never knew we had.

This chapter in our lives was one of the most significant times that revealed the colossal power of Faith.

My husband, Al, and I had been on a relationship retreat; our marriage was coming up to the ten-year mark, we had three kids and expecting our fourth, and our marriage was on the roughest ground it had ever been. Not doing well was an understatement.

We finished the weekend course, and the following morning unexpectedly, Al's Father called to tell him he had just been diagnosed with terminal cancer and given only a couple of months to live. That was the first time Al and his father both said, "I love you." His father had just come back from a two-week bike trip, was in great shape when they found his liver was full of cancer, and that was the secondary cancer. Without any hesitation, we decided Al's family needed him. He left that week with two of the kids, and I joined with the youngest a couple of weeks later. We put them in school halfway across the country in eastern Canada, a couple of blocks away from Al's homestead (Grade 3, Grade 1, and Preschool), and we helped hospice Al's father alongside his mom and family.

The kids got to know their papa-Keith (grandpa) and grandma. It was hard to see him slowly degenerate, yet it was such a gift of time.

Our marriage was still struggling, as we had grown apart through values going such different directions. Al was career-driven with business partners who were about success at any cost. Al was the company's face as he is one of the most trustworthy people you could ever meet.

His partner's true colors came through, as there was no official contract and partner agreement. Long story short, we ended up losing everything, including our home, as the partner moved all the assets around while we were away from September to December. We had a dear friend who was a partner in a law firm who was more than happy to help us. He let us know it would be an uphill battle for a few years. It was millions of dollars in assets, and it would jeopardize all the investors involved. We decided to walk away and start over.

Al's father passed away on December first. I flew back to my hometown when school was out, seven months pregnant and with three little ones. My husband stayed behind to help his family.

I moved back in with my parents because our house was still rented out from while we were away. I remember walking in their home all decorated. I just let go in tears; the stress has been so much.

Al ended up driving thirty-six hours straight to make it to us for Christmas Eve.

This was the first time I had spent that much time with my parents in some time, having taken huge pride in buying my first home after I retired from the Olympics. I was grateful to have a roof over our head with our three kids as I had contractions two months early from all the stress. I remember my parents sitting us down, saying, "you're going to kill each other from the stresses between the two of you right now." We had the biggest fight and got out all the emotions that had been bottled up inside.

We knew healing this relationship wasn't something we could do on our own; we had to both decide we wanted to fight for it and that we needed help. It was the best decision we made, and that was the first day starting on the healing path.

Our fourth baby, Amazing Grace, was born on February twenty-fifth. I needed to be induced as the baby was under stress, and her heart rate was dipping. The doctor told me I had a minor heart attack when I had her from all the stress.

Fast forward two years ahead: We were still getting our heads back above water and in a rental property working to repurchase a home. Proud of the healing and the growth journey we had been on, I was also proud that Al had made sure that every investor he had brought into his previous company had saved their investment and even made profits. His integrity and word were something he stood beside.

We still had a way to go.

We were also beyond grateful for a dear friend who gifted us the funds to keep our kids in their activities, knowing that it was the best space and energy to be in through challenging times. With Al and I both being late bloomers and becoming Olympians, we never wanted the pressure on them. It has never been about podium for our children; it has been about the growth, community, and positive environment through sports and activities.

We had finally saved up enough money to buy a second vehicle to get everyone where they needed to go. While driving to school one day, a fight broke out in the back seat of the car, you know the one, "…she touched me,"

"…no he touched me first!"

I'm like, "Ok! Let's change the environment. Let's plan a family trip. We haven't done anything for ages. Where would you like to go for a fun family trip?"

Growing up in a blended family of ten kids, my mom taught me there is always a way.

I thought that with our kids being ages ten, eight, six, and two they would want to go to Disneyland. Instead, they were like, "We want to go to Mexico!"

You see, my birth dad lived in a bit of a fishing village in Mexico six months of the year. The kids had gone with us a few years earlier. Some children lived behind him, in little shanties, dirt floors, bare feet, and no toys. Our kids had made friends with the kids, playing with a ball they had brought.

"Mom, we could go to Mexico and bring more toys for the kids. Maybe we could get some of our friends to collect more toys with us, and we could bring more. Mom, could you imagine if we just all shared what we have? No kids would be without."

"Mommy, we are going to need a plane."

Our house was still in boxes as we were in a rental property, working to buy back into the market again.

That day after school, Alissa came running up the stairs with a CD in her hand, saying, "Mom listen…this could be our theme song." It was of a young boy named Billy Gillman who had been on Oprah. The song was *One Voice.*

"Some kids have, and some kids don't, and some of us are wondering why? Mom won't watch the news at night; there is too much making her cry. A thousand words, a million prayers. One voice was heard."

We can call it "A Gift of Love," she said.

We have always told our kids you could do anything you put your mind to, and they set on this vision.

We reached out to a couple of friends, and before you knew it, the next day, we were down at an airline's head office with the kids presenting their idea. In minutes, the executive team turned to us, "You have a plane" My mouth dropped.

In the next six weeks, miracle after miracle happened. Whenever questions came up, *how are you going to do this?*, I would say, *I'm not sure, but I know it is happening.*

We ended up having seventy children ambassadors from twenty-two schools who collected over 3,000 packages of loved toys, gently worn shoes, school supplies, and a note for each of the kids. We had friends who worked in Mexico and lined us up with the Army, Navy, and Rotary women, who sourced all the special needs schools and orphanages for us.

We had a Boeing 737 for thirty-six hours packed to the rim with loved packages, right down to the last little red trike. These young ambassadors hand-delivered 3,000 boxes to kids in orphanages and special needs schools. Such a powerful experience; kids connected, knowing that they cared about each other.

The world did not know that we didn't know how we were making rent the next month, and in the middle of this came A Gift of Love.

What I also know is that our kids never felt like they were without love.

Inspiring Possibilities are in every one of us, no matter our age or background. When something is more significant than ourselves, and we add unstoppable Faith. Miracles happen!

MICHELLE CAMERON
COULTER & AL COULTER

About Michelle Cameron Coulter: Michelle is an Olympic gold medalist, entrepreneur, mother of four, community leader raising millions of dollars for charities, global inspirational leader, and founder and CEO of Inspiring Possibilities.

About Al Coulter: Al is a two-time Olympian in volleyball, captain of Team Canada, world record holder in matches representing one's country in any sport, with over 735 matches, entrepreneur, father of four, and personal best coach, specializing in relationships, team, and resilience.

Michelle and Al are the embodiment of today's leaders. Strong and empowering, they embraced life's challenges with strength and courage. They bring insight, compassion, depth, and inspiration to the table with multiple world championships, three Olympics, an Olympic gold medal, marriage, and four children.

They are sought-after inspirational leaders. Through their speaking, workshops, and retreats, their gift and passion is to inspire possibilities and support people to embrace their greatness in a real, authentic, healthy, and vibrant way—creating thriving community, connection, and one's own gold medal results.

Author's website: *www.MichelleCameronCoulter.com*
Book Series Website & Author's Bio: *www.The13StepsToRiches.com*

Michelle Mras

FAITH: YOU'RE NOT DEAD YET - GET UP!

Have you ever taken the time to watch a toddler at the early stages of walking? They pull themselves up by grabbing furniture, pant legs, or any object that appears larger than themselves. They rely on their strength while holding Faith, per se, in the object they use to become upright. We watch them, smile, and have admiration for their tenacity.

It was May 2014 when my lesson of embracing the tenacity of a toddler became the catalyst of what I believe saved my life. Prior to then, I was living the life I perceived to be expected of me. I was an above-average student, played sports, had a large group of friends, attended college to get an engineering degree, married my high school sweetheart, became a mother, kept our home practically perfect, and made well-rounded meals every day. I maintained an overactive level of participation in our children's school activities, baking cookies, and working every event possible, all while maintaining a job outside of the home. I was in full *Wonder Woman* mode until I wasn't.

On that auspicious day in May, I was in an automobile accident that left me with what we thought was a slight concussion. Twelve days after the accident, I lost my ability to form sentences and, shortly afterward, the ability to walk without assistance. My life changed forever. I went from doing everything to needing assistance to wash and feed myself. I was on a regime of pain killers and brain therapies. After a year spent trapped in this state of being, I discovered that I had a Traumatic Brain Injury (TBI) that affected four areas of my brain. The therapy to have my brain communicate more effectively increased. I was fully cognizant inside my mind without the ability to communicate through writing or speech.

Every time I showed signs of improvement, something would occur, and my brain would lock down again. This was my idea of Hell. I became severely depressed because of the lack of independence and the increased inner-critic thoughts that bombarded me daily with all my shortcomings. I had lost Faith in God and the possibility of ever regaining any semblance of who I was. That is when the suicidal thoughts joined the chorus.

My ability to recognize the passing of time had also left me, but I distinctly remember sitting on my couch. I was guided there every morning by a family member. I would remain there until someone came home to move me or feed me.

This particular day, I was alone. I meticulously played suicide scenarios through my mind. I became increasingly agitated because all plans I concocted were undoable simply due to the fact I couldn't move without help. In frustration, I screamed in my mind to God, "If you hate me so much, kill me already!" to which I heard the response, "You're not dead yet, get up."

I don't know if you have ever had an experience like that, but I assure you, it was a voice you cannot ignore. It reverberated throughout every cell in my body and through every molecule around me. When I heard the command, I saw myself in every moment in my life when I had felt abandoned or left to suffer as if they were movie scenes. In each instance, I was held by an unseen hand. To this day, I can't honestly explain it in words. I felt a wave of peace and acceptance wash over me. The next thing I knew, I was on my knees in the middle of the living room, several feet from my couch. I was saying, "Thank you for every experience. Thank you for my life."

When my husband returned home, he found me sitting at the office computer, insisting that I needed to speak. He said, "How are you speaking? How did you move to the office?" Two activities entirely out of my abilities for the past two years. Yet, there I was.

My journey to the woman I am today was not instantaneous. I had fantastic days and very challenging days. There were times I could perform daily tasks without assistance and others when I couldn't leave my bed for weeks. I would walk, then have vertigo attacks. Pull up, then fall. Speak coherent sentences, then revert to playing charades to ask for water. Recovery was not easy, nor was it linear.

I found a renewed love for life. I stopped viewing the challenges before me as punishments for my inadequacies. Instead, I considered the challenges to be circumvented and conquered. I smiled through my pain, not because it didn't hurt.

I smiled because I had the gift of waking up to complain. I laughed at my shortcomings and figured out other ways to complete a task. In short, I had reverted my mindset to that of a toddler.

Every day I become better. I still have days when I can feel my brain's short circuit, and that's okay. It simply means I need to throttle back and approach my day differently. It has become part of my life to adjust and reset.

How about you? Do you allow circumstances, situations, and people to throw your day off? Do you get frustrated when what you expect to happen doesn't? How about when someone doesn't do what you want them to do? Do you get frustrated with yourself?

There is a quote by Byron Katie that comes to me daily. It reads, "There are only three kinds of business in the universe: mine, yours, and God's." Control what is in your sphere of control—YOU. How does this quote guide me daily? How can it guide you to success? Whenever you feel overwhelmed or unable to control a situation, ask yourself, "Who am I attempting to control?" Once you realize the answer isn't, "Myself," back off.

Faith comes into play throughout every aspect of life's ups and downs. In my experience, I lost Faith in God and in myself. That lack of belief kept me from getting back up. Once I realized I am not alone, my confidence rejuvenated. I had my much-needed preverbal object to hold on to when I felt unstable and ready to fall. Now, when I fall, I have the tenacity of a toddler to do everything within my power to find a way back up. I have Faith in myself that there is a way.

I found that the key to getting back up after a pitfall is to keep Faith in God or a higher power while maintaining confidence in yourself. Throughout my TBI journey, I have met many individuals who are experiencing life challenges. They wonder why they aren't recovering or are more successful. They have Faith in God or a higher power, but they lack confidence in themselves. To move to your next level, be it health, relationships, career, etc., you must have Faith in both.

My mentor, Paul Scheele of Scheele Learning Strategies, shared an observation that holds regardless of your stage of life. "We, as humans, are created to fall. From the time we learn to walk, we fall, we get back up, we fall again, we get back up. We are designed to fall and get back up." The importance of falling is to learn from the fall, adjust to repeat what worked, and not repeat what doesn't -You must have Faith that you will find a way.

Remember that you are a toddler in an adult body. You will fall. Train yourself to have Faith that there is something more significant at play. You can adapt and grow to whatever you desire to accomplish. Embrace your toddler mindset.

"Get up. You're not dead yet!"

MICHELLE MRAS

About Michelle Mras: Michelle is an International Award-Winning Speaker, Communication Trainer, Success Coach, co-Host of the Denim & Pearls podcast, the Author *of Eat, Drink and Be Mary: A Glimpse Into a Life Well Lived* and *It's Not Luck: Overcoming You,* and Host of the MentalShift show on The New Channel (TNC), Philippines.

Michelle is a survivor of multiple life challenges including a Traumatic Brain Injury and her current battle with Breast Cancer. She guides her clients to recognize the innate gifts within them, to stop apologizing for what they are not, and step into who they truly are. She accomplishes this through one-on-one and group coaching, Training events, Keynote talks, her books, Podcasts and MentalShift television show.

Awarded the Inspirational Women of Excellence Award from the Women Economic Forum, New Delhi, India; the John Maxwell Team Culture Award for Positive Attitude; She has been featured on hundreds of Podcasts, radio programs, several magazines, is in a few SyFy movies, and does audiobook narration and has a habit of breaking out into song.

Michelle's driving thought is that every day is a gift. Tomorrow is never promised. Every moment is an opportunity to be the best version of you... Unapologetically!

Author's Website: *www.MichelleMras.com*
Book Series Website & Author's Bio: *www.The13StepstoRiches.com*

Mickey Stewart

YOUR 'SWITCH' OF FAITH

If you've ever visited the United Kingdom, you would have undoubtedly noticed that our electrical outlets work quite differently than those in most other countries. In addition to plugging your device into a power outlet, there's also an 'ON/OFF' switch you manually need to press before your device will work or before your battery will charge.

Although it's somewhat embarrassing to admit, I can't tell you the number of times (after 20+ years of living in Scotland) that I've plugged my phone in to charge overnight, only to wake up the following day to realize I FORGOT TO TURN THE SWITCH TO THE 'ON' POSITION! And, as if the initial disappointment of realizing my mistake isn't enough, I'm left with the realization that I now have to 'wait' for my battery to charge!

Surprisingly, this has become a metaphor for my FAITH.

To me, Faith has always meant 'trusting in something or someone bigger than ourselves; that invisible, higher power many of us refer to as God, the Universe, or Source.' While the actual term we each use might differ, I believe the overall essence is the same.

Although it's easy to have Faith when things are going our way, it's inevitable for life to throw us curveballs, and rarely do we EVER see these curveballs coming. Whether it's the initial shock of its first blow, or later, when we're doing everything possible to try to recover from its impact, our Faith (unfortunately) is often what makes the biggest hit of all, with our trust left damaged, shattered into pieces, sprawled out everywhere on the floor.

In August 2018, I awoke to excruciating head pain, a headache, unlike anything I have ever experienced. I was soon to discover I was suffering from an undiagnosed traumatic brain injury that not only made it unbearable for me to sit up, but impossible for me to stand. It appeared that a spontaneous tear in my dura (the toughest, outermost membrane covering my brain and spinal cord) was causing cerebrospinal fluid to leak into my body. The result? My brain was (literally) sagging into the back of my head.

I suffered for months before being diagnosed, and the 'not knowing' was terrifying. On the days I somehow managed to force myself to crawl to the bathroom to get washed, I'd ultimately end up on the floor of my shower, crying, feverishly willing myself not to vomit from the pain. It was during these dark moments that I often found myself consumed with the thought, "*Oh my God! Is this going to be my life?*" I wasn't even fifty years old yet, and it was starting to look like my husband was now going to have to be my caregiver for the rest of my life.

I gradually found myself feeling depressed and emotionally heartbroken by this betrayal of my body. It's only in looking back now that I can also see how angry I was; angry at my body, angry at my life, and angry at the Universe because it was supposed to have my back. When one doctor suggested that, "Perhaps it's just a bad migraine," I wanted to punch him in the face. I believe that this anger was the coping mechanism I used to mask my fear.

While I might have always prided myself in continually being 'plugged-in' or 'connected to my higher power,' it was now glaringly clear that, at this particularly dark point in my life, I had forgotten to TURN MY FAITH SWITCH TO THE 'ON' POSITION.

This realization is what provided me the smallest glimmer of hope I so desperately needed. After recognizing what was happening, I manually flipped my FAITH switch to the ON position—the easy part—and prepared myself to enter the hard part—the waiting.

But do you know what happened while I waited? It was the most beautiful thing imaginable! It was during one of these most extreme, darkest hours, sitting limply on the floor of my shower, crying, waiting for my Faith battery to recharge when the words of Napoleon Hill rang true in my ears. *"Within every adversity is an equal or greater benefit."*

I knew those words as truth.

Throughout my trips in and out of hospital (during my lumbar puncture, CT scans, MRIs, and various other tests) my higher power sent me an incredible team of people whom, today, I refer to as my 'earth angels':

The doctors at my local health center didn't delay when all the signs started pointing toward a brain aneurysm similar to what my dad had experienced.

My hospital doctor went to battle to get me an appointment with a top neurologist within 24 hours, when there were no appointments available.

That top neurologist who immediately knew what was wrong with me (even though most GPs never come across such a case during their entire careers and the majority of people go undiagnosed for years).

The anesthesiologist who did my blood patch procedure convinced me that the blood patch would work with every fiber of his being. He phoned two days later to give me full permission to get on with my life.

My Kundalini yoga teacher, who, during my year-long recovery, helped me heal my connection with myself (physically, emotionally, and spiritually).

Interestingly, it was after deciding to manually flip my switch (remembering to choose to have Faith) and by purposely entering into my waiting period (as my doctors began to unfold their findings) that the amazing domino effect (back to health) began to take place. During this entire process of identifying what was WRONG with me, I began to have Faith that all would be RIGHT gradually. My Faith battery was finally on its way to becoming fully charged!

As for my "greater benefit" of having gone through such adversity? It came in the form of a HUGE wake-up call. I DON'T have all-time in the world. My time here on earth is limited. There are still so many things I want to create, to experience. This life-changing event planted a fire deep within my soul, resulting in a renewed sense of urgency to live life, NOW!

Understandably, our connection to our higher power can appear broken when we're experiencing such times of fear and despair. And it often feels as if ALL our worries and ALL our thoughts are taking part in one huge, competitive battle inside our brain, shouting at us so incredibly loudly that they drown out what our higher power is trying to communicate to us:

"Trust me! I'm here and ready to help."

FLIP THAT SWITCH!

I'm so excited to have this new, simple exercise (connect to my power source / remember to flip the switch / wait / identify the greater benefit) to use as a tool to help guide me through the inevitable, upcoming curveballs of life, regardless of whether they come in the form of a small, one-ounce golf ball or large 16-pound bowling balls.

I invite you to do the same!

MICKEY STEWART

About Mickey Stewart: Born in Cape Breton, Canada, Mickey Stewart is a musician, coach, and author who has been a player and instructor of the snare drum and bodhrán for forty years.

Responsible for heading up the drum program at Ardvreck School in Perthshire, Scotland since 2002, Mickey is in high demand to teach throughout the U.K. and North America.

Creator and founder of BodhránExpert.com, her YouTube videos have received more than two million views from students and fans from every country throughout the world.

Over the past eight years, she's been involved in the TV and film industry as a supporting artist. Even more recently, she's begun following her newest passion, which is teaching others how to share their talents with the world.

Stewart lives in Crieff, Scotland with her husband of twenty-four years, Scottish musician and composer Mark Stewart, along with their 16-year-old son, Cameron, who is also a piper.

Author's Website: *www.MickeyStewart.com*
Book Series Website & Author's Bio: *www.The13StepstoRiches.com*

Natalie Susi

TWO SIDES OF THE SAME COIN

As a teacher, entrepreneur, and single woman well into my late 30s, I've had to call on Faith a lot. Most of us are trained to believe that working hard and grinding away are important, necessary factors in creating the life we want. While we need to be proactive, we also need to learn how to set intentions, take inspired action, and then surrender and trust in our Faith that the exact right person, place, or thing will show up to help us produce the result we are seeking. It takes patience and a high degree of self-worth and empowerment to use Faith as a tool, but once you start learning what it looks, sounds, and feels like to live and act from Faith, you will begin to see how much more quickly and easily you can manifest your ideal life.

I will share one of my most important stories about finding Faith and allowing it to work in my life. As I share this story, I encourage you to start thinking about a moment where it may have felt like you were pushing a boulder up a hill, or a period when you were searching for answers, solutions, or healing, and you couldn't seem to gain any clarity or relief. If you want to uncover how you might individually move through finding your Faith, you could journal about these moments and write the story out just as I do below. When you write about your experiences, you often start to see patterns that will help you identify some of the actions or mindset shifts that work for you.

Faith in Business

When I was 23, I started my first business called Bare Organic Mixers. This is a very long story, but I'll give you the most relevant highlights. I had an idea to create a low-calorie cocktail mixer, and it launched the same day as Skinny Girl Margarita, a brand that ended up selling for many millions of dollars. I launched my brand at just the right time in the marketplace, but I had zero knowledge about developing a product, building a business, or creating a brand in one of the most competitive industries on the planet. I wore all the hats and performed all the jobs right down to delivering the product out of the trunk of my Hyundai.

I spent eight years of my life on this business, and in the process, I lost a boyfriend, a business partner, and my life savings. I learned all of my lessons the hard way. By year seven, I was exhausted. It felt like I was pushing a boulder up a hill all the time. In the midst of all of this, my boyfriend of four years broke up with me, and seven days after the breakup, I turned 30. A few days after that, all three of my jobs to keep my head and business above water fell through. I was brought to my knees, doubled over, and crying from heartbreak and loss, so deep that I never thought I'd recover. At that moment, I was forced to find my Faith.

One day, after another lengthy cry-fest, I kneeled on the floor, put my hands up, and I said out loud, "I am done. Please show me what to do next." I didn't realize what I was doing at the time, but I was in the act of surrendering. I let go, and I let God. I chose to step out of fear and into Faith. I recognized that all of my relentless pushing to make something happen was not bringing me the intended results, and I knew somewhere in my heart that the universe, God, divine (whatever you'd like to call it), made everything fall apart at the same time so that I could rebuild differently. I was at last released, and the answers finally showed up.

Like magic, a few days after my surrender moment, a man named Max (someone who had previously been interested in my business) reached out to reconnect on a call. And a few months after this call, Max helped me sell the company. All of my wishes for the brand were realized. Max is an extraordinary mentor and friend to me, and I still call him "my domino" because he was the person who set all the pieces in place for me to release my business and move on to my next life adventure. Many moments and key players ultimately fell into place after my surrender moment; like one of my other mentors, Cheryl, stepping in to help me close the sale of the business. I was very blessed and guided after I finally stopped pushing and started acting in Faith.

Faith and Fear are Two Sides of the Same Coin

You cannot experience both at one time. You have to turn over fear to find Faith. You have to throw your hands up in challenging circumstances, and instead of saying, "I give up," you say, "I give in. I trust. I surrender."

Faith is the act of trusting that everything is working out in your favor, no matter how challenging the circumstances. It's knowing that the business will always come, the heartbreak will always heal, and the layoff will always lead to better and more aligned opportunities. Faith is about knowing what you know, even if you don't always know how you know it. It's about being so clear in your mind, body, and soul that a greater power has your back, so you can stop searching for answers and start trusting that all of your desires are just on their way. When referring to Faith, you can call it God, Divine, Allah, Spirit, or Higher Self. You can name it whatever feels best as long as you call on it at some point.

To help with this, I'd encourage you to start creating a process around how we find Faith when it feels impossible to do so. If you'd like to try that, write out 2-3 stories where life pushed you to build your Faith muscle. Write out the whole story as I did. Who were the players? What was the situation? What challenges and hardships did you experience? When did you put your hands up and decide to give in, trust, surrender, and find

Faith? What did that process look like for you? How did the situation end up working in your favor? What miracles and magical things showed up?

Having Faith is simple, but it is not always easy. Life is always encouraging us to strengthen our Faith muscle, so we will continue to be presented with opportunities to learn, build, and grow into a greater version of ourselves.

NATALIE SUSI

About Natalie Susi: Natalie has more than 14 years of experience as a teacher, speaker, entrepreneur and mentor. Currently she's a 5-year UCSD professor focusing on communications and the Pursuit of Happiness. As an entrepreneur, she founded and grew Bare Organic Mixers beverage company for 8 years resulting in an acquisition in 2014.

After selling the company, Natalie combined her educational background as a teacher and her experience as an entrepreneur to provide personal development coaching and consulting to individuals, businesses, and creative entrepreneurs. She developed a program called Conscious Conversations and utilizes a step-by-step process called The Alignment Method to support leaders in cultivating conscious teams and businesses through a process of self-reflection, self-discovery, and self-ascension that ultimately increases profits, productivity, and the growth of the individuals personally and professionally.

Author's website: *www.NatalieSusi.com*
Book Series Website & Author's Bio: *www.The13StepsToRiches.com*

Nita Patel

FAITH

We have a 50% meter on Faith. When things happen in our favor, we say, "I knew it would!" When they don't happen in our favor, we say, "Why? Everyone else gets what they want. Why not me?"

Faith is having complete trust, belief, confidence in God, the universe, a higher power, whichever term resonates most with you, that the thing you've set out for will happen for your highest good.

For your **'highest good,'** that's where we get confused. We think we know what's best for us, and when we don't get it, we're disappointed, often distraught.

For me, Faith was learning to pray for the best outcome, knowing that whatever happens will be for my highest good. Of course, this doesn't mean sitting around doing nothing else but praying. Life is about being in motion. Even Faith requires taking action.

This is how I've learned to live my life daily now, but it wasn't always like this.

I was 39 years old. I got a call from my Gynecologist one day asking me to see him. I thought, "That's odd. Maybe he needs me to take some additional tests or something." After all, life had been extremely stressful.

Anything could be possible. I already had multiple procedures at this point, many of them included having ovarian cysts removed throughout my 30s. I assumed this was related to something similar.

I was eagerly awaiting whatever it was that he was going to tell me. He walked into the room with my chart. He paused, looked into my eyes and said, "Well, we've detected pre-cancer cells in your bloodwork. But don't worry, it doesn't mean anything." He rambled on for a bit while I was still stuck at the first five words that came out of his mouth. "Wait, what?"

"What do you mean?" My voice started to tremble as I asked, "Can you explain this to me again?" My heart started pounding, my palms were sweaty as I realized I need to understand what he was saying, so I told myself to stop freaking out and breathe.

He responded with, "Well, you can have full-blown cancer in the next 30 days, so we're going to need to monitor you. Don't worry about it though, just come back and see me in 30 days, and we'll do some additional testing and discuss what's next." My face must've looked like I had seen a ghost at that moment. He looked at me and knew I wasn't comprehending what he was saying. Concerned, he said, "Why don't you come see me in a week?"

I vaguely heard anything after that. All I could think of was, "I could have cancer, and he's telling me not to worry, and he wants to wait an entire month to see what happens. Are you out of your mind? He just said I could die in a month!" Although that's not exactly what he said, that's how I translated it in my head. His voice faded. I saw him making some notes in my chart as he walked out of the room.

I gathered myself, and as I was closing the exam room door behind me, in that split moment, I declared, "I'm DONE with this!" As I walked out of the building, I put my hand on the handrail to walk down the ramp towards my car. Suddenly I had a flashback: Fourteen years ago, I had fallen apart holding that very same handrail. Right after I found out that it would be my baby or me, but both of us would not make it.

The difference was, this time, I was able to decide that I wasn't going to succumb to self-pity. The past was not going to determine my future.

I wasn't going to come back. No more surgeries. No more doctor visits. No more allowing my emotional state of mind to dictate sickness to my body. Those days were over. Starting today, I was regaining control over my health and my life, and I was no longer going to be an innocent bystander. I decided that I was done being poked and prodded. I decided THIS was not going to happen to me.

When we make these declarations, we want it to happen 50% of the time, and the other 50% we hope it happens. Yes, we often take action towards our decisions, but FAITH's magic formula brings everything together.

I had Faith that whatever God had decided for me was going to be for the best for me. For the first time in my life, I was so sure. Some people call it the power of belief. Others refer to it as prayer. Call it what you may, but when you declare, decide, and know that it will be, the universe conspires to put you in the right place, at the right time to make it happen.

Now when I say a prayer, I don't mean praying from a sense of desperation. The best way to pray for me is to do it with a smile. With a sense of joy, no matter how dark the circumstance is. And the key here is to surrender once you pray. It's not to question or bargain with God about what you will do if things go your way. It is to speak your truth and know that everything is always for your best.

I have learned that no matter how badly you want something or how hard you work for it, if you don't surrender, you will never see your efforts come to fruition. When you surrender, you get to ride the wave. I never knew what that meant until I surrendered 100%, and ever since then, I finally learned what it means to ride the wave. Sure, every great accomplishment comes with great challenges and obstacles. And yes, determination and persistence must be applied. But when all of that comes with Faith, it typically works out.

The next time I went to see my doctor, I was 41. Not because I was afraid, but because I was so caught up in changing how I was living my life that I lost track of time.

Faith = Surrender

Faith = Belief Faith = Trust

What does Faith mean to you?

For me, it meant every time I launched a business, and it failed; every time I applied for a job and was rejected, every time I launched a service that didn't quite work out, I fought the current, I took all the stress upon myself until I remembered to surrender. And every time I let it go, a better idea, a better opportunity, and amazing results came to me.

Why?

Because what we want for ourselves is so small compared to what God has in store for us. When we learn to surrender and trust in that statement, what Napoleon Hill referred to as the snowball effect, starts occurring.

Goodness starts expanding in all areas of your life at an exponential rate, and you wonder where it's been all this time. And when that happens, remember, it was because you had Faith. When you surrender and take inspired and planned action, God will do His part to make it better than you ever imagined it could be.

As I shared in the previous book, when I saw that image of Le Louvre, I cut it out and thought to myself that when the time is right, I'm sure it'll happen. Meanwhile, I kept taking action and kept my focus on the current plan. There was no timeline assigned to the surrender process. And less than twelve months later, I walked into Le Louvre thinking, "Wow! My work is in the same building as the Mona Lisa!"

Just like when I went to see the doctor a year and a half later, I thought to myself, "Wow! How do I apply this to all areas of my life every day, not just when I receive a death threat?"

As for all of us, the true test of Faith is waking up with an intention every day to provide value, to be present, to find joy and gratitude in the small and big things, and celebrate daily successes without judging ourselves.

With Faith, we can all live our best lives.

NITA PATEL

About Nita Patel: Nita is a Best-Selling Author, speaker, and artist who believes in modern etiquette as a path to becoming our best selves.

Through her professional years, Ms. Patel has 25 years of demonstrated technology leadership experience in various industries specifically with a concentrated focus in health care for 14 of those 20+ years. She's shown her art across the world to include the Louvre in Paris. She's a best-selling author and performance coach, pursuing her master's in industrial organizational (I-O) psychology at Harvard. Her investment in psychology theory and practice is what led her to a deep interest in helping others. She has become deeply and passionately devoted to nurturing others and in building their confidence and brand through speaking and consultative practices.

Author's website: *www.Nita-Patel.com*
Book Series Website & Author's Bio: *www.The13StepsToRiches.com*

Olga Geidane

5 RULES TO NURTURE & STRENGTHEN YOUR FAITH

"Be crystal clear about what you want, do what you can, and just have Faith that it will work out!"

Every time I would mention these words to someone for the first time, they would roll their eyes at me and add:

"Olga, this is so wishy-washy! The world doesn't work like that!" Let's just have a look at your life here!

How do you start your day?

You start your day with waking up and, if you are like me, then you have an alarm for a specific time of the morning you would like to be up. So here is my question. "Do you think about whether you will wake up AT ALL tomorrow or not, when you set your alarm?" Out of all the people in the world, there surely are some with very severe stages of terminal illnesses who are not sure whether they will wake up or not, and most likely, they stopped using the alarm long ago, anyways!

So the bottom line is you set up an alarm in the evening because you KNOW, because you have Faith, that you WILL wake up in the morning.

If you have Faith and believe in waking up, without any guarantee, then you CAN have Faith in your dreams, goals, and the best outcomes if you choose to.

Having Faith in meeting the love of your life. Having Faith in getting the career of your dreams.

Having Faith your passion turns into a money-making machine. Having Faith in the people that surround you, trusting them.

It's very easy to choose to settle for second best, not fulfilling, and boring just because something didn't show up in your life just yet. But when you have Faith, you WILL be patient. You will trust the processes to happen.

And the truth is, having Faith or not depends on what you were exposed to growing up.

If in your family it was quite normal to believe in yourself, believing in dreams and goals, then most likely you would never even question yourself about having Faith. Subconsciously, you will just naturally believe in it and will already have it and practice that.

If you grew up with a negative mindset in the family, with very analytical and critical parents, then you will question the whole subject about Faith, unless you consciously decide to make a change to your own thinking.

However, if you have Faith but it is not nourished and supported by yourself and others, you will only have ashes of regrets left of it.

Having Faith in your goals, targets, your super power, and your mission in life means guarding the entrance of your mind with the strongest antivirus program! That means following these Five Rules of Faith:

Having only inspiring and supportive people in your life. You are the average of five people you speak most to, so now ask yourself, "Am I happy to be the average of my five?" Those who are positive and into personal growth and learning surely will support you with your dreams and goals. They will be the ones helping you find solutions and the best ways to achieve what you want. Those who are not ambitious, negative, and complaining will be jealous and will help you only with finding the excuses and reasons why you shouldn't do what you intend to do.

Write a list of at least ten people with whom you regularly stay in touch, whether it is on the phone, face to face, working together, or meeting as a friend. Include your partner if you have one, by the way. When you write their names, list a few bullet points about them describing their main characteristics. If the list has more than ten names, that's fine. Write them all down and circle those with whom you spend MORE time one way or another. Once you complete the list, ask yourself, "Who must stay and who should go, based on their characteristics? Are they part of my new, bright future, or not?"

Remember, it's about doing everything to help you to have Faith. So, are they helping you with that?

Carefully selecting what you are reading, online and offline. Reading your goal-oriented information will be strengthening your Faith versus reading negative stories. One negative word said to someone requires forgiveness and an explanation of why those words were said. And even after, that the person most likely would still hold a grudge. So that means every negative requires approximately three positives to shift the energy up.

Go back in time as far as you can in your memories (it can be just today or it can be a week) and check what you have been reading? What have you been listening to? Was the information you allowed to enter your subconscious supportive of your Faith, or not? Have you learned something new, something useful that will help you to achieve your goals, or have you just wasted your time on scrolling down on social media, liking one post after another? Make a list of at least five information sources you allowed yourself to be exposed to, visually or auditorily. Ask yourself, "Will THAT information take me to the next level?" If it's a YES, then do MORE of it. If it's a NO, make a choice to reduce it if you really wish to reach your goals.

Remember, it is about supporting your Faith into your dreams, so make sure what you expose yourself to is aligned with your desires!

Choosing to visualize your own reality vs. real circumstances. I know what you are probably thinking right now, "But how can I ignore my outside circumstances?" You CAN and should ignore your current outside circumstances at least for those moments of visualization when you expose yourself in your mind to what you WANT. Why is that? Because the minute you start shifting your feelings inside of you, that will up level the world around you. Remember, what you see outside is a mirror of what you CHOOSE to feel inside of you.

Let's do this exercise: write down how a situation in your life right now is in one of the areas you would like to make a change. It could be relationships, work, friendships, social life, hobbies, health and wellness, anything really. Once you have finished your "factual reality", turn the page around or take a new sheet of paper and in a very detailed way, describe how you would like the situation to be. Make sure you include what you see, hear, taste, feel, and touch. When all five senses are involved, it becomes easier to trick your subconscious. Once you finish, reread that on a daily basis, ideally in the mornings and in the evenings. Add more details and remember, even when you deal with the tasks and things in your factual reality, do it from the space and embodiment of the New You, not the old version of you.

The more you practice the new reality AND stay open minded and receptive to the guidance and opportunities, the quicker you will get to what you want.

And if you really want to make a huge leap towards what you desire, then start living your life as if what you want has already happened! That means waking up, having breakfast, doing other activities of the day, walking, speaking, and even wearing the clothes of that NEW you and the NEW level that you want to be at. It sounds a little bit like "fake it until you make it", you might think, but the truth is, this is NOT faking. This is levelling yourself up and embodying your desires being a reality. Yes, it might feel weird in the beginning, but it's only because your mind is busy comparing. So choose to keep it busy with Rule Number Three: Your Own Reality.

There is a saying, "You can take a person out of the village, but you can't take the village out of the person." What happens very often is that people are shifting through their lives as a result of their personal development, without recognizing it and as a result, they are forever in a state of "once I get there." It is a very tiring and endless journey. It's a lot easier to practice you ALREADY being there and experiencing the joy and satisfaction of bliss.

Embodying the new version of you and having those emotions inside of you will make your Faith a lot stronger.

Let it go. I can imagine you being totally puzzled. "Olga, what do you mean 'let it go' after all that you suggested?" Yes, dear, let it go after you have done all of that, because this is what Faith is all about.

What happens when you chase the cat? It runs away. When you have what a cat wants, then it will come to you. So you doing all of the above is "having what a cat wants" and all you have to do is expect to receive.

Have you noticed that when you expect the worst to happen, it happens, including you taking money out of your "rainy day" moneybox?

So follow all five rules of Faith from above, let go, and then just know that you will receive—just like you know you will wake up tomorrow.

To your success!

OLGA GEIDANE

About Olga Geidane: Olga is an Executive Mindset and Performance Coach, International Speaker, a Best-Selling Author, and a Regional President of the Professional Speaking Association. She is a host of Olga's Show and A World-Traveler. "Change your mindset = change your life" is Olga's favorite quote and she truly walks her talk: being a divorcee and a single mom at the age of 24, she came to the UK from Latvia with no spoken English, just £100 in her pocket and a 2.5-year-old son. Her success in life is based on continuous growth and transformation of her mindset and habits.

Being an expert in mindset transformation, Olga knows how to challenge and press the right buttons in order to achieve the best results for her clients. Her non-judgmental and confidential approach helps people to dive deeper into the darkest alleys of their minds whilst being supported and walked through the journey by Olga, not only during the coaching/advisory sessions, but also in between them. She will not only elevate you, but also transform you and will help you to live the life you desire!

Author's Website: *www.OlgaGeidane.com*
Book Series Website & Author's Bio: *www.The13StepstoRiches.com*

Paul Andrés

CREATING FAMILY & TESTING FAITH

And so it begins…

In the fall of 2010, what was supposed to be a non-committal daytime date in Seattle, ended up being three days of non-stop sharing between two souls. We spent hours sharing every life experience and then laying on turf in a public park; I realized this was also the moment I proved my Faith and met my future husband. We said, "I Do," just under four years later and officially became Paul and Jamie Trudel-Payne.

Jamie, a devilishly handsome All-American Senior Account Manager and freelance writer, came from a tightly woven and kind household. While I, Paul, a cute (ish) bi-racial (Mexican/ Caucasian) Designer and Business Coach, came from a somewhat intrusive, rambunctious, and huge Hispanic family. Six months later, after saying, "I do," we began the adoption process, wearing rose-colored glasses and nothing but exciting insight.

With Jamie's writing skills, my marketing skills, and being a highly sought-after professional photographer, we had a winning combination to make a strong connection to a Birthmother. A few months passed since we made our profile live, and we were matched with and talked to a birthmother who was six months pregnant with a baby girl. The fairytale went into hyperspeed, and we were decorating a nursery, filling her closet with every adorable little girl outfit, and fighting over baby names, just like every other parent-to-be. Fueled purely by Faith and excitement, we pushed forward.

A nightmare dressed as a daydream...

There were some red flags along the way that we blindly ignored, but then her 9th month of pregnancy came, and we were hit with a flag that was so large, there was no way we could ignore it. We received a text message that asked us for a large sum of money so that she could purchase a home. Then one last request, to not mention this to the agency, or she would have to move on to another family.

You can't imagine the feeling of someone asking you to put a price on a child that already felt was your own. We felt paralyzed. There was no way we could give up this child, but the alternative of illegally purchasing a baby felt just as unfathomable. We contemplated every possible outcome for our dilemma, but after a few days, we knew there was only one decision we could ethically and legally make. We contacted our agency and made the insanely tricky decision to stop the adoption along with the communication. And with that decision, our test of Faith felt lost.

A nightmare dressed as a new dream...

A few weeks had passed when we received another message. The birthmother was in labor and wanted to give us the daughter. We were shocked, confused, and ecstatic! We dropped everything and flew out to PA on the first red-eye we could book, and spent the next four days in the NICU with a beautiful baby girl. We named her, fed her, changed her, and learned how to bathe her. We held her hand and calmed her cries and never once thought about how we had also mourned her just a few weeks prior. The moment she was born, the birth mother decided not to be involved. She was done, just like she had said. But it was OK because we were there every day, never once leaving her side.

We scheduled to sign all the final adoption documents with the birthmother at 11:30 am on day four. At 11:01 am, we received a call from the hospital's social worker. The birthmother had changed her mind, which meant the adoption was over. Paralyzed again, our Faith was obliterated. We let the excitement of a dream coming true get the best of us. The social worker apologized but said there was nothing we could do. We called our lawyers to plead our case. But they, too, quickly confirmed there was nothing we could do. And at that moment, I watched my husband break. Silently, at first. A state of shock just overtook his face. But slowly, the breaking became so painful and heavy that tears poured from his eyes like heavy rainfall, and his cries of loss were cavernous as they bellowed out from his stiffening and hunched body.

Surviving the nightmare…

I don't know how or where it came from, but I decided to go numb. I couldn't let grief, loss, anger, or any other emotion that I was feeling escape from my body. If we wanted to make it out of there with any chance of recovery from this heartbreak, it would require a strength found only in emptiness. It required a desolate lack of feeling. So shedding no tears, I quickly packed our things, and we left immediately.

We drove to the hospital to grab any remaining items and were allowed to give one quick kiss goodbye each to that baby girl. Then, groggy and stunned, we booked seats on the first flight back to Seattle. After we boarded, I found myself awake and alone. I made my second decision for survival that day. With Jamie passed out from grief next to me, I decided to bury this experience beneath all of my shame, anxieties, worries, and darkest secrets. In the stillness of that flight, alone with only my thoughts, I set aside the numbness. For just a few brief minutes, pain engulfed me, and I let myself cry into the sleeve of my coat and say goodbye to the daughter we had just lost for a second time.

Healing and hope…

For about six months after returning home, I decided not to be involved in the adoption process. For me, Faith was gone, but luckily that wasn't the case for everyone. In the spring of 2016, the agency's marketing manager asked if he could come over to talk to us. He wanted to make some suggestions to refresh our profile and ensure that we hadn't yet just given up on Faith.

I reluctantly agreed to meet but made no promise of moving forward. Fortunately for me, he convinced me to try again and renew our profile, along with our hope and Faith. Shortly after that meeting, we were matched once again. The birthmother, Trisha, was about five months along, and we arranged to fly out and meet her. We knew from the moment we connected, this would be different. She introduced us to her daughter and grandmother, and let us know the baby would be biracial (African American/Caucasian). Before we said our goodbyes, she told us how good she immediately felt when first meeting us and how she could already tell from even our texts back and forth that we would be amazing fathers to "our" baby. She couldn't afford another person in the home but wanted this child to have a chance at a life she couldn't give him. And that's how we learned we were going to have a baby boy.

A daydream with no nightmare insight…

It seemed like we had only just returned home when we received a call from Trisha's grandmother, informing us that Trisha had gone into labor early, by a few weeks. It was August 1st and nearly two years from the start of our adoption journey. We dropped everything and began the quest once again to meet a baby that could become our own. We arrived and were taken straight to Trisha's room to meet our son. After hugs and some tears, we took our son to our room, where the medical staff had set up a new parent room just for us. The nurse showed us everything in the space, from diapers to formula, to extra blankets. She asked our baby's name. She smiled, wrote Alexander Reneé Trudel-Payne on the board, and said goodnight.

We checked out after a few days in the hospital. Michigan adoption laws do not allow adoption finalization for 30 days, so we opted to stay in a hotel for the first month after the birth, just in case any hiccups arose during the finalization. It was a fun adventure to learn how to parent together in a small hotel room. We fell in love with our son more and more each day. A few days before the 30th day, we received the call that all the papers were processed and finalized. We were officially the parents of a baby boy, and we were free to go home.

And so it ends...

Ander is what we decided on as a nickname for Alexander who is now five years old. He's handsome, kind, loves being the center of attention as much as he loves being alone flipping through books or playing with cars. He's meticulously clean, full of energy, and overflowing with personality. He's full of giggles and life, and there hasn't been one day since the first time we saw him that we have forgotten how lucky we are to be his fathers. Even though our Faith was tested, I can say not to be afraid to rely on those around you to help keep your Faith alive. We can all go through difficulties that test our Faith and even times where we feel no Faith at all, but that does not mean Faith is gone. It might just be that someone close is carrying it for you until you are strong enough to carry it again on your own. Our adoption journey was far from rosy, but every time I look into Ander's eyes or hear him giggle, it doesn't come anywhere near the feelings of love and joy we now hold as a family of three with our adoption journey finally complete.

PAUL ANDRÉS

About Paul Andrés: Paul is an award-winning conscious entrepreneur, visual storyteller, and intuitive coach. From digital and interior design, to business clarity and personal growth coaching, to social justice advocacy and volunteering, Andrés is proof that aligning your passions with your purpose is the true magic to success. He currently devotes his time to helping awakened entrepreneurs and heart-centered creatives design the life they deserve through personal and professional coaching and consulting, as well as shedding light on uncomfortable topics that bring awareness to the social justice issues of today as the host of his video podcast,

In Your Mind. Andrés is also a two-time #1 best-selling author. You can catch him as a featured guest speaker at events across the country.

"Home is so many things, but ultimately, it's where life happens. It's where we sleep and grow a family, it's where we play and grow professionally, and it's where we learn and grow within. Each home plays a key role in helping us design a whole life—the life we all deserve." — Paul Andrés

Author's Website: *www.PaulAndres.com*
Purchase Book Online: *www.The13StepstoRiches.com*

Paul Capozio

RAW AND REAL FAITH

Here is a warning to all before reading this chapter. I've decided to do this in a very raw and real fashion. Faith is so guttural and truly encompassing when it is left to be what it is meant to be. Only when we look to define, control or prepackage it is where you lose the power. It's the ability to create abundance. I'm not going to try to soften any language or worry about people with different beliefs because then I will be defeating the true meaning of this chapter's purpose. So, I ask for your understanding and call on your ability to see the bigger picture. Your view is most likely different from mine, so what you should gain from this chapter is its nature, core, and essence, and then take away from that what you will. This power fits to where you are, at your current Faith level and acceptance, and it can only get better. When you feel yourself judging me, put your present understanding on the back burner, or you will miss it. Do not be offended if your beliefs differ. I do not feel I need to be converted, nor should you, but you need to change in order to advance and unleash your Faith. What you should take away from this chapter is strength, power, and courage. Use it to your greatest advantage. Ignoring this because of a minor difference of opinion only costs you success and abundance.

I have gone through a journey with "Faith," starting as a little boy growing up in New Jersey. I was raised in a Roman Catholic family home where religion was an enormous part of my life, not that I had much choice. I believe that was ok as it was a foundation I built upon, even if I needed to dismantle most of it completely. I had strict religious education from kindergarten throughout high school, and there was not one aspect of that education that was not influenced by the Roman Catholic Church's teachings somehow. Sports and clubs were influenced, too.

While there were some metaphysical aspects in my structured religious education, practicing the Faith itself was considered man-made and gave me some red flags. My parents were hardworking, blue-collar people. My dad spent money he didn't have to give my two brothers and me an education that my parents' Faith demanded of them. This sacrifice made by my parents was more of an education in Faith and belief to me than the actual education on which they spent their hard-earned money.

I am not exaggerating when I say my parents spent money they didn't have. I recall a story I only recently learned of, about how my parents struggled financially for years to provide for us that life. I spent weekends at my grandparents' home at the Jersey Shore, and they had only $5 in their pocket in 1969. The story of how they had no clue how they would have gas money to get home ends with my dad finding $10 in the pocket of an old bathing suit he had left there the year before. That created one of the most incredible weekends we all spent together. My parents and their Faith made sure that we, as kids, had no idea that we were a poor family. My father knew there was no way he left ten bucks in that bathing suit, or anywhere else for that matter. Every penny was always accounted for, and nothing could be wasted. The Faith on their part was divine intervention; pure and straightforward. Start collecting your Faith stories. Go back as early as you can remember.

Faith related to strength, belief, and unwavering commitment was taught through discipline in those places, not emotion. But my parents' money was well spent.

When does education stop producing results? If you are still having realizations influenced by that education 40 years later, was it not effective? Even if you rejected it at the time. Through the Bible stories' teachings, I gathered so many people who have Faith have obtained. Think of Noah and the flood, Abraham, and his son. The unwavering commitment to something. That deep down belief that transcends ridicule, fear, and loss of life.

As time goes on, these stories take on new meaning for me. Noah was always a story of Faith and trust, but is it not a story of preparation? Did Noah wait until he felt the first drop of rain to begin to prepare?

As I grew older, then came the stages of so-called "enlightenment," which I believe many of us are in now. We feel that Faith and God are not genuine, and life is nothing more than Darwinism. Not some guy on a throne, in a cloud bank throwing lightning bolts.

The sun rises every day and sets. Without question, life goes on just because it does what it does, and the grand design is the luck of the big bang. My explanation was that God is just an energy field. What a weak way to sound smart! We convince ourselves all that nonsense was necessary in more primitive times when people had fears of everything. Lousy weather, failing crops, famine were all some punishment for our lack of proper worship and adoration. God has a God Complex.

We are wiser now, aren't we? No need to believe such nonsense. So we disengage ourselves from traditional religion, and we believe that we are more enlightened and more empowered just knowing that this all works as it should because we're so damn lucky.

I lived in that state for many years up until about a year ago. That belief system allowed me to find significant financial freedom and many successes, way more than I expected. Maybe you feel that your Faith is more in yourself. Hey, you are highly successful already, so don't fix it if it's not broken.

But I will tell you, I started to understand that there's something more and something greater within you, within everyone. There is something that connects us all regardless of what we choose to call it, and if you embrace that genuine Faith, you will unleash the unlimited power of true riches.

So my evolution was that of structured, organized religion to this freethinking nonbeliever to a person of Faith. Yes, the process I went through was one of stripping down some of the trappings of organized religion and understanding that some energy and the higher power controls us. It connects us all, and it is God. I tell you that putting a name back at the beginning of it all is what unleashed me and empowered me because it's now confirmed. Faith is not just us alone; Faith requires courage. Faith will deliver more and help you maximize any other chapter we share with you in this book series. Your Faith is the very core of your capability. Without Faith, there is no ability to recharge. Without Faith, there is nothing you can count on when no one else is there for you. Faith is the never-ending source of your power, your energy, your ability to renew. You need to accept it for what it truly is and get rid of constructs.

You can now let your mind wander a little bit into what you want to call Allah, God, Jesus. You may worship the Son or the SUN. You could be an atheist. But if you ever had anyone in your family taken ill or experience trauma and you said, "God help me," you understand the need for Faith. NO, it is not just an expression; it is in your DNA! Find your Faith and grow your Faith, but understand that it will only deliver unconditionally, consistently, and at levels of abundance you cannot at this moment comprehend until you realize it is not yours to define or dilute. You cannot pick and choose. You need to commit and know it to the bone, or you are only living a half-life. You can do this! I have Faith in you and God!

PAUL CAPOZIO

About Paul Capozio: Born in Hoboken, NJ, and grew up on the streets of Hudson County. His bedroom window looked out at the skyline of New York City, and he knew he would make his mark there one day. Husband of 32 years to his wife, Linda. Father, and grandfather.

At 35, he was recruited to be the President of Sales and Marketing for a 350-million-dollar Human resources firm. In 7 years, he drove the top-line revenue of that firm to over 1.5 Billion.

Mr. Capozio owns and operates Capco Capital Inc., an investment and consulting firm. The majority of Capco's holdings are manufacturers and distributors of health and wellness products and Human Resources Firms. Capco provides sales consulting and training, helping companies increase sales through traditional and direct sales disciplines. Making the invisible, visible, and simplifying the complex is his stock and trade.

A dynamic public speaker, he provides motivation and "meat and potatoes" skills to those in the health and wellness field who do not consider themselves "Salespeople," allowing their voices to be heard above the "noise." He can be reached thru his website Paulcapozio.com.

Author's Website: *www.PaulCapozio.com*
Purchase Book Online: *www.The13StepstoRiches.com*

Robyn Scott

FAITH VERSUS ALL

I am sure you have read this quote from the Bible more than a few times in this book already. I will follow suit and add my perspective.

"I say to you, if you have Faith as a mustard seed, you will say to this mountain, 'Move from here to there,' and it will move; and nothing will be impossible for you." (Matthew 17:20)

Here, Jesus Christ reveals the power of Faith. In a complicated and often chaotic world, something as simple as Faith can change everything. Think about the great men and women throughout history who have changed the world for the better - Abraham Lincoln, Martin Luther King, Jr., and Mother Teresa. Without their Faith in God and their courage to act on it, where would we be today? It is only through Faith that we can see the world as it ought to be.

I was part of an amazing conversation at a mastermind a few weeks ago. What is the opposite of Faith? Fear? Courage? Doubt?

We are going to look at all three.

Faith vs. Fear

*"Now Faith is the substance of things hoped for, the evidence
of things not seen."* (Hebrews 11:1)

Growing up was an interesting time for Faith and fear for me. I put them
together usually because I believed that if I was faithful enough, I would
not feel fear. If I did not have Faith, I had better fear my God then. In my
child's mind, I had often put my Faith right next to my fear.

Fear is the derailing emotion most of us automatically go into when we
find ourselves in new situations. It is our enigma working diligently to do
its job and keeping us alive. The problem with that is we are not always in
danger when we feel fear. Have you heard the saying, "What we want is on
the other side of fear?" I have changed my views on fear, and I challenge
you to do the same! In your body, you can feel the emotion of fear! The
fear is real. You have created it somewhere along your journey, and now
it is time to shake things up and get out there to conquer your fears! If
you feel that feeling, then think of being nervous about being on stage,
nervous to talk to that client, nervous to make those sales calls. If you use
the word, nervous, it feels more manageable and not so scary. Nervous
and scared feel the same in your body. Use that feeling to move forward!
This is crucial. As you feel fear, let your mind brush over the idea that you
are EXCITED!

Can you get excited about that sales call? HECK YES!

Can you get up on that stage and deliver an extraordinary speech of
motivation and inspiration? YOU BET YOUR SWEET BIPPY YOU
CAN!

The first thing to do when you feel fear (or every emotion, actually) is
STOP! Stay in it for a minute. Sit in that emotion and feel it. Where do you
feel it in your body? Can you turn it into excitement? Fear is the body's

way of telling you to do the exact thing that is causing you to fear! Of course, I am not telling you to stand still like a statue feeling fear if a bear is charging you! The fears in our heads that we create are the deepest fears we want to identify. Where did that fear come from? Is it still true for you? Are you truly afraid? These may seem like straightforward questions. They are. Life is not supposed to be so gosh dang darn complicated! It is as simple as asking your higher self, "Am I afraid?"

You see, I am going to give you a new acronym of fear. I have looked, and there are A LOT of fantastic acronyms for fear. This is the one you need to remember: Fear is FREAKING EXCELLENT ACCORDING TO ROBYN! Yep, the next time you feel fear, remind yourself that F.E.A.R. is giving you a clue to what it is you may need to do next! Fear is a liar, and it thinks it has your best interest in mind. It does not. It's only when you take the time to observe, analyze and respond instead of reacting that you can change your fear into a Faith of the unknown. (Cue Elsa!)

Faith vs. Courage

One of my sweetest friends sent me a quote from John Wayne, and it said, "Courage is being scared to death and saddling up anyway!" It's perfectly timed, and I believe Faith is what we can use to increase our courage. Opposite? Maybe not exactly. Let's use it in an example: You have prepared, practiced, and feel ready to get up on that stage. In the wings, though, is the familiar feeling in the pit of your stomach. You start to feel the fear. You are standing still, breathing deep and turning that fear into excitement. The next step is to remember "Why are you on that stage?" You are presenting a new program you have developed. You announce your new company, or maybe you are teaching about suicide prevention and cannot wait to help people in business and in their lives! You know this will be an answer to prayers for others! It is so much easier to have Faith and be courageous when you know with conviction that your amazing, needed program, group, or app will change others' lives for the better! Why do you want peoples' lives to be better? People will be happier. Why does it matter that people are happy? When people are happy, they have less stress. Why is it important to have less stress? I get angry faster and more often if I am overwhelmed and stressed. People will want others to be happy because they are. Why is it important that we care about each other? Love thy neighbor as thyself. We are all in this together on this earth. It is important to uplift and boosts each other to be the best versions of who they are.

I love the Marianne Williamson quote: "Our deepest fear is not that we are inadequate. Our deepest fear is that we are powerful beyond measure. It is our light, not our darkness that most frightens us. We ask ourselves, 'Who am I to be brilliant, gorgeous, talented, fabulous?' Actually, who are you not to be? You are a child of God. Your playing small does not serve the world. There is nothing enlightened about shrinking so that other people won't feel insecure around you. We are all meant to shine, as children do. We were born to make manifest the glory of God that is within us. It's not just some of us; it's in everyone. And as we let our own light shine, we unconsciously give other people permission to do the same. As we are liberated from our own fear, our presence automatically liberates others."

Now that takes courage! I asked my mentor once, "Why was this an accurate statement?" She paused for effect and said, "Jesus showed us how to shine, and they killed him for it." I instantly knew this was entirely true for me. I have decided I am going to shine as much as I can. It will take Faith AND courage.

Faith vs. Doubt

This one may be the most common. The Faith you absotively and positutely sure, doubt you are not sure. Pretty simple concept. I have been encouraged to "doubt my doubts before I doubt my Faith." I like this because the "Faith" I have is in more than just God. I have Faith in myself and my abilities! I have Faith in my drive and commitment to be successful! I have Faith that my husband and children support me! I have Faith that you, the reader, will get what you need from this book! Is this more optimism than Faith? I feel that Faith and optimism are incredibly similar in this instance. Faith can interchange with optimism. The same could be said about doubt and pessimism.

In conclusion, we have 3 steps to Faith;

1. Fear is FREAKING EXCELLENT ACCORDING TO ROBYN! Use that energy to build Faith!

2. 5 WHY's deep (thank you, Elise Smith)

3. Doubt your doubts before you doubt your Faith!

Everybody talks about Faith, but few take the time to define it. The Bible offers a definition: Faith is not merely holding to certain teachings, such as that God exists, but rather it is a strong conviction that the world around us is part of a more excellent plan, God's plan.

Even when the world looks chaotic and uncontrolled, with Faith, we feel deep down that this chaotic world is not where we truly live—instead, God guides our existence with strength and power.

The world is more than just a wild place of cruelty and power struggles, of seemingly meaningless deaths and hardships with Faith. We are more than mere animals with animal desires. A world seen through the eyes of Faith is a world in which each of us has meaning as a part of a great plan. Faith means that there is more to the world than what we see with our eyes.

Moreover, Faith is not just a mental agreement. As the rest of Hebrews 11 illustrates, Faith drives action. If we believe there is more to life than what we see, true Faith will drive our values, decisions, and actions to align with our belief." -https://www.thenivbible.com/blog/what-is-faith/

What do you have Faith in?

ROBYN SCOTT

About Robyn Scott: Robyn is the Chief Relationship Officer for Champion Circle. She manages the prospecting program for Divinely Driven Results. Scott is a Habit Finder Coach and has worked closely with the president, Paul Blanchard, at the Og Mandino Group. She is also a certified Master Your Emotions Coach, through Inscape World. Scott is commonly known in professional communities as the Queen of Connection and Princess of Play. She has been working hard for the past 9 years to hone her skills as a mentor and coach.

Scott strives to teach people to annihilate judgements, embrace their own stories, and empower themselves to rediscover who they truly are. Scott is an international speaker and also teaches how to present yourself on stage.

Her first book, *Bringing People Together: Rediscovering the Lost Art of Face-to-Face Connecting, Collaborating, and Creating* was released in August of 2019 and was a bestseller in seven categories.

Author's website: *www.MyChampionCircle.com/Robyn-Scott*
Book Series Website & Author's Bio: *www.The13StepsToRiches.com*

Shannon Whittington

FAITH: THE UNQUENCHABLE FLAME OF DESTINY

If you were to ask me what I consider to be a powerful quote regarding success, it would be this simple sentence by the Welsh philanthropist Ann Cotton: "Have faith in your intuition and listen to your gut feeling."

As professionals, we put so much stock into the recommendations and opinions of those we consider more successful than ourselves. We witness their accomplishments and treat everything they say as gospel ("Always do this, never do that, only do these three things, etc."). While listening to the advice of successful individuals is often helpful, what is most important is trusting our "gut feeling" – that tiny voice inside us that lets us know when we are on the right path, that something bigger than or beyond us has our back, if only we put a little bit of trust in it.

I grew up in the Southern Baptist Church, and when I say my parents took me to church all the time, I mean all the time. Every Sunday morning, every Wednesday night, revival service, Saturday night rehearsals, I was there. One Sunday morning, when I was no older than four, I was sitting on the second pew holding my tiny little Bible, listening very intently to the preacher. He said something I will never forget. "All you need is faith the size of a mustard seed," he said, quoting Matthew 17:20. "If you have faith no bigger than a single mustard seed, you can move mountains. A speck of faith can change the world."

As I let the preacher's words settle in, I thought to myself, "Wow, a mustard seed? That's it? That's almost nothing! Just a little bit of faith, and I can move mountains? Wow! This is amazing!" So I decided to put my preacher's words to the test. I started asking God for little things while having Faith they would come to fruition. SOMETIMES, IT WOULD START TO RAIN when I attended outdoor events like picnics, barbecues, or sporting events. In those moments, I had Faith that the rain would go away, and nearly every time, the rain stopped, and the sun would come out. I would smile to myself inside, knowing beyond all belief that the sun came out because of *my* powerful little mustard seed of Faith.

When I got older, I attended college. Because I lived off-campus, I would often have to find rare parking spots on side streets or shell out ludicrous amounts of money for on-campus parking. So whenever I drove to class, I would have Faith (some days truly the size of a mustard seed) that I would find a parking spot so I could save my hard-earned money. And sure enough, every single day, I found one. If you were to ask me how, I couldn't tell you. I just felt led to where the parking spot was and latched onto that feeling – that Faith – and I'd find it.

After graduation, I found myself living in many different places. To this day, I've lived in three other states and four different countries. That much relocating can cause even the most extroverted person to feel lonely or insecure. Whenever I began settling into each new place, I had Faith that I would make a new friend, that I'd meet someone genuine and kind who would help me feel a little less alone. Within a few weeks, I would meet someone amazing, and just like that, I had a new friend! I'm still in touch with many of these literally "faithful" friends to this day.

Throughout my life, I used this hidden power of Faith to make my dreams a reality. By honing in on my gut feeling, I found myself empowered to make the best decisions, which led to me accumulating success in material and emotional ways. Make no mistake, hard work and perseverance are vital to success, but it all starts with that tiny little mustard seed of Faith.

Please do not conflate my personal experience as an intention to convert you to Christianity, or any other religion for that matter. However, I believe there is an intangible force that exists beyond us (whether you want to call it God, Jesus, Allah, the universe, destiny, time, or something else) and that force is interconnected with each one of us. Whatever "it" is, it's essentially just a bigger part of yourself, and having Faith is nothing more than realizing and affirming that the same energy that created the universe exists inside of you.

Later in life, I realized that having Faith was about more than just me. It could save peoples' lives. As a nurse, I worked on a cardiology floor, and I would always make a habit of introducing myself to all my new patients at the start of my shift. Sometimes, I can't explain precisely how or why, I would interact with a particular patient and have a gut feeling that something was wrong. They wouldn't exhibit any external signs of distress, but I had an inkling deep inside me that they might code, which means that their heart would stop beating in medical terms. Whenever this feeling would kick in, I would move all the patient's furniture out into the hallway (the chair, the bedside table, etc.) because when a patient codes, we need as much room as possible to run the code. Sure enough, nearly every single time I had this feeling, the patient would code. This happened so often that my colleagues started jokingly calling me "the witch nurse," as if I had supernatural premonitions. But ultimately, I truly believe that I prevented many deaths by being so proactive and by trusting my gut.

When I was working as an in-home care nurse, I visited a patient who seemed fine.

Her vital signs were stable, but something about her didn't seem right. I couldn't put my finger on it. She complained that her belly hurt slightly, which could have been a symptom of constipation or something else relatively small. I palpated her stomach, and I didn't feel anything hard, but my gut told me something was wrong. Even though I had no substantiation, I called the hospital to inform them that I would be sending her in for an examination. In a few hours, her son called me and said, "Nurse, you saved my mom's life." It turns out she had been complaining about abdominal pain for about a week, but nobody had paid it any attention because everything "looked" fine. But, as I knew all too well, Faith doesn't work by trusting just what's on the surface. Because I listened to my gut and sent her to the hospital, the doctor located six abdominal abscesses, which they could successfully treat. My Faith saved this woman's life.

Some of you more rational-focused readers might sneer at these anecdotes; you may assert that Faith is for children and that logic, and logic alone, is the key to success. While I believe that logic and rational thinking have their places, I would ask such readers, "Do you experience love? Do you love your spouse, your parents, your children? If so, why exactly do you love them?" Sure, you might be able to explain specific things about them that you like, but that's not the same thing as loving *them*. If you think about it, we don't have good reasons for feeling the love. We just do. Love has nothing to do with logic, and yet it's such a vital part of our existence as humans. To quote the Bengali polymath Rabindranath Tagore, "A mind all logic is like a knife all blade. It makes the hand bleed that uses it." From my perspective, if we can loosen our grip on logic to experience love, we can (and should) do the same thing to experience Faith.

I also seek to clarify that success is not dependent on Faith *alone*, that it is simply the spark that turns into the unquenchable flame that is our destiny. It is not enough to have Faith that something will happen; you must also have Faith that *you* can make it happen. You must have Faith in your ability to work just as hard as those you admire, to create a detailed and structured plan of action, to persevere despite every obstacle in the world in your path, and to adapt and regroup when necessary. This is what my preacher meant when he said a mustard seed of Faith could move mountains. That when you trust your gut, you can realize that you have endless potential and are empowered to make your dreams a reality. No matter what you believe or don't believe, all I ask is that you believe in yourself, that whatever exists outside of you has your back. All you need is that tiny little mustard seed. Now go and move that mountain!

SHANNON WHITTINGTON

About Shannon Whittington: Shannon (she/her) is a speaker, author, consultant, and clinical nurse educator. Her area of expertise is LGBTQ+ inclusion in the workplace. Whittington has a passion for transgender health where she educates clinicians in how to care for transgender individuals after undergoing gender-affirming surgeries.

Whittington was honored to receive the Quality and Innovation Award from the Home Care Association of New York for her work with the transgender population. She was recently awarded the Notable LGBTQ+ Leaders & Executives award by Crain's New York Business, as well as the International Association of Professionals Nurse of the Year award. Whittington is a city and state lobbyist for transgender equality.

To date, Whittington has presented virtually and in person at various organizations and conferences across the nation, delivering extremely well-received presentations. Her forthcoming books include *LGBTQ+: ABC's For Grownups* and *Kindergarten for Leaders: 9 Essential Tips For Grownup Success.*

Author's Website: *www.linkedin.com/in/shannonwhittington*
Book Series Website & Author's Bio: *www.The13StepsToRiches.com*

Soraiya Vasanji

THE GIFTS OF FAITH

At first mention of the word Faith, I think about spirituality, religion, trust, and source. I was born believing in a higher power, something unseen but internally felt, where you put your Faith into it, and it also provides you with Faith. There is the Faith in oneself, which is about genuinely trusting ourselves, and then there is the Faith in the universe, God, source, or whatever rings true for you. Personally, they both go hand in hand, and as one strengthens, the other strengthens too, and both facets of Faith are necessary.

When I think of Faith, I immediately think of my mom. Her belief, trust, and surrender to God are inspiring. She has unwavering Faith in God, a deep understanding of the importance of nurturing our soul, having a daily practice in Faith, and trusting that what is meant for our growth and happiness is what will come about. She once shared with me that she never thinks to ask or receive anything in return from the people or things she serves. She expects nothing from others and instead trusts that God and the universe will provide all the lessons and opportunities to experience growth and abundance. For me, this is on a whole other level of receiving from the universe that I had not acknowledged up until now. I dedicate this chapter to my amazing, loving, and Faith-FULL mama, Rozmin Lavji.

I grew up with strong Faith, but that's not to say that I have not had moments where I lost my Faith or questioned why something was happening to me. There will be struggles in life. Growth occurs through tumultuous, transformative processes that are uncomfortable and that stretch us beyond what we think we are capable of. And then when we emerge, we think, "Well, that wasn't as bad as I thought it would be," or "Wow, I survived that!" When we are provided these learnings, we must continuously dig deeper into ourselves and the unseen. There is an inner knowing that we can align with, and when you tap into this space, the courage to move through a calamity or tragedy is accessed.

"What did I do that I'm being punished by losing not one, but both my babies?" This was a real thought that crossed my mind over and over again. I could not comprehend what and why things were happening in the way they were because I had always believed and trusted that when I put my energy into something and worked hard for it, then no matter what, I was going to get it. Because if it is up to me, I am scrappy as ever and will find a way. But this is where control meets its match—because we are not in control. I remember looking out from our balcony overlooking the San Francisco Bay, unable to reconcile the deep grief in my heart, and how could that same God create such a glorious and magnificent world? How could the sunrise bring such great majesty and warmth to my body and my heart be completely broken into a million tiny shards continuing to burn and make more internal scars? My trust was knocked out when I lost our twins; both the trust and Faith in God (albeit momentarily) and my inner confidence that I can do anything, that my body could do anything. I was angry at God for allowing me to experience the miracle of being pregnant and then taking them away with no warning or reason that I could understand at the time. In an instant, I had a choice in whether to abandon all Faith or go deeper. When I saw the beauty of the world that God created, I knew that while I didn't understand why this is happening, I must lean into my Faith. This is the moment I really chose in. It was much later when I realized that my story and one of the many gifts the girls gave me was an insatiable way to love up women struggling with their fertility journey, loss, grief, or choices. I know I am destined to lift these women up: to bring light, love and peace to the darkness and isolation of neonatal loss and fertility loneliness. When I chose in, I was rewarded by a quadrupling of my Faith in myself and the world. The strength of Faith is that when you choose a little bit, it lifts you up tremendously.

Our vision for a happy, healthy family grows, and as we jump through the hoops of in vitro fertilization (IVF), we are met with more and more challenges and opportunities. (Because every obstacle is merely a possibility in disguise!) As I write this draft, I am undergoing another round of IVF and am enrolling my mind, body, soul, and spirit in the possibility and probability of becoming pregnant. Every fiber of my being is choosing it, is surrendering to it, and is trusting. I am choosing to trust that what is meant to be for my family is what is best. We don't know why things happen or don't happen, but my Faith has me place trust and surrender in the universe and God that the best things are yet to come. And I get to do my part and be on my side. Play big, dream big, and surrender to it. I have Faith that the immense love I have inside will be shared with a child or children in the world that are meant to know true unconditional love.

There are moments in our lives when we feel like we don't have Faith or we've lost our Faith. And in those moments, it's when we dig deep within ourselves and look for courage, acknowledgment, grace, and compassion for ourselves and others. To know that we are human and we will make mistakes, and sometimes we don't know why or what's next. In these moments, it is crucial to connect to the source, the divine, and/or the universe within and ask ourselves what we get to create? To learn? To let go of? So we can reinvent ourselves into the next best version of ourselves.

Faith allows you to overcome and move through grief where it not only lessens the pain, with time of healing, but where we can see the gifts of the painful experience. Losing the twins was horrific and a tragedy, and it was also the single greatest gift to know my purpose in this world and truly understand how precious life is. How precious having a child is and that they are a gift, and when you are lucky to have a child, they come first, and they get to know they matter and are loved. My mission is to support moms and children to know they matter, that they get to give and receive love. I have felt the absence and know what is missing is love. So I get to be what is missing and am love wherever I go. I also got to see how there are so many people in this world struggling in silence. On the outside, it may have felt like others have an easy time creating their family. I could have been bitter and angry and dwelt in "How come it's so hard for me to get pregnant?" But the inner wisdom that was revealed was the empathy and compassion for others, knowing that as a coach, I can bring that love, care, and consideration for somebody, to hold their hand, hold their heart and support them through their dark time. I received all these gifts to give back in a more significant way. I was called for in a way that I was here to make that difference.

Faith is truly believing to the deepest extent, even when there is no reason or evidence to have it happen. This is why it is referred to as a 'leap of Faith'. As I finalize this chapter a month later, I share that our IVF attempt was unsuccessful. I don't know why none of the embryos survived. I don't know why the whole physically painful process leaves me with a deeper level of emotional grief to process. Is this the end? Well, it is the end of this cycle. And while I am disappointed, sad, and frustrated, I am choosing to surrender to God and trust that these steps are not for my lasting pain, but to blossom other seeds and put amazing opportunities in the path that I am on. I know for sure that I don't know what will happen in life, and I know that I will always have Faith.

SORAIYA VASANJI

About Soraiya Vasanji: Soraiya is a Certified Professional Coach (CPC), Energy Leadership Index Master Practitioner (ELI-MP), and has a Master's in Business Administration (MBA) from Kellogg University. She inspires women to be present, not perfect, ditch what doesn't serve them, and create their best messy life now.

She loves sharing her wisdom on mindset, the power of language, self-love, self-worth, and leadership principles. She is the founder of the Mommy Mindset Summit series, where she interviews experts on topics that interest moms so they can create a life of authenticity, abundance, and joy and show their kids how to have it all too.

Soraiya is married to her soul-mate, has a four-year-old daughter, and lives in Toronto, Canada. She is a foodie, a jet-setter, and loves collecting unique crafting and stationery products!

Author's Website: *www.SoraiyaVasanji.com*
Book Series Website & Author's Bio: *www.The13StepstoRiches.com*

Stacey Ross Cohen

THERE IS NO SUCCESS WITHOUT FAITH

"Desire backed by faith knows no such word as impossible."
Napoleon Hill, *Think and Grow Rich*

The first book in this series explored the importance of desire, an emotion Napoleon Hill defined as "the starting point of all achievement." But desire alone isn't a potent force. You also need to sincerely believe that you're able to make that desire—whether it's becoming a billionaire or a Best-Selling Author - into a reality. In short: You also need *faith*.

Faith is a powerful tool that allows us to overcome obstacles, complete the most difficult of tasks, and weather dire situations. In this chapter, we'll explore faith: what it is, how to build it, how to maintain it, and how it fuels success. But first, a personal story about the importance of faith in my own life.

My Mother, Faith

Faith is a tool for all of us. And for me, it's also something a lot more personal: My mother's first name. My grandmother named my mom "Faith" because she almost lost her life on the delivery table. And throughout her whole life, my mother lived up to her name. There's one experience that really captures this. At age 48, my mom got severely ill while vacationing with friends. A local doctor dismissed her symptoms as a mere stomach virus, and prescribed a soak in the bathtub. But after 36 hours, there was no improvement. My father took Faith to the nearest hospital by ferry and learned the true diagnosis was severe. My mom had suffered a massive heart attack, had lost 70% function of her heart, and had just three months to live.

But my mom ended up living until age 65. Why? Because Faith had faith. She spent the next 17 years wearing heart monitors and visiting emergency rooms, yet always believed she would be okay. She was incredibly positive and I rarely heard her complain. In fact, she lived selflessly, from inviting "strays" to Thanksgiving, to covering her hospital roommate's television fees, to countless other kindnesses. My mom's own faith granted her an extra 17 years with her family, and also taught us the importance of faith.

Put Faith in What Matters

From early on in my professional life, I had a burning desire to launch my own PR and marketing agency. I wanted to lead a thriving firm where every member of the team would be encouraged to learn and grow, and where every client's story would be heard and celebrated. This desire grew even more when I worked at CBS and other corporations, which required extensive travel despite my having two young girls. So I put my faith in what mattered: Launching my own firm, which would also grant me more time with my family.

When my daughters, Amanda and Kelsey, were both toddlers, I took that leap of faith and and launched my company, Co-Communications, from a spare room in my house. Starting your own business always takes faith, but I especially needed it, since my husband, Bruce, was opening his own law practice at the same time. Giving up two stable paychecks might not have been prudent, but I had faith that we'd be successful. Why? Because I had placed my faith in myself and what mattered most to me.

Faith Takes Work

There's a misconception that faith is passive or that it doesn't take work to find it or fuel it. The truth is, faith is active. You need to work at it every day.

Fortunately, my parents instilled a "can do" attitude in my sisters and me from an early age. My parents didn't have the luxury of attending college, but still inspired us to be avid learners and high-achievers. Today, my two sisters have doctorates and I have an MBA.

I've gifted my daughters Amanda and Kelsey the power of a "can do" attitude After all, a mother's faith can inspire children to achieve things they never thought possible.

"If at first you don't succeed, try, try again" was my mantra from the time my daughters took their first steps. And so today, I am the proud momma of two "can do" independent and successful young ladies. Kelsey recently graduated as an engineer and is working at a big four consulting firm implementing technology projects at Fortune 500 companies, and Amanda is working at a major financial services corporation where she was fast-tracked to Vice President at age 25. (Even in elementary school, the girls took it upon themselves to RSVP for their friend's birthday parties to help their full-time working mom.)

I've also brought this culture of "can do" to Co-Communications. My team knows that there are two words that are not permissible in the office: "I can't." If my colleagues are having difficulty securing media coverage for our clients, I use an old adage. "Go in the front door, and if that doesn't work, go in the back door." I encourage everyone to be a problem solver, not a problem spotter. That's faith.

In the early days of Co-Communications, one of our clients asked if we could run an advertising campaign. Even though we were just PR professionals at the time, my answer was, "Yes, we can!" My very next call was to my friend in advertising, who helped us glean the expertise we needed. The result? We evolved from strictly a PR agency into a multi-million dollar integrated marketing firm with multiple service offerings. Again, that's faith.

In all these examples, faith isn't something lingering in the background — it's the force propelling us forward, toward success. It's the force that energizes us, pushes us, and allows us to manifest our desires.

Keeping the Faith

Sometimes, even when you have faith in spades, things don't work out. And you may find yourself asking, "Are faith and failure compatible?" The answer is yes.

Successful people regularly embrace challenges, try new things, make mistakes, and deal with unexpected situations. And they fail often. That's okay. Why? Because failure is often a stepping stone towards success. You need to embrace it. As long as you can improve through each successive failure, then you've created a stronger platform for eventual success and wealth in the future. Let each failure build your faith, rather than sap it.

If you find your faith faltering, identify a pattern of self-limiting thoughts (for example, "I can't do this." or, "It's too hard.") Then, replace this negative inner monologue with "I can." Whatever it is that we focus on in life, we get more of. If we focus on problems, we live solely in those problems and have difficulty moving past the negativity. Alternatively, when we focus on positivity and seek out solutions, we can resolve our problems and move toward success.

How to Fuel Your Faith

As we've discussed, faith is about believing in yourself. And this can take a lot of energy. I can tell you firsthand, because my colleagues have nicknamed me "Taz," short for Tasmanian devil. And my husband, Bruce, tells me frequently that I have "Shpilkes," a Yiddish term which essentially means my "motor is always running."

So where can you find the energy to keep the faith? About 10 years ago, I was out for a romantic Valentine's Day dinner with Bruce. As I was eating the last chocolate covered strawberry, he presented me with a gift card for a meditation program. This gift of mindfulness was life-changing. A decade later, I now practice meditation and visualization regularly and am exponentially more present, focused, and in sync with my desires and objectives. It essentially allows me to "keep the faith" and accomplish what I want in business, personal life, and health.

Don't just take my word for it. Some of the most successful individuals, including Arianna Huffington, Oprah Winfrey, and LinkedIn CEO Jeff Weiner, claim that meditation has played a significant part in their success.

Slowing down may seem to contradict faith. Shouldn't you be out there *doing*? Doesn't constant action fuel faith? Not so. When you step away from the hustle and bustle of life, you can hone your focus on what really matters. And don't worry—you needn't shut yourself off from the world for hours at a time. I personally prefer coupling my meditation with a walk, adding exercise to the equation. If that sounds right for you, you can find 30-minute walking meditations on YouTube.

As I finish writing this chapter, I see the small wood block on my desk that simply reads "Faith." It's a short but powerful reminder that we all need to hold onto the expectation of greater things to come. Exercise your faith muscle regularly. Lean into your faith, embrace it, and then activate it.

STACEY ROSS COHEN

About Stacey Ross Cohen: In the world of branding, few experts possess the savvy and instinct of Stacey. An award-winning brand professional who earned her stripes on Madison Avenue and major television networks before launching her own agency, Stacey specializes in cultivating and amplifying brands.

Stacey is CEO of Co-Communications, a marketing agency headquartered in New York. She coaches businesses and individuals across a range of industries, from real estate to healthcare and education, and expertly positions their narratives in fiercely competitive markets.

A TEDx speaker, Stacey is a sought-after keynote at industry conferences and author in the realm of branding, PR, and marketing. She is a contributor at *Huffington Post* and *Thrive Global*, and has been featured in *Forbes, Entrepreneur, Crain's* and a suite of other media outlets. She holds a B.S. from Syracuse University, MBA from Fordham University and a certificate in Media, Technology and Entertainment from NYU Stern School of Business.

Author's website: *www.StaceyRossCohen.com*
Book Series Website & author's Bio: *www.The13StepsToRiches.com*

Teresa Cundiff

WHERE IS YOUR FAITH

I am a Wordy Nerd!

My media company is Wordy Nerds Media.

I have a community on Facebook called Wordy Nerds Academy, where I introduce a new word every day to help the members improve their vocabularies. Words matter to me. Words have meaning and shouldn't be used lightly. You should know what all the words mean that you are using. You're probably sitting there wondering, "Why is she saying all this?" The answer is simple. Many people often speak without understanding the full weight of their words.

In this second book of the 13 Steps to Riches series, we are talking about FAITH! It's a word that means so much to me. The American Heritage Dictionary defines faith as:

A confident belief in the truth, value, or trustworthiness of a person's idea or thing;

1. Belief that does not rest on logical proof or material evidence;

2. Loyalty to a person or thing;

3. Belief and trust in God and the doctrines expressed in the Scriptures or other sacred works; conviction;

4. A system of religious beliefs;

5. Any set of principles or beliefs.

6. So I ask you, how many of these apply to you? What do you believe in? Where does your Faith lie?

Consider my chapter of this book an exercise in figuring out what you put your Faith in.

Some of you already know, but some of you may not. If you read my chapter in Book 1, you know that I am a Christian. Napoleon Hill said, "Christianity is the single greatest force which influences the minds of men." The basis of Christianity is our Faith in the shed blood of Christ on the cross to forgive our sins. This Faith comes from hearing the Word of God as the scripture teaches us. But you're like, "That's a bunch of hooey, Teresa! I don't believe that!" Okay then! What do you believe?

Let's say you have Faith in yourself. You get up every day and go to work and believe that your efforts will support your family. That's good.

You have Faith that your job is going to be there for you every day as well. Or you don't go to a job, and you trust your skills as an entrepreneur/ business person to carry on as they have and that you will continue to prosper and make money. You believe in your stockbroker. You believe in the stock market. You believe in your investment banker. You believe in status. You believe in possessions. You believe in beauty.

Stop right now and take stock. What do you believe in?

I will share with you some more about me. I used to want material things very badly. We used to carry debt to have nice cars. But I looked around and took stock of the things that truly mattered to me. Possessions are just things, and I had given them a place of importance in my life that they didn't deserve! It was materialism! I came to the conclusion that "stuff" didn't matter when we moved back to the United States from England in 1997 and were separated from our household goods for about three months.

The movers pack up your things and bring in what we called "stick furniture" for you to live on prior to your actual departure so that your goods can get on a slow boat back to the U.S.

You have what's called "hold baggage", which are essentials that you keep behind that will be flown for you as your departure date draws closer. Once we were in the States, we were further displaced while waiting for our quarters to be ready with the Navy at Great Lakes, IL, because the Army didn't have much housing at Ft. Sheridan, IL. The husband reported to work and stayed in billeting while the boys and I stayed in Green Bay, WI, with the grandparents. We were blessed to have a lovely place to be displaced in for so long.

I've explained all this to tell you that I was without my whole house and all my possessions for three months and didn't miss any of it. I had my family with me, and that was all that mattered. Clearly, one needs things to live, and we had those, but it truly opened my eyes to materialism, and that putting my Faith in "stuff" was misguided and misplaced.

Have you figured out what it is that you believe in? Do you know where you place your Faith? Do you consider yourself as having Faith? You see, I cannot write this chapter about Faith without talking to you about my Faith. Since I was a girl, I have been a Christian, so I have never known a life without Faith and trust in God. I have always had a relationship with Him. I quit going to church during my later high school and college years, but He brought me back to Him in my mid-20s. You see, God never moves. It is we who move away from God.

I have lived through terrible tragedies in my life, but I know God loves me. I have Faith in Him, even when I cannot have Faith in myself.

Napoleon Hill says, "Love and Faith are psychic; related to the spiritual side of man." This makes perfect sense to me because God is love, having given His Son for the redemption of man; Faith is the assurance of things hoped for, the conviction of things unseen. (Hebrews 11:1) They are psychic in the way the supernatural, all-powerful, Almighty God alone can make manifest.

In all our moves in the military, God has always provided for us. We have never worried about where we will live, who our neighbors will be, where we will go to church, if the kids are in a good school district, or any of that stuff. The husband would always make an advanced trip to the new city to house hunt WITHOUT me! That's right!

Some of you might be laughing and think THAT is the greatest act of Faith! LOL! Right? But I trusted him to find us a house, or if we thought it was best, to get on the list for housing. We usually rented off post because the waitlist was always too long to get on post.

God's hand was always on us, and here's the thing: Faith begets Faith! If you don't believe me, just try it. The hubs get orders, we know our move date, he plans his trip, he finds a house, we get our new address, I forward the mail (oh yeah, don't forget that little piece of business!), and the list goes on. We step out in Faith every time, knowing that the Lord will order our steps because we are believers and have put our trust in Him to do so. It's just as simple as that.

I wish I could tell you that everything about me comes as easily to me as my Faith. I still have insecurities, even though I shouldn't.

The world isn't suddenly simple or easy just because one is a believer. That's just silly to think! I sometimes forget that God is still interested in the little things about my life and don't talk to Him about them, but He is interested. It's so mind-blowing to think how the God of the universe loves and cares for me, but scripture is replete with verses telling me just that. After all these years of reading them, you'd think that it would finally sink in, but I am a flawed human, after all.

I realize that my writing isn't as elegant as the other authors in this book and that I don't wax poetic across the page, but my heart is in this chapter. A person's Faith is a very deep and personal thing.

I am just asking you to examine yourself to see where your Faith lies. I will confess that I struggle to have Faith in myself and my abilities, but I surround myself with a truly remarkable group of people who support me, lift me up and love me, which helps me in so many ways. I have a family who loves me and believes in me, and whom I treasure and adore.

I pray that you have the same thing, too. But if you don't, find yourself that amazing circle of friends who will love you like family. And lastly, my Faith rests in Almighty God, Maker of heaven and earth who gave His Son and ransom for many. I've shared with you where my Faith lies... where is your Faith?

TERESA CUNDIFF

About Teresa Cundiff: Teresa hosts an interview digital TV show called Teresa Talks on Legrity TV. On the show, she interviews authors who are published and unpublished— and that just means those authors haven't put their books on paper yet. The show provides a platform for authors to have a global reach with their message. Teresa Talks is produced by Wordy Nerds Media Inc., of which Cundiff is the CEO.

Cundiff is also a freelance proofreader with the tagline, "I know where the commas go!," Teresa makes her clients' work shine with her knowledge of grammar, punctuation, and sentence structure.

Teresa is a two-time International Best-Selling Contributing Author of 1 Habit for Entrepreneurial Success and 1 Habit to Thrive in a Post-COVID World. She is also a best-selling contributing author of The Art of Connection; 365 Days of Networking Quotes, which has been placed in the Library of Congress.

Author's Website: *www.TeresaTalksTV.com*
Book Series Website & Author's Bio: *www.The13StepsToRiches.com*

Vera Thomas

GOD IS IN CONTROL

God is in control Get out of the way
This is what he wants to say

God is in control
He is the lamp unto our feet We must concede
He is the light until our path Only what we do for him will last

God is in control
We must acknowledge our role Which is to walk the path
He has ordered our steps to take On our own there
May be anxiety depression Heartache and mistakes

We may experience mental angst When we rely on ourselves
When we succumb to our whelms

God is not a God that He would lie His Word is the answer
Where we must abide His Word is the same
Yesterday today and forever
His Word is here to eliminate pressure
The joy of the Lord IS our strength.
"Peace be still" without restraint.
We are transformed by the renewing of our mind

It is in His word where we find The answers to whatever
May come our way

We have but to ask when we pray Believing
He always, always, always Makes a way
No matter what Come what may

He did not promise
A road without challenge Heartaches or sorrow

He promised to be there
with us yesterday, today, and tomorrow

Put your trust in Him who is able to keep us from falling
Have faith is in His Word Hear him calling
On all of us to let Him control

Be a light Have mercy
Do justice Have faith
Those are our roles!

Vera Thomas 8/13/19

What Faith means to me is trusting God's Word, His promises, and the Holy Spirit inside me.

I know when I get out of the way and allow God to lead, guide, and direct me, things are in divine order. When I decide to control, things may go awry.

I was a Preacher's Kid. We were in church more than we were not. However, I did not recognize the power of a letting a relationship with God control me until I was older and on my own.

While He is with us all the time, I first recognized His presence while in Los Angeles. I was working in downtown L.A. and lived in South L.A., and it was a November evening after 6 pm. While riding the bus home, a rider got on and did not pay. The bus driver was so upset, and he did not hear when I pulled the cord for my stop. Los Angeles blocks seem at least a mile long. It was dark. There was a parking lot on the side where I needed to be. As I was crossing the intersection, a car full of guys pulled up to the intersection. Instead of continuing on their way, they started following me in the parking lot. I did not know what to do except start reciting the 23rd Psalms, "The Lord is my Shepherd; I shall not want…." As I was reciting, the car hit something in the parking lot and busted a tire.

They stopped. I ran and continued to recite the 23rd Psalms. All I could say was, "Thank you, Lord."

I have been to LA twice. (No, I did not seek God's guidance when I made both those moves). The last time was with my ex-husband. I shared that story in my first chapter. The day I was leaving LA, I was offered a job. I told them, "As we speak, I am walking out the door to leave." They begged me to stay. I told them, "I will call you back." I got my Bible and prayed, "Lord show me through your Word what I should do. Whatever you say, I will do". I opened the Bible to "Go home to thy friends and tell them what great things the Lord has done and how he has had compassion upon you." (All of which was true). I called the company back and went home. God knew what was best. The plan was to stay in Ohio for no more than two years and then leave again. I did not want to be in Ohio! However, EVERY TIME I prayed about leaving, no matter what Bible I would look in, it was ALWAYS, "Stay where you are…" for 25 years!

God also has a sense of humor. I had applied for a job that I just knew I would get. I did say, "Lord, if this job does not come through, I am leaving Ohio." The job did not come through! When I received the rejection letter, I stood in the bathroom with tears in my eyes, looked in the mirror and said, "Lord, you keep telling me to stay here. If you want me to hear, you need to make a way!"

Within minutes, the phone rang. I was offered a position 25 miles away and still in Ohio! At that point, I said, "Lord, I meant leave Ohio, not just this city!"

At one point, I considered the Orlando, Florida, area near my brother.

The year I was considering, we went to surprise my brother for his 50th birthday. While there, I was seriously exploring the option. We were there for a week. As I was contemplating moving there that Tuesday, it was dropped in my spirit that this was not where I was to be. That Wednesday, during a church service, the minister, as he delivered his sermon (it was as if he was looking directly at me), said, "Sometimes the Lord wants you to stay where you are!" Confirmation!

Both of my sisters were diagnosed with cancer at the same time. I traveled back and forth between Ohio and Kentucky as they went through their ordeals. After returning to Ohio from Kentucky, as I was sitting on my couch, I picked up my Bible and asked, "Lord is it time?" When I opened the Bible, on both sides of the page was the word "Go!" I was in shock. I said, "Really? You are telling me I can leave?"

I did not trust what I had seen. A few days later, I was sitting on my bed, picked up my Bible and said, "Lord, I know you said I could go. Can you please confirm through your Word that this is what I am to do?" I opened the Bible and it said, "Pack your bags…."

I moved to Kentucky and continued to travel back and forth for my sisters. The transition to Kentucky was one of the smoothest I ever experienced. The challenge in Kentucky was dealing with toxicity. I relied on the scripture "Peace Be Still" to get through some contentious times. He gave me the peace I needed to care for my baby sister regardless of the situation!

My sister in Ohio lost her battle in 2015. Five years later, my sister in Kentucky lost hers. My purpose for having been there was complete.

My son suggested we all move to Atlanta. I prayed about it. I was shown several times that I should make that move. There was a point where there was a sense of urgency to get to Georgia. I felt it, but did not understand. We were to stay with a cousin until we could get settled. When we arrived at her home that Sunday evening, we learned that she had a headache all that day. She had refused to go to the hospital. When I saw her condition, I took her to the hospital. She was transported to another hospital over an hour away from there, and then air flighted to Atlanta. The doctors told me that had she not gotten to the hospital when she did, she would be dead! Hence, that sense of urgency!

This transition was not as smooth as the one to Kentucky. Everything that could go wrong, did. We were not able to find a six-bedroom house promptly. The job my son got in Atlanta transferred him back to Ohio.

God kept telling me that this is where I was to be. I think God got tired of me questioning what He told me. I remember saying to him, "Lord, if this is where you want me to be, why are things so difficult?" I heard, as clear as day, "Look, I told you, this is where you are to be. Do what you want to do!" When you have a relationship with your higher power, you hear that still, small voice. Some people have dreams or visions. I hear His voice, or He speaks to me directly through His Word.

I stayed in Georgia. I am convinced that writing this book would not have happened if I had decided to leave Georgia.

These are just a few examples of how God's plan will be revealed when we trust our Faith and do not walk by sight!

VERA THOMAS

About Vera Thomas: As a Life Coach, Speaker, Trainer, Mediator, Poet, and Producer of a weekly podcast/radio show called "The Vera Thomas Show," Vera has worked with companies, non-profit organizations, schools, and churches customizing and delivering training and leadership programs.

Enduring physical, emotional, and mental abuse as a child, rape, homelessness and surviving as a battered wife leaving her husband when her son was only 6 months old, Vera has organized a program called the "Father's Walk!" This program would focus on fathers walking their child to school on a specific date. Impacting over 10,000 fathers who took part in the program, it allowed the movement to change systemic attitudes and behaviors towards fathers in family court, child support, and children services.

Author's Website: *www.VeraThomasCoaching.com*
Book Series Website & Author's Bio: *www.The13StepstoRiches.com*

Yuri Choi

FAITH: TRUSTING THAT YOU WILL GET OVER THE RAINBOW

Have you ever had moments of feeling alone or hopeless in your journey towards your big goals and dreams? Have you ever found yourself feeling lost in darkness as you launch yourself into the unknown and new possibilities?

The day I am about to share with you was one of those days for me. Even though this day was many years ago now, I remember it like it was yesterday. And it was an important day because from that point on, I developed complete Faith in the Universe.

But before I tell you about that day, let me give you a bit of context. A month before that day, I had just quit my well-paying corporate sales job and became an entrepreneur with no steady income for the first time in my life. My mom, my only family left in the U.S., had moved back to Korea days before. I had just invested in my first coach and in some courses to support my big dream of becoming a coach that inspires and impacts millions to live more fulfilling lives. And all these changes happened shortly after my dad's passing after years of battling cancer.

That day, I was sitting in my parked car, in the driver's seat, feeling lonely, hopeless, and lost in my journey towards my dreams.

I had just spent yet another full day studying, learning from courses, writing, and working on building my coaching business. I didn't know how it was supposed to happen or what I was supposed to do, but I knew I had to do anything and everything I could think of to take even a tiny step towards my vision of serving millions of people to live a life leading with L.O.V.E. (laughter, oneness, vulnerability, ease). All I had was this big dream of helping people live a happier, more fulfilled, and meaningful life, and building my coaching business to make this happen.

I went on this path to serve people upon my dad's passing, as I had learned one of the most significant spiritual lessons that changed the course of my life. I had never witnessed anyone close to me pass on before that point in my life. After I got the call, I remember getting to the hospice, and I walked into his room to witness my dad's lifeless physical body. His physical body was there, but it was clear that he wasn't there. His *soul* wasn't there. So who was *he* all along, if he was not his body that was left behind? Who am *I*, really, if my body is not who I really am? It became clear that my physical body was merely a container and a vehicle for my soul. It became real to me that I also have an expiration date for my physical body and that my soul will eventually transcend one day.

Until then, I had not thought much about my death. I realized that I do not have to live out my dreams and follow my soul's purpose forever. For the first time in my life, it became urgent that I get to live my life to the fullest, to do all the things I had been scared of doing and only dreamed about. I started to dream bigger than I ever had before. I wanted to impact millions of people, be a coach that changed peoples' lives, a spiritual teacher, a coach, an author, a speaker, an entrepreneur, and a healer. I wanted to create my reality in my own way and leave a legacy in the world.

Ironically though, the clearer and the bigger my dreams got, the scarier the road ahead of me started to feel. So, from grieving the loss of my dad, in the midst of this existential crisis; taking a huge leap of Faith of quitting my job and making an investment in myself to work with a coach; having no guaranteed income; following my dream, with no familial support system anywhere on the continent, mixed with the bigness of my dreams; it created a perfect storm that day as I sat in my car. My heart and my soul were exhausted. I felt like I was on a little boat, rowing, and rowing in complete darkness, with no light in sight. I felt fear in my chest as I found myself sitting with these racing thoughts.

Can I really do this? Will this ever get better? Will I ever find my way to find the light again and make it to my dreams? Do I really have what it takes to create this vehicle of transformation for others who want to live a truly happy life? Is this really even my destined path? If so, why does it feel so scary and hard right now?

Instead of sitting in these thoughts, I decided to pray to my dad in heaven and the Universe.

Dad, are you there in heaven? I miss you. I feel so lost. Please help me. Your life, and your death, gave me the gift of courage to go on this journey to help people. I was so sure that this is exactly what I am destined to do. Yet, today, right now, right here, I feel so lost and scared. Can you please give me a sign that I am on the right path? Dad, Universe, God, whoever can hear me first, please let me know I will be okay because this all feels...

Then, at that very moment, I heard my intuition gently whisper, "Yuri, listen to the lyrics of this song." So I paused, praying to tune into this familiar tune, *Somewhere Over the Rainbow*, that came on the radio.

"... dreams that you dream of, really do come true."

These lyrics struck a chord in my heart. It was the very confirmation and the sign I had just prayed for. It was the confirmation that my dreams would come true and that I would get over the rainbow one day after this storm.

So that's why I had burst into tears that day. They were tears that I had held back for so many weeks. I cried so hard. It was exactly the energetic release I needed, and something magical happened.

Just like that, all the fears, anxiety, and stress that I'd been holding in my chest burst out into the ether and left my body. I started to feel at ease in my body again, and I was breathing more deeply. I felt this energy of courage sprouting from deep within my heart. The inspiration started to blossom from my soul. During that song, I found myself transmuting my fears into something beautiful that would take me on a magnificent journey of helping many people over the years. I was able to transform my despair into Faith. And that Faith is what carried me through all these years. Without this Faith, I would not have been able to build my coaching business these last four years, changing many lives and the mindsets of powerful leaders, C.E.O.'s and high achievers to live fulfilling lives and achieve their full potential in their businesses. I have inspired many through my words as an author, YouTuber, and speaker. I have impacted millions of people with my talks and teachings as an official designated coach for the largest mental health YouTube channel, Psych2Go. I have created location freedom while serving my amazing clients and have lived the last year in Asia. I am making more money than I ever did in my corporate world. I credit all of this back to the moment that day in my car, where my Faith became my new foundation for everything I do.

Faith is the foundation for hope and eternal resilience. Faith is the constant that fuels our souls back onto our path whenever we start to let any doubts creep up. Faith is the evidence that there are unseen forces or divine guidance that are supporting you, always. Faith is the complete surrender and a trust fall into the Universe. Faith activates the knowing that there is a force light-years bigger than us, supporting us to become all that we are destined to be. Faith is the portal to infinite possibilities and miracles. Faith makes what seems impossible, possible. With Faith, we become unstoppable.

And so, now you know why on that day, I was sitting in the driver's seat of my parked car in tears as I listened to this song. And after this song was over, I wiped my tears, decided to turn on the ignition, and started to drive again. But this time, with hope, unshakable Faith, and a smile.

As I was working on my last edits for this chapter in a hotel room by the ocean in Korea, I was streaming a random playlist, and it started to play *"Somewhere Over the Rainbow."* So I smile, yet again, for the millionth time, feeling infinitely supported and loved with my Faith in the Universe!

YURI CHOI

About Yuri Choi: Yuri is the Founder of Yuri Choi Coaching. Yuri is a performance coach for entrepreneurs and high achievers. She helps them create and stay in a powerful, abundant, unstoppable mindset to achieve their goals by helping them gain clarity and understanding, leverage their emotional states, and create empowering habits and language patterns.

She is a speaker, writer, creator, connector, YouTuber, and the author of Creating Your Own Happiness. Yuri is passionate about spreading the messages about meditation, power of intention, and creating a powerful mindset to live a fulfilling life. She is also a Habitude Warrior Conference Speaker and emcee, and she is also a designated guest coach for Psych-2Go, the largest online mental health magazine and YouTube Channel. Her mission in the world is to inspire people to live leading with L.O.V.E. (which stands for: laughter, oneness, vulnerability, and ease) and to ignite people's souls to live in a world of infinite creative possibilities and abundance.

Author's Website: *www.YuriChoiCoaching.com*
Book Series Website & Author's Bio: *www.The13StepsToRiches.com*

GRAB YOUR COPY OF AN OFFICIAL PUBLICATION
WITH THE ORIGINAL UNEDITED TEXT FROM 1937
BY THE NAPOLEON HILL FOUNDATION!

THE NAPOLEON HILL FOUNDATION
WWW.NAPHILL.ORG

Global Speakers Mastermind &
Habitude Warrior Masterminds

Join us and become a member of our tribe! Our Global Speakers Mastermind is a virtual group of amazing thinkers and leaders who meet twice a month. Sessions are designed to be 'to the point' and focused, while sharing fantastic techniques to grown your mindset as well as your pocket books. We also include famous guest speaker spots for our private Masterclasses. We also designate certain sessions for our members to mastermind with each other & counsel on the topics discussed in our previous Masterclasses. It's time for you to join a tribe who truly cares about *YOU* and your future and start surrounding yourself with the famous leaders and mentors of our time. It is time for you to up-level your life, businesses, and relationships.

For more information to check out our Masterminds:
Team@HabitudeWarrior.com
www.DecideToBeAwesome.com

BECOME AN INTERNATIONAL
#1 BEST-SELLING AUTHOR & SPEAKER

Habitude Warrior International has been highlighting award-winning Speakers and #1 Best-Selling Authors for over 25 years. They know what it takes to become #1 in your field and how to get the best exposure around the world. If you have ever considered giving yourself the GIFT of becoming a well-known Speaker and a fantastically well known #1 Best-Selling Author, then you should email their team right away to find out more information in how you can become involved. They have the best of the best when it comes to resources in achieving the best-selling status in your particular field. Start surrounding yourself with the N.Y. Times Best-Sellers of our time and start seeing your dreams become reality!

For more information to become a #1 Best-Selling Author
& Speaker on our Habitude Warrior Conferences
Please send us your request to:
Team@HabitudeWarrior.com
www.DecideTobeAwesome.com

Hardback ISBN: 978-1-63792-117-3
Paperback ISBN: 978-1-63792-122-7